TRAILBLAZERS, HEROES, AND CROOKS

TRAILBLAZERS, HEROES, AND CROOKS

STORIES TO MAKE YOU A SMARTER INVESTOR

BY STEPHEN R. FOERSTER

WILEY

Published by John Wiley & Sons, Inc., Hoboken, New Jersey.
Published simultaneously in Canada.

For general information on our other products and services or for technical support, please contact
our Customer Care Department within the United States at (800) 762-2974, outside the United States
at (317) 572-3993 or fax (317) 572-4002.

Wiley also publishes its books in a variety of electronic formats. Some content that appears in print
may not be available in electronic formats. For more information about Wiley products, visit our
web site at www.wiley.com.

Library of Congress Cataloging-in-Publication Data is Available:

ISBN 9781394275922 (Hardback)
ISBN 9781394275939 (epdf)
ISBN 9781394275946 (epub)

Cover Design: Wiley

SKY10081012_080524

CONTENTS

CONTENTS

PREFACE

Quintus Fabius defeated Hannibal through masterly inactivity. A hostage crisis in 12th-century Venice led to the birth of government bonds. Sir Isaac Newton had a dreadful case of FOMO and lost a fortune. A 16-year-old boy caused havoc on an Aeroflot flight when he unknowingly disengaged the autopilot. The New York Mets are paying Bobby Bonilla $30 million *not* to play baseball. Cristiano Ronaldo removed Coca-Cola bottles at a press conference, and caused the stock to lose $4 billion in value in a single day—or did he? After a salad oil swindle almost destroyed American Express, Warren Buffett swooped in to make one of the best investments of all time.

We'd all love to invest like Warren Buffett. We can't all be Warren Buffett, but understanding the lessons behind his story and many other historic events can make you a smarter investor. Smart investors understand the fundamentals and sound principles of investing, like what drives the price of stocks, bonds, and other securities; why diversification is important; and how you can preserve your purchasing power. Smart investors are more attuned to avoiding pitfalls and don't let their emotions get in the way. They simply make better investment decisions.

The goal of investing is trying to achieve the highest level of expected return for a given level of risk. The bedrock of any sound portfolio starts with stocks and bonds. Why do our portfolios start with these traditional investments? It comes back to expected return and risk, and finding the right balance. Trailblazers were the pioneers who came up with models to help us think about investments or the approach to how we invest. Trailblazers were also practitioners who helped create products for how we invest, or who encouraged a better way to invest.

Unfortunately, we may not act as smart as we can when it comes to investing. We often let our emotions and biases get in the way of sound investment decision-making. Investing success requires that we act rationally. Yet evidence suggests we don't always act that way. For example, we often get excited and look at investment opportunities through rose-colored glasses and we're overconfident in our stock-picking abilities. We conclude that we should invest in a company simply because it makes cutting-edge products, yet we ignore how expensive the stock currently is. We convince ourselves that we have to buy a stock now because if we don't and the price goes up, we'll regret it later. Yet we don't have to let our emotions and biases get in the way. We can become smarter investors. We can learn the lessons that history teaches us.

As in life, there are heroes and crooks in the investment world. Along with the trailblazers, this book is about their stories. What they have in common is that both heroes and crooks understand the impact of emotions and biases on our investment decision-making. Crooks like Bernie Madoff play off our emotions and biases. They cause us to make poor investment decisions, ones in which only they stand to gain. On the other hand, heroes like Buffett find ways to counter emotions and biases. Some heroes look for investing opportunities when emotions have caused prices to diverge from what a security is truly worth. Other heroes take our emotions and biases totally out of the investment equation, so that we can make sound investment decisions regardless of how we feel.

What you'll learn from the stories in *Trailblazers, Heroes, and Crooks* is that it pays to be diversified and start your portfolio with a strong foundation of stocks and bonds. Then be mindful that crooks are trying to play off your emotions and biases. Don't be enticed by their false promises. On the other hand, it may pay to emulate the strategies and approaches of investing heroes. Whether you are a novice investor or a professional, you can become a smarter investor. You can learn the lessons that history teaches us to develop a sound investment philosophy. These stories about investing trailblazers, heroes, and crooks will help you to do that. And you'll also enjoy simply reading the fascinating stories.

The stories cover over two thousand years, and originate in various locations around the world. They're set in the Roman Empire in the second century BCE; in Venice in 1172; in the UK in 1720; in Switzerland and France in 1759; in Massachusetts in 1780; in New York City in 1907, 1987, and again in 1999; in New Jersey in 1963; in Africa in 1974; on an Aeroflot flight from Moscow to Hong Kong in 1994; in the jungles of Indonesia in 1996; and at a European soccer tournament press conference in Budapest in 2021. Buckle up because we'll be hopping back and forth through time and space. Along the way we'll meet seven trailblazers: Harry Markowitz, Bill Sharpe, Jack Bogle, Charley Ellis, Jacob Bouthillier Beaumont, Lawrence Sperry, Doge Vitale Michiel, and legislators for the Commonwealth of Massachusetts; eight heroes: Quintus Fabius, Muhammad Ali, Bobby Bonilla, Dennis Gilbert, Harry Markopolos, Hetty Green, Warren Buffett, and Karsten Mahlmann; and six crooks: Bernie Madoff, Sam Bankman-Fried, John Blunt, Tino DeAngelis, a promoter from Cornhill, and (alleged crook) Mike de Guzman.

I hope you enjoy the stories, and the lessons you take away that make you a smarter investor.

Stephen R. Foerster
London, Ontario
April 2024

CHAPTER ONE

DID RONALDO MOVE THE STOCK MARKET?

W ho's the best soccer player in the world? Well, it depends on how you ask and whom you ask. Asking who's the best player of all time may elicit a different answer than asking who's the best active player. And of course, the answer will be subjective. In 2022 prior to the World Cup, one list[1] had the top three active players as Lionel (Leo) Messi, Cristiano Ronaldo, and Neymar da Silva Santos, Jr. (known simply as Neymar). Born in Argentina, Messi was named the Fédération Internationale de Football Association (FIFA) world player of the year six times, and, by the time he was only 24, had scored 233 goals for Barcelona to become the fabled club's all-time leading scorer.[2]

Ronaldo, born in Portugal, was a five-time FIFA world player of the year, and in the 2017–18 season, playing for Spain's Real Madrid, scored 44 goals in 44 games.[3] Neymar, born in Brazil and one of the country's most productive scorers, played for Barcelona between 2013 and 2017 and was a chief contributor to the club's success.[4]

Who's the greatest social media influencer in the world? If we narrowly define what we mean by *influencer*, this question has a more objective answer. Based on Instagram followers as of 2024, it's not even close. And it turns out to be one of the three top soccer players. Messi had 496 million followers. But Ronaldo was a clear number one with a whopping 616 million followers—now that's influence! (In case you were wondering, Selena Gomez was in the number-three spot with 429 million followers.)

RONALDO AND THE COKE BOTTLES

Here's a story you may have heard about that speaks to Ronaldo's influence beyond the soccer pitch. This headline from the *Washington Post*, on June 16, 2021, said it all: "Cristiano Ronaldo snubbed Coca-Cola. The company's market value fell $4 billion."[5] The article referred to an incident at a press conference on June 14, 2021, during the 2020 European Championship (postponed until 2021 due to the Covid-19 pandemic). At the start of the press conference in Budapest, before Portugal played Hungary, Ronaldo proceeded to remove two bottles of Coke that were prominently displayed on the table in front of him. This was shocking because Coca-Cola was one of the tournament's official sponsors. He replaced them with a bottle of water, saying, "Agua. No Coca-Cola." It was immediately big news. A YouTube video of the incident has been viewed over 22 million times.[6] (Portugal went on to beat Hungary three to nil, with Ronaldo scoring late in the match on a penalty kick, and another one in stoppage time.)

The *Washington Post* article was very conclusive: "The simple gesture [of moving the Coke bottles] had a swift and dramatic impact: The soft drinks giant's market value fell $4 billion, highlighting the power and impact that celebrities and influencers can have on the market." That implies a clear cause-and-effect. The cause was the action by Ronaldo, a celebrity and influencer, snubbing Coca-Cola by removing Coke bottles. The effect of Ronaldo's action was a substantial drop in the market value of Coca-Cola. Case closed! Or was it? Let's take a closer look.[7]

ANOTHER EXAMPLE OF CAUSE AND EFFECT: EX-DIVIDEND DAYS EXPLAINED

But first, an important digression and explainer of another example of cause and effect. This one doesn't involve influencers. Established companies like Coca-Cola pay regular cash dividends, usually on a predictable quarterly cycle. The timing of upcoming dividend payments isn't a surprise to the market because companies announce their plans ahead of time. There is a cutoff point, known as the ex-dividend date, and that's announced in advance as well. After that date, anyone who becomes a new owner of shares doesn't receive the imminent dividend.

Here's a simple hypothetical example. On May 1 a stock is selling for $10 per share. There's an upcoming dividend of $1 per share to be paid on May 15. The ex-dividend date is May 2. The stock is priced at $10 in anticipation of the upcoming $1 dividend. If you own the stock on May 1, you'll be getting the upcoming dividend. Then on May 2 the stock trades ex-dividend, which means anyone buying shares on that day or later won't be receiving the upcoming May 15 dividend. So, unless there's new information relevant to the stock's value, we would expect the stock to drop by $1 on May 2, the ex-dividend date.

Here's a real example. June 14, 2021, was an ex-dividend date for Coca-Cola.[8] That meant that anyone who first bought the stock on that date wasn't eligible for the $0.42 per share dividend that was going to be paid on July 1. With 4.3 billion shares outstanding, that's a total cash payment of about $1.8 billion. So, absent any other relevant information, we would expect Coca-Cola's market value (stock price times the number of shares) to drop by that amount on the ex-dividend date. For anyone who owned the Coca-Cola shares *prior* to June 14, 2021, the anticipated share price drop wouldn't affect their overall wealth since they were entitled to the upcoming cash dividend. June 14 just happened to coincide with the day of Ronaldo's press conference.

WHAT REALLY HAPPENED ON JUNE 14, 2021

Now let's see what was *really* happening with Coca-Cola's stock around the time of the infamous snub. On Friday, June 11, Coca-Cola's stock price closed at $56.16 a share. The company's shares had an overall market value of $242.6 billion. On Monday, June 14, when the market in New York opened for trading at 9:30 a.m., the stock was at $55.69. That price was down $0.47 a share since Friday's close, or a market value decline of $2.0 billion. In the absence of any major news over the weekend, we would have expected the stock to drop by $0.42 a share, the amount of the upcoming dividend, or overall by the total cash payment of $1.8 billion. That's fairly close to what actually happened. The S&P 500 index, a broad measure of the overall U.S. stock market, hadn't moved much between its Friday close and Monday opening. It was up just 0.02 percent, and so that didn't seem to impact on Coca-Cola's opening price.

Coca-Cola's stock price continued to drop during the next several minutes, from $55.69 at the 9:30 a.m. open to $55.27 at 9:43 a.m. By that time, the overall Coca-Cola stock value had declined by $3.9 billion since the Friday closing value. That sounds like a lot of money. But to put that in perspective, it's just 1.5 percent of the Friday value. Furthermore, half of that amount (0.75 percent or $0.42 per share) was because of the ex-dividend date effect. Subsequent to the June 14 market opening, the S&P 500 index declined only slightly, so we can conclude that there was some other reason that caused the unexplained drop of about 0.75 percent. Perhaps it was related to the outlook for Coca-Cola or the beverage industry. But that's not surprising. New information and changes in investor expectations cause stock prices to move all of the time.

What's important is that Coca-Cola's stock price drop occurred *prior* to the start of Ronaldo's press conference. Ronaldo removed the Coke bottles at 9:43 a.m. (New York time). From 9:43 a.m. through the remainder of the trading day, Coca-Cola's stock price actually *rose*, both in absolute terms as well as relative to the overall market. It went from $55.27 to $55.55. So how about this for a revised story headline: "Cristiano Ronaldo snubbed Coca-Cola. The company's market value *then rose by $1.2 billion*." If that was the new headline, would we then try to infer cause-and-effect and conclude that Ronaldo was a past-his-prime-has-been and no longer an influencer?

Let's go back to the *Washington Post* headline: "Cristiano Ronaldo snubbed Coca-Cola. The company's market value fell $4 billion." Taken literally and separately, each sentence is a true statement. There's no question that Ronaldo's removal of the Coke bottles and his statement "No Coca-Cola" was a deliberate snub. And based on the change in Coca-Cola's closing stock prices between Friday, June 11, and Monday, June 14, Coca-Cola's market value dropped by more than $4 billion. But placed together, the implication is that one thing caused the other. That's clearly not what happened.

Correlation describes the extent to which two things are related to one another. Is there a correlation between the snub and the stock price decline? Yes, as they both occurred on the same day. But the evidence indicates that within that particular day, the snub didn't *cause* the drop in the stock price. What we do know—and is well established—is that Coca-Cola's stock going ex-dividend was the primary cause of the price decline at the opening of trading.

A few days later, an *Associated Press* article was much more accurate than the *Washington Post* article when it stated, "A drop in Coca-Cola's share price this week was attributed by some to Ronaldo's snub, but without any evidence that the two things were connected."[9] Understanding the ex-dividend date effect and examining intraday prices on June 14, there's no question that Ronaldo's press conference snub didn't *cause* Coca-Cola's stock price to drop that day. There's an important distinction between correlation and causation, yet we often confuse the two.

THE SUPER BOWL INDICATOR

Classic correlation versus causation examples abound. Here's one that connects sports with stocks. It isn't very often that the prestigious academic publication the *Journal of Finance* publishes a paper about sports. One such paper, in the June 1990 issue, was titled "An Examination of the Super Bowl Stock Market Predictor."[10]

The Super Bowl dates back to January 15, 1967, when the American Football League (AFL) and the rival National Football League (NFL) agreed to have their respective champions play in the first World Championship Game (as it was initially called). The NFL's Green Bay team defeated the AFL's Kansas City team 35 to 10.

As early as 1978, a pattern was detected. *Sporting News* noted that between 1967 and 1977, whenever one of the original NFL teams won the

Super Bowl, played in January during that era, the stock market rose over the remainder of the year and ended higher overall for the year. The reverse was true if an original AFL team won the Super Bowl.[11] This happened in each of 11 consecutive years.[12] The 1990 paper updated the analysis through 1988 and found that the predictor was correct 20 out of 22 times, for an accuracy rate of 91 percent. The average annual return differences for the S&P 500 index were astounding: 15.3 percent if an NFL team won, versus –10.9 percent if an AFL team won.

So what's happened to the Super Bowl predictor *since* 1988? According to one study, between 1989 and 2016, the predictor's success rate dropped to 61 percent.[13] And if we account for the more recent Super Bowls through 2023, that percentage drops to a near-coin-flip 51 percent (18 out of 35). In other words, it's not much of a predictor. But we shouldn't be surprised. It's hard to come up with a solid argument why a Super Bowl win by an original NFL team should *cause* the stock market to go up.

THE FACTOR ZOO

Correlation analysis plays a major role in investing strategies known as factor investing. Factor investing is a strategy that tries to identify stock investment opportunities by looking for relationships between stock price movements and quantifiable measures. For example, a stock's returns might vary as overall market returns vary: if the S&P 500 index goes up, then Walmart's stock might go up as well, and vice versa if the market declines. Other factors might be related to a firm's earnings. For example, "value investors" look for stocks that might be reasonably priced relative to current earnings, while "growth investors" look for stocks with expectations of hyper-growth in revenue or profits. For value investors, a firm's price-to-earnings ratio is an important factor to consider when buying a stock. For growth investors, expected growth is an important factor.

The idea behind factor models can be traced to Nobel laureate Harry Markowitz in his 1959 book *Portfolio Selection*.[14] Markowitz's investment model showed that as long as stock prices don't move in lockstep, there are benefits to being diversified—in other words, owning a portfolio of stocks rather than just one or two. That's because while one stock might be down on a given day or week, others might move up, and so the overall portfolio will be less volatile. He showed that there actually is a free lunch. With a portfolio, you can get a better overall return relative to risk.

Factor models were popularized by his protégé William (Bill) Sharpe, with whom Markowitz shared the Nobel Prize in Economics. In his 1963 paper, Sharpe created a simple model with one factor. Security returns were related to one another only through some basic underlying factor such as the overall stock market, gross national product (GNP), or "any other factor thought to be the most important single influence on returns from securities."[15] In Sharpe's 1964 paper, he created an equilibrium model that became known as the capital asset pricing model or CAPM. Instead of assuming a single factor, he derived it. It turned out to be the market portfolio of all investable assets.[16]

In Sharpe's model, the best way for investors to act was to put all of their money in this market portfolio, and then borrow or lend depending on risk preference. If you were well-diversified, then it really didn't matter how risky one stock was on its own. All that mattered for that stock was how risky it was *relative* to the overall market portfolio. A measure of that relative risk became known as beta. In the mid-1960s, there wasn't any mechanism to efficiently invest in a market portfolio. Today we have low-cost index funds.

There's an important implicit cause-and-effect in the models like Sharpe's. An increase in the overall stock market *causes* an individual stock to go up by a certain proportion. For example, if there is some unexpected good news on how the overall economy has been performing, investors may revise upward expectations for future profits for particular companies. But the relationship isn't necessarily one-to-one.

The popularity of factor investing has increased as quantitative data related to stock characteristics has become more readily available. John Cochrane, former president of the American Finance Association, coined the term "factor zoo" to describe the proliferation of factors in these models that try to develop an investment strategy that will outperform.[17] Sample factors include dividend-to-price ratios, unexpected earnings, leverage, price momentum, and volatility, to name just a few. Some models have dozens of factors that are used to explain and predict future stock returns. Unlike Sharpe's theory-based capital asset pricing model, most of these models are developed by back-testing strategies on historical data. Quite often, the back-test results look much more promising than actual results once a strategy has been implemented. That's no surprise, and it gets at the heart of correlation versus causation. If 100 factors are tested and five seem to be good predictors of future stock returns, it may be that those five showed statistically significant relationships just by happenstance—like the Super Bowl indicator.

CORRELATION VERSUS CAUSATION: DON'T BELIEVE EVERYTHING YOU READ

What are we to make of all of this? Here are short captions from a nerdy cartoon that distinguishes between correlation and causation.[18]

Person 1: "I used to think correlation implied causation. Then I took a statistics class. Now I don't."

Person 2: "Sounds like the class helped."

Person 1: "Well, maybe."

Proving a particular factor causes stock price movements is very difficult, as stock prices are driven by all kinds of information. Some factors may impact the overall market, like economic news, and some are specific to a particular firm, like its earnings. At best, we can look for evidence of correlation coupled with a plausible explanation that is isolated from other possible explanations. But even that isn't a guarantee. In the case of the Ronaldo snub, the *Washington Post* and many other news outlets overlooked important information, the missing link related to the ex-dividend date.

The *Washington Post* reporter who wrote about Ronaldo's snub covered breaking news and national stories and wasn't a finance expert.[19] She wasn't deliberately trying to create "fake news." The message here isn't to distrust mainstream news outlets but rather to gather as much relevant information as you can before jumping to any conclusions, or making any decisions. Correlations are all around us, and in particular in the world of investments. It doesn't hurt to start from a skeptical perspective. Then, based on extensive evidence, you'll need to be really convinced of a causation story.

There's no conclusive evidence that by moving the Coke bottles, Ronaldo destroyed Coca-Cola shareholder value. Even if he succeeded in getting his followers to drink more water, it's not even clear what impact that would have had either. According to the *Guardian*, the bottle of water that Ronaldo replaced the Coke bottles with was also a Coca-Cola product.[20]

NOTES

1. Delanty, Gavin, "Top 10 Best Soccer Players in the World," Lineups.com, https://www.lineups.com/articles/top-10-best-soccer-players-in-the-world/.
2. Britannica, Lionel Messi, https://www.britannica.com/biography/Lionel-Messi.
3. Britannica, Cristiano Ronaldo, https://www.britannica.com/biography/Cristiano-Ronaldo.

4. Britannica, Neymar, https://www.britannica.com/biography/Neymar.

5. Villegas, Paulina, "Cristiano Ronaldo Snubbed Coca-Cola. The Company's Market Value Fell $4 billion," *Washington Post*, June 16, 2021, https://www.washingtonpost.com/sports/2021/06/16/cristiano-ronaldo-coca-cola/.

6. "Cristiano Ronaldo HATES Coca-Cola," YouTube, June 14, 2021, https://www.youtube.com/watch?v=_nw7FOgOgtA.

7. Facts relating to what happened that day were described in Nuno Fernandes, "A Post-Truth World: Why Ronaldo Did Not Move Coca-Cola Share Price," *Forbes*, June 19, 2021, https://www.forbes.com/sites/iese/2021/06/19/a-post-truth-world-why-ronaldo-did-not-move-coca-cola-share-price/?sh=59fa67fefbb.

8. Nasdaq, "Coca-Cola Company (KO) Ex-Dividend Date Scheduled for June 14, 2021," June 11, 2021, https://www.nasdaq.com/articles/coca-cola-company-ko-ex-dividend-date-scheduled-for-june-14-2021-2021-06-11.

9. "UEFA Warns Euro 2020 Teams to Leave the Coke and Heineken Bottles Where They Are," Associated Press, June 21, 2021, https://www.marketwatch.com/story/eufa-warns-euro-2000-teams-to-leave-the-coke-and-heineken-bottles-where-they-are-01624301933.

10. Krueger, Thomas M., and William F. Kennedy, "An Examination of the Super Bowl Stock Market Predictor," *Journal of Finance* 45, no. 2 (1990): 691–697, https://onlinelibrary.wiley.com/doi/abs/10.1111/j.1540-6261.1990.tb03712.x.

11. Koppett, Leonard, "Carrying Statistics to Extremes," *Sporting News*, February 11, 1978.

12. The 11 for 11 accuracy depends on the definition of the stock market. It is true based on the New York Stock Exchange (NYSE) index, but slightly off based on the S&P 500 index. This is because in 1970, when Kansas City won the Super Bowl, the indicator predicted markets would decline. As predicted, the NYSE index was down, by 2.5 percent, while the S&P 500 index was essentially flat, up by only 0.1 percent for the year.

13. Schmidt, Bill, and Ronnie Clayton, "Super Bowl Indicator and Equity Markets: Correlation Not Causation," *Journal of Business Inquiry* 17, no. 2 (2017): 97–103.

14. Markowitz, Harry, *Portfolio Selection: Efficient Diversification of Investments*, Cowles Foundation for Research in Economics at Yale University, Monograph 16 (New York: John Wiley & Sons, 1959), 96–101.

15. Sharpe, William, "A Simplified Model for Portfolio Analysis," *Management Science* 9, no. 2 (1963): 277–293.

16. Sharpe, William, "Capital Asset Prices: A Theory of Market Equilibrium Under Conditions of Risk," *Journal of Finance* 19, no. 3 (1964): 425–442.
17. Cochrane, John, "Presidential Address: Discount Rates," *Journal of Finance* 66, no. 4 (2011): 1047–1108.
18. xkcd webcomic, https://xkcd.com/552, CC BY-NC 2.5.
19. "Paulina Villegas," *Washington Post,* https://www.washingtonpost.com/people/paulina-villegas/.
20. "Coca-Cola's Ronaldo Fiasco Highlights Risk to Brands in Social Media Age," *Guardian,* June 18, 2021, https://www.theguardian.com/media/2021/jun/18/coca-colas-ronaldo-fiasco-highlights-risk-to-brands-in-social-media-age.

CHAPTER TWO

MASTERLY INACTIVITY: THE ART OF NOT ACTING

T he term "masterly inactivity" may conjure up an image of laziness or procrastination, but it's much more nuanced than that. It's a versatile concept, applying to a broad number of contexts such as warfare, the boxing ring, soccer, medicine, and investments. Let's start with a definition for masterly inactivity from Fine Dictionary: "The position or part of a neutral or a Fabian combatant, carried out with diplomatic skill, so as to preserve a predominant influence without risking anything."[1] Simply and more broadly stated, masterly inactivity is the art of knowing when *not* to act.

QUINTUS FABIUS

That dictionary definition refers to the successful strategy employed during the Second Punic War (218–201 BCE) by the Roman dictator Quintus Fabius. He was known as Fabius Cunctatus or "the Delayer" and we'll see why.[2] He also earned the nickname "Maximus" among Romans—akin to calling rock star Bruce Springsteen "The Boss." Fabius showed how a weaker party can patiently overcome a stronger one.

Fabius was a cautious, composed, soft-spoken child. He was nicknamed *ovicula*, "the little sheep." His cool temperament and dispassion were initially misinterpreted as signs of a mental disability. Yet he eventually became one of Rome's ruling elite.

In the early third century BCE, both Rome and Carthage had expanded their territories in the western Mediterranean area. That put them on an inevitable collision course of superpowers. They fought a lengthy war between 264 BCE and 241 BCE without resolving longstanding issues between them. In 219 BCE, Carthaginian Hannibal Barca emerged as one of the greatest military commanders in history, with the capture of Saguntum, a recent ally of Rome in present-day Spain. At age 28, the young Hannibal assaulted, enslaved, and slaughtered the people. Rome was furious and sent its legions to defeat Hannibal. He eluded them by invading northern Italy, famously crossing the Alps with war elephants.

Hannibal's army ravaged Italy in victory after victory, both in skirmishes and major battles. Despite huge losses, many Roman senators felt the best strategy was direct confrontation with Hannibal's army. That played into the Carthaginian's plan: not to capture Rome, but to occupy as much territory as possible before forcing a peace. Realizing that Hannibal's forces were superior, Fabius decided to deny Hannibal the battles he was looking for until the Roman army could be reinforced.

Fabius was appointed dictator, with vast powers. He took personal command and encamped his troops at Aecae, a town in the Apulia region in southern Italy. When Hannibal learned of their nearby encampment, he resolved to terrify the Romans by attacking. But as his army approached and prepared for a great battle, there was no response from Fabius. Hannibal's army retreated to their camp.

Fabius knew that his army was inferior, and so his strategy was to bide his time rather than risk defeat in battle. Fabius reasoned that his army was on home turf and close to supplies and more men. By waiting he could amass a larger army. His tactic was to engage in the occasional skirmish in order to maintain morale, but to avoid a frontal battle until he felt the time was right, in a low-risk, high-gain scenario. Eventually his patience paid off, and Fabius was able to secure an unexpected military victory. Masterly inactivity was born.

MUHAMMAD ALI

One of the greatest boxers of all time, Muhammad Ali, employed a Fabian strategy in the boxing arena against George Foreman. (You may recognize Foreman's name for another reason. Post-retirement, Foreman was a promoter of the iconic grill that bears his name and that made him richer than through all of his boxing fights.) Their famous World Heavyweight Championship bout occurred on October 30, 1974, in Kinshasa, Zaire (now the Democratic Republic of the Congo), and became known as the "Rumble in the Jungle."[3]

Ali, born Cassius Clay, had been the world champion until 1967. As a conscientious objector, he refused to serve in the U.S. Army during the Vietnam War. He was imprisoned, lost his boxing license, and was stripped of his championship title. In 1970, he was back in the ring, and handily defeated Jerry Quarry. Then Joe Frazier beat Ali in 1971 in the "Fight of the Century." Over the next three years, Ali then beat Frazier, lost in a split decision to Ken Norton, and racked up a total of 13 wins. At age 32, Ali was clearly past his prime, more flat-footed and less of a dancer in the ring. He entered the fight against Foreman as a 40-to-1 longshot with some bookmakers. Many feared for Ali's safety against the younger (age 25), heavier Foreman, who also had a longer reach.

With a thunderstorm advancing, Ali arrived at the outdoor stadium—once used as an execution chamber for dissidents—wearing a white satin robe with an African blanket trim. Nearly 60,000 spectators looked on. Foreman was the reigning champion, unbeaten in 40 fights and with 37 knockouts. His opponents hadn't lasted more than three rounds before getting knocked out. Only one other person, Floyd Patterson, had been able to regain the heavyweight title, in 1960. This was clearly an uphill battle for the underdog Ali.

In the first of the scheduled twelve rounds, Foreman pinned Ali to the ropes and slammed punches with both hands to Ali's rib cage, with Ali protectively covering up. At the end of the round, sitting on a stool in his corner, Ali winked at Foreman. In the second round, Foreman chased Ali and pinned him against the ropes. Ali appeared to be wobbly. In the third round, Ali lay on the top rope and let Foreman punch away at him.

At the end of the round, instead of resting on his stool, Ali went over to a ringside TV camera and, hamming it up, made a face. In the fourth round, Ali again lay against the ropes while Foreman jabbed at him. Foreman's legs started to look weary. The fifth round proceeded much like the others, with Ali on the ropes. Before the sixth round, an official was trying to tighten the top rope where Ali had been laying against, but inadvertently loosened it. So Ali avoided that section.

By the seventh round, Foreman was stumbling. He chased Ali, but Foreman's face had become puffy, especially around his right eye, which he had cut during training. In the eighth round, Ali suddenly hit Foreman with a left-right combination. Foreman veered and collapsed on the canvas, with his dazed head rising briefly. Ali had delivered a stunning knockout. Soon after the fight finished, dawn broke, and a heavy rainstorm poured down.

Ali had deployed an unusual strategy that became known as rope-a-dope. Foreman threw 461 punches to Ali's 252, and landed 194 to Ali's 118.[4] Instead of meeting Foreman in the center of the ring, Ali leaned back against the ropes, protected himself, and let the elastic ring ropes absorb much of the force from Foreman's blows. Like Fabius centuries earlier, this was one of the greatest examples of masterly inactivity.

MASTERLY INACTIVITY AND SOCCER

Arguably the most exciting play in soccer (or football to our non–North American friends) is the penalty kick. It occurs either when one team commits a serious offence close to the goal, or when a game is tied after regulation and extra time. The ball is placed 12 yards from the goal. The goalkeeper must remain on the goal line until the ball is struck by the kicker. Four-fifths of penalty kicks result in a goal. That's significant because on average there are only 2.5 total goals scored in any given game.

Since it takes less than 0.3 seconds for the ball to reach the goal line, the goalkeeper has to decide on inaction or action, such as diving to the left or right, at the same time as the ball is struck. So, what *should* the goalkeeper do? And what *does* the typical goalkeeper do? A fascinating study found that among a sample of elite goalkeepers and penalty kicks, the optimal strategy was actually to stay in the center—masterly inactivity![5] However, most goalkeepers deviated from this rational decision-making. Only 6.3 percent of goalkeepers chose to stay in the center. The authors speculated that the goalkeepers' intuition for not staying in the center was because diving left or right was viewed as the norm. If the goalkeeper dived and was scored on, then they were thought to simply be unlucky. However, remaining in the center and being scored on would amplify negative feelings among spectators rooting for the goalkeeper's team. Why didn't they do *something*?!

MASTERLY INACTIVITY AND MEDICINE

Imagine you're a physician with a vocal patient demanding action, such as wanting a prescription or a test. The doctor may determine that the ideal approach is masterly inactivity—letting the body naturally cope with an ailment while monitoring the patient. And yet, according to Dr. François Mai, patients and society pay a huge price for the short-sighted approach of ordering unnecessary prescriptions and tests.

In a paper title "Masterly Inactivity: A Forgotten Precept"[6] in the *Canadian Medical Association Journal,* Mai argued that sometimes the best therapeutic option is just to wait and do nothing. Our bodies have natural coping mechanisms to combat disease and waiting can help the healing process. On the other hand, a patient may be worse off if unnecessary tests are undertaken, or medical procedures are poorly performed. According to a survey of over 2,000 doctors conducted by the *American Medical Association*, one-fifth of overall medical care was unnecessary, including 22 percent of prescription medication, 25 percent of tests, and 11 percent of procedures.[7] Common reasons for overtreatment were fear of malpractice, patient demands, and difficulty of accessing prior medical records. Society would be better off if more doctors practiced masterly inactivity.

MASTERLY INACTIVITY AND INVESTING

Now that we've seen the challenges—and successes—of masterly inactivity, let's turn to the world of investing. John (Jack) Bogle founded the Vanguard Group in 1975. He was the first to offer index mutual funds. Vanguard became known for its low-cost index funds. The firm had over $5 trillion in assets under management at the time of his passing in 2019. According to Bogle, "When you hear news that moves the market and your broker calls up and says, 'Do something,' just tell him my rule is 'Don't do something, just stand there!'"[8] Bogle referred to investing for the long-term in low-cost index funds as a "winning strategy."

Action bias suggests a tendency for investors to make decisions that will impact on their portfolio, such as reacting to news like a large drop in the stock market by immediately liquidating stocks and moving into cash. As investors, is there a potential price we pay for knee-jerk reactions and ignoring masterly inactivity? Let's look at the 10 worst days for the broad U.S. stock market index, the S&P 500, back to 1962. Imagine that after each of these 10 worst days, investors ignored masterly activity and sold their stock investments in a panic.

The worst 10 days occurred in 1987, 1997, 2008, and 2020. The one-day drops ranged from –20 percent to –7 percent. The median (or mid-range) daily loss was –8.9 percent. Panic selling would have locked in these losses. Alternatively, how would masterly inactivity have played out? Over the subsequent 10 trading days, in 7 of the 10 cases, the market was up, in one case the market was flat, and in only two cases did the market continue downward. In both those continued downturns the market corrected soon after the 10 trading days. Overall, the average median short-term rebound was 5.5 percent. So, related to extreme negative events, on average, masterly inactivity pays off.

It's one thing to get out of the market when facing a severe downturn, but it's another thing to know when to get back in. Some of the best days' returns occur shortly after the worst days. So here's another thought experiment. If we were on the sidelines and missed out on some of those bounce-backs, what would be the impact?

The average annualized returns (ignoring dividends) on the S&P 500 since 1962 was 7.2 percent. (Adding in dividends, annual total returns were around 10 percent.) If we exclude just the 10 best trading days, the average annual return drops to 5.8 percent—and that's just eliminating 10 days out of 15,170, or 0.07 percent of the sample! Excluding the 30 best days drops it down to 4.0 percent, and finally excluding the best 50 days drops the annualized price change to 2.6 percent, or just around one-third of returns since 1962.

Of course, masterly inactivity in investments doesn't mean *never* taking action. For example, you might have a minimum portfolio value needed to meet certain goals. In that case, a drop below a certain threshold might require risk reduction and liquidation of risky assets like stocks. The point is to actively monitor your portfolio and be *prepared* to take action, when necessary, but not in a knee-jerk manner. Have a plan in place, and think before you decide to jump. Often, doing nothing can be a winning strategy, just as it was for Quintus Fabius, Mohammed Ali, and Jack Bogle.

NOTES

1. "Masterly inactivity," Fine Dictionary, https://www.finedictionary.com/Masterly%20inactivity.html.
2. Accounts of Fabius are from Holmes, James, "Fabian Strategies, Then and Now," *War on the Rocks*, September 15, 2015, https://warontherocks.com/2015/09/fabian-strategies-then-and-now/; and Brand, Steele, "The Reluctant Warrior: How Fabius Maximus Became Rome's Greatest General by Avoiding Battle," Military History Now, January 29, 2020, https://militaryhistorynow.com/2020/01/29/the-reluctant-warrior-how-fabius-maximus-became-romes-greatest-general-by-avoiding-battle/.
3. Unless otherwise noted, accounts of Ali, Foreman, and their famous fight are from Anderson, Dave, "Ali Regains Title, Flooring Foreman," *New York Times*, October 30, 2014; and Mitchell, Kevin, "Rumble in the Jungle: The Night Ali Became King of the World Again," *Guardian*, October 29, 2014.
4. "George Foreman vs Muhammad Ali Stats," Boxstat.co, https://boxstat.co/bout/127824/george-foreman-vs-muhammad-ali.

5. Bar-Eli, Michael, Ofer Azar, Ilana Ritov, Yael Keidar-Levin, and Galit Schein, "Action Bias Among Elite Soccer Goalkeepers: The Case of Penalty Kicks," *Journal of Economic Psychology* 28, no. 5 (October 2007): 606–621, https://www.sciencedirect.com/science/article/abs/pii/S0167487006001048.

6. Mai, François, "Masterly Inactivity: A Forgotten Precept," *Canadian Medical Association Journal* 186, no. 4 (2014): 312, https://www.ncbi.nlm.nih.gov/pmc/articles/PMC3940585/.

7. Lyu, Heather, Tim Xu, Daniel Brotman, Brandan Mayer-Blackwell, Michol Cooper, Michael Daniel, Elizabeth C. Wick, Vikas Saini, Shannon Brownlee, and Martin A. Makary, "Overtreatment in the United States," *Plos One*, September 6, 2017, https://journals.plos.org/plosone/article?id=10.1371/journal.pone.0181970.

8. Lo, Andrew, and Stephen Foerster, *In Pursuit of the Perfect Portfolio: The Stories, Voices, and Key Insights of the Pioneers Who Shaped the Way We Invest*, Princeton, NJ: Princeton University Press, 2021.

CHAPTER THREE

OPPORTUNITY COST: WHY PAY BONILLA *NOT* TO PLAY BASEBALL

I f you're a long-suffering fan of the New York Mets, whose last World Series championship was in 1986, then you probably suffer a bit more when July 1 rolls around. That's the day, known in infamy as Bobby Bonilla Day, that commemorates the former Mets player. In 1999, Bonilla had the remaining year of his contract bought out for $5.9 million, and each July 1 he collects his annual $1.19 million paycheck. He's been receiving these checks since 2011, and will continue receiving them through 2035. That's a total of $29.8 million—*not* to play baseball. This sounds like the deal of the century, or even better. The contract that created the annuity stream was recently auctioned for $180,000—like a gift that keeps on giving. It's even been turned into a non-fungible token (NFT) known simply as "The Contract." The NFT website, promoted by his former agent, refers to it as "the most famous sports contract of all time."

How did Bobby Bonilla's agent, Dennis Gilbert, negotiate a contract that 25 years later allows a long-retired player to collect an annual salary that's more than what a third of the recent roster gets?[1] Perhaps a case can be made that it's the most *famous* sports contract of all time but does it make it the *greatest*? The secret to answering that question is understanding a simple three-letter initialism: TVM, which stands for time value of money. TVM (along with a related concept called opportunity cost) is probably *the* most important investing concept, and explains what drives the value of stocks and bonds. So let's step up to the plate, have some fun with the Bonilla contract, and swing for the (investing) fences!

BOBBY BONILLA, THE PLAYER

Roberto Martin Antonio (Bobby) Bonilla was born in the Bronx, New York, in 1963, of Afro–Puerto Rican heritage. His father was an electrician, and his mother a psychologist. His parents divorced when Bobby was eight. He grew up living with his mother, but his father lived close by. Bonilla was motivated to work hard on achieving a baseball career when he saw how hard his father worked, and the dangers of his job. Sports also helped Bonilla to stay away from drugs and gangs. His high school coach, Joe Levine, had a positive impact. Levine went above and beyond, including fundraising to help pay for Bonilla to be part of an all-star team that played in Scandinavia.

Bonilla was known for his neon smile.[2] He played his 1986 rookie season for the Chicago White Sox. Midseason, he was acquired by the

Pittsburgh Pirates. In 1987 he hit a superb .300 average. (In Major League Baseball, getting hits 3 out of 10 times is elite level. The batting average is usually around .250.) Bonilla finished in second place in the National League's Most Valuable Player (MVP) voting in 1990, and in third place in 1991. In 1992, the Mets signed him to the most lucrative contract in the Major League, $5 million a year for five years.

With expectations sky-high, he disappointed early. He hit only .130 in May and .249 for the season. On the defensive side, Bonilla was often prone to errors. Legendary Los Angeles Dodger broadcaster Vin Scully commented about Bonilla, "Sometimes it seems like he's playing underwater."[3] Fans seethed at his high salary and underperformance. Bonilla also had run-ins with the media. His next three seasons were better, but he was traded in 1995. In 1997, Bonilla's new team, the Florida Marlins, surprised pundits and won the World Series. In 1998 he was traded to the Los Angeles Dodgers and, after the season, back to the Mets. He signed a two-year contract.

But in 1999, he agreed to have his 2000 contract bought out in return for a deferred salary or annuity stream of payments. He played for Atlanta the next season. In 2001, the St. Louis Cardinals became the last team he played for, at age 38. After 16 years in the Major League, Bonilla retired with a career batting average of .279; 2,010 hits; 1,084 runs; 1,173 runs batted in; and 287 home runs. During his career, he appeared on six All-Star teams and received three Silver Slugger awards.

DENNIS GILBERT AND DEFERRED SALARY CONTRACTS

Bonilla's 2000 salary buyout was converted into what's known as a deferred salary contract. This is an agreement made between the player and the owner to have money owed to the player deferred and paid at a later date. It's often in the form of an annuity, or stream of equal payments. The benefit to the baseball team's owner is that the money that would have been paid to the player can be used for other purposes, such as compensating existing players more in order to retain them, or acquiring new players. From the player's perspective, the deferred salary allows the player to have a secure revenue stream in the future, even after they have retired. The amount of each payment is negotiated and stipulated in a contract agreement. That agreement also reflects the promised rate of return to compensate the player for agreeing to the deferred salary.

Bonilla's agent, Dennis Gilbert, was a former minor league baseball player and a successful insurance professional. Gilbert became an agent in 1980 by forming Beverly Hills Sports Council.[4] The firm represented baseball stars Barry Bonds, José Canseco, George Brett, Mike Piazza, Brent Saberhagen, and Danny Tartabull, among others. Bonilla's 1991 contract for $29 million, during his first stints with the Mets, was the richest in baseball at the time. Chicago White Sox chairman Jerry Reinsdorf commented, "As a player representative, Dennis was always one of the toughest negotiators we faced."[5]

Gilbert remarked about the famous contract, "From the first day Bobby became a client, all our conversations revolved around saving money for the future. A lot of my friends [from the minor leagues] who went to the big leagues were retired and broke. It's just taking money out of the bank today and putting it in the bank tomorrow."[6] When Gilbert presented Bonilla with the deferred contract idea, "Bobby always asked a lot of questions. He was very curious about everything. Being in the insurance business, I was very persuasive, and Bobby actually got it. He was very much on board with it, way more so than many of my other clients."[7]

TIME VALUE OF MONEY (TVM) AND BONILLA'S CONTRACT

Simply stated, TVM means that a dollar today is worth more than a dollar tomorrow. Having money today matters more than having money tomorrow (or some other time in the future) because you can invest the money today and have it grow. The crux of TVM is the opportunity cost. It's expressed as an interest rate percentage that reflects the expected return you could get by investing the money. For example, if you know you can invest that dollar today and have it grow by 8 percent over the next year, then you would expect to have $1.08 a year from now. We call it an opportunity cost because you're giving up the opportunity to spend that dollar today. You'd only be willing to do so if you expect to get more than a dollar later.

Bonilla gave up the opportunity to earn, and spend, $5.9 million in 2000. He was only willing to do so in return for receiving more cash in the future. According to the contract, Bonilla's guaranteed return or opportunity cost was 8 percent. That's what he required in order to give up his 2000 salary. On the other side of the same coin, Mets' owner Fred Wilpon was willing to provide Bonilla with that guaranteed return of 8 percent, and at the same time save paying him $5.9 million in 2000. According to the contract, Wilpon agreed to provide Bonilla a stream of payments of $1,193,248.20 starting in 2011, and for each of 25 years through 2035, when Bonilla turns 72, for a total of over $29.8 million.

Let's look at what's behind that precise annual payment to see how TVM works. Bonilla gave up his $5.9 million salary in 2000, for something in return: a promise of 25 annual payments of $1.193 million from 2011

27

through 2035. For that first promised payment in 2011, that was worth an equivalent $511,764 to Bonilla in 2000. That's the amount Bonilla could have invested for 11 years with a guaranteed annual return of 8 percent, growing to $1.193 million in 2011. For that second promised payment in 2012, that was worth an equivalent $473,855 to Bonilla in 2000. That's the amount Bonilla could have invested for 12 years with a guaranteed annual return of 8 percent, growing to $1.193 million in 2012. If we add the equivalent amounts, known as present values (as of the year 2000), of all 25 future payments, that gives us precisely $5.9 million.

THE OPPORTUNITY COST

Now let's return to the opportunity cost. We can also think of it as an alternative use of the money. Without knowing the conversation that went on between Bonilla's agent, Gilbert, and the Mets' owner, Wilpon, we can make an educated guess at how the 8 percent was arrived at. Let's go back to the summer of 2000. Long-term Treasury bonds were yielding 5.9 percent. Historical average annual compound returns of large U.S. stocks (between 1928 and 1999) were 11.9 percent.

With that in mind, an opportunity cost of 8 percent was not outrageous. Bonilla could have used the $5.9 million to invest in Treasury bonds with no risk, but a lower return, 5.9 percent. He could have invested in stocks with more risk, but with a higher expected (but not guaranteed) return, say around 10 or 12 percent. Or he could have invested in some combination of the two perhaps. It was astute for Gilbert and Bonilla to negotiate a guaranteed rate above the going risk-free Treasury rate at the time. So, considering risk and expected return, a guaranteed 8 percent rate sounds like Goldilocks's just-right porridge.

Now let's look at this from the perspective of Wilpon. By not having to pay Bonilla's salary in 2000, he was able to make other deals to help the team, and consequently to potentially increase ticket sales, as well as enhance the long-term franchise value. With cash freed up from Bonilla's salary deferral, the Mets were able to sign such players as Derek Bell, Todd Zeile, and Mike Hampton. The short-term payoff was that the Mets won the National League title in 2000. We can speculate that this might not have happened if the Mets paid Bonilla $5.9 million that year.

"THE CONTRACT" NTF

Gilbert kept his copy of the famous Bonilla contract, and like a collector of rare baseball cards, it paid off decades later. In August 2022, the contract was auctioned off in the collectibles marketplace Goldin.[8] Within 50 minutes, bids went from below $23,000 to $180,000, the winning bid. In addition to the contract, the lucky winner received a 30-minute Zoom call with Bonilla, another with Gilbert, a signed baseball, a game-used bat from Bonilla's personal collection, and a Bobby Bonilla contract NFT. The NFT was like a virtual baseball card.

Bonilla, Gilbert, and another sports agent, Rick Thurman, tried to capitalize on the NFT craze by issuing NFTs to commemorate the famous contract. They capped the number of available NFTs at 1,193, part of the infamous dollar amount that Bonilla receives each year. The NFTs were only available for sale until the day before Bobby Bonilla Day in 2023.

SHOHEI OHTANI'S CONTRACT

Here's another baseball contract with a nifty TVM story. In late 2023, Japanese professional baseball player Shohei Ohtani signed a contract that was trumpeted as the "biggest deal in sports history."[9] Like Babe Ruth,

Ohtani was the rare player who excelled as both a pitcher and a hitter. He was regarded as a once-in-a-generation player. The story was that Ohtani signed with the Los Angeles Dodgers for a 10-year $700 million deal. While $700 million is an incredible sum, now that we understand time value of money, what's the contract *really* worth? There seemed to be confusion in the media on that point.

Like Bonilla's deferred salary contract, most of what Ohtani was to get was after he retired. In fact, during his 10-year playing contract, from 2024 through 2034, he was only going to receive $2 million each year, for a total of $20 million. That gave the Dodgers financial flexibility to build a solid team around him. Not to worry that Ohtani would only draw a miserly salary of $2 million a year—he made a lot more than that through endorsements, so he didn't need the cash. The remaining $680 million of the contract was to be paid to him between 2034 and 2043.

Muddying the story, Major League Baseball (MLB) has a Competitive Balance Tax, also known as a luxury tax, applicable if a team spends over a certain threshold on total salaries. To determine the amount of tax to charge, MLB estimated what the salary would be if Ohtani's contract amount was paid over the 10-year term of the contract rather than the actual 20 years. According to the *Wall Street Journal*, the amount of Ohtani's contract for luxury tax purposes was actually $460 million, and not $700 million.[10] That lower number was purported to represent an MLB-determined amount equivalent to Ohtani receiving $46 million each year of the 10-year contract. The $460 million total amount was simply adding up $46 million a year for 10 years.

To get the $46 million a year equivalent, the MLB luxury tax procedures dictated it use a discount rate of 4.43 percent, which was the prevailing federal midterm rate (determined by the Internal Revenue Service) as of October 2023. That happened to be close to the 10-year Treasury yield at the time, which we can use as a more intuitive proxy for the technical federal midterm rate. If we consider that 10-year stream of annual $46 million payments, and use the 4.43 percent discount rate, we can do a present value calculation of the contract. That works out to around $365 million. We could also have arrived at that same present value amount based on the actual stream of payments: $2 million annually for 10 years, followed by $68 million for 10 years. Another interpretation of the $365 million: if Ohtani received that money as a lump sum payment, and if he invested it at 4.43 percent, he could pay himself a stream of $2 million annually for the next 10 years followed by $68 million for the subsequent 10 years.

There's another TVM issue the media overlooked. The 4.43 percent discount rate wasn't Ohtani's true opportunity cost. Rather, it was an arbitrary IRS number. Recall that in Bonilla's, case, the opportunity cost of 8.0 percent was explicit in the contract, but not so for Ohtani. When Bonilla signed his contract, long-term Treasury yields were about 1.5 percent higher than when Ohtani signed. Let's suppose Ohtani's actual opportunity cost was around 6.5 percent, which like in Bonilla's case was about 2 percent above the long-term Treasury yield. Using that 6.5 percent opportunity cost as the discount rate, the present value of Ohtani's contract drops to $275 million. That's still a lot of money, but a far cry from the headline amount of $700 million.

Here's one more wrinkle. It's quite feasible that Ohtani may envision retirement in his home country of Japan. For decades, Japan had much lower interest rates than most countries, including the U.S. In the fall of 2023, long-term Japanese government bond yields were just below 1 percent. So adding 2 percent as in the previous examples, that would result in Ohtani's opportunity cost of 3 percent. Using that as the discount, the contract's present value is around $450 million. The lower the opportunity cost, the higher the present value.

TVM AND VALUING BONDS AND STOCKS

So what can we take away from this? Back to Bonilla. If we understand TVM, then Bonilla's deferred salary contract probably wasn't the deal of the century, as is sometimes claimed. But it was an attractive deal in terms of the opportunity cost as of 2000, relative to the risk-free rate at the time. Bonilla gave up the use of money, and Wilpon fairly compensated Bonilla for giving up the use of money. In return, Wilpon got something of value when the Mets won the National League title in 2000.

TVM has broader applications, so it's a very important tool. For example, what a bond is worth today can be determined by TVM applications. A bond's yield to maturity is just like the opportunity cost or guaranteed return that Bonilla received. If we know that, then a bond's price is simply the present value of the stream of coupon payments—an annuity just like Bonilla is receiving—plus the present value of the face value of the bond, received at the time of the bond's maturity.

Another example of TVM is the application to stocks. Think of a company like Walmart, which has consistently paid dividends for decades. Those dividends have consistently grown over time. The value of Walmart's stock today can be estimated by applying a particular present value formula (known as a growing perpetuity). We could estimate what future dividends Walmart might pay out, and then find their present values. Adding up those present values tells us what the stock should be selling for. Broadly speaking, the value of *any* security is just the present value of expected cashflows.

When owning a stock, it matters when we anticipate that the company is going to be generating profits—according to TVM, the sooner the better. It also matters what that opportunity cost is, which in turn often depends on the overall level of interest rates. If interest rates are really low, like in 2009 to 2016, and 2020 to 2022, then there's not as much of a gap between distant and near profits. That's often when so-called growth stocks with high expected earnings growth tend to do well. It all comes back to TVM.

CONNECTION TO A FRAUDSTER

There's an interesting footnote to the Bonilla story. It may also explain why Wilpon agreed to guaranteeing Bonilla a rate of 8 percent. It turns out that Wilpon and his family were heavily invested in a fund that was providing steady annual returns of over 14 percent between January 1990 and June 1999. The fund was managed by a well-respected investment professional named Bernie Madoff. As Wilpon was to find out, the fund was actually based on a Ponzi scheme, one of the greatest swindles of all time, and the apparent returns weren't real. More on Madoff in our next story.

So if you're a Mets fan, perhaps a better understanding of TVM takes a bit of the sting out of the next Bobby Bonilla Day. And the one after that. And the one after that. And the one after that. . .

NOTES

1. "New York Mets 2022 Payroll," Spotrac, https://www.spotrac.com/mlb/new-york-mets/payroll/.
2. Biographical information is from Souder, Mark, "Bobby Bonilla," Society for American Baseball Research, June 1, 2017, https://sabr.org/bioproj/person/bobby-bonilla/.
3. Mitchell, Houston, "Here are Some of Vin Scully's Most Memorable Calls and Quotes," *Los Angeles Times*, August 3, 2022, https://ca.sports.yahoo.com/news/vin-scullys-most-memorable-calls-045918616.html.

4. "Former Agent Gilbert Joins White Sox," AP News, November 28, 2000, https://apnews.com/article/913c2b807a1fbeee0ccd85634b7623bf.

5. Ibid.

6. Heyman, Jon, "Bobby Bonilla's Old Agents Selling NFT's to Celebrate Infamous Contract," *New York Post*, July 1, 2022, https://nypost.com/2022/07/01/bobby-bonillas-old-agents-selling-nfts-to-celebrate-contract/.

7. Verlander, Ben, "Meet the Mastermind Behind 'Bobby Bonilla Day' and a Most Unusual MLB Contract," Fox Sports, July 2, 2021, https://www.foxsports.com/stories/mlb/bobby-bonilla-day-mets-dennis-gilbert-mlb-ben-verlander.

8. Hajducky, Dan, "Bobby Bonilla's Infamous New York Mets Contract Sold for $180K at Auction," ESPN, August 7, 2022, https://www.espn.com/mlb/story/_/id/34361023/bobby-bonilla-infamous-new-york-mets-contract-sold-180k-auction.

9. Wexler, Sarah, "$700M Stunner: Ohtani to Dodgers on Biggest Deal in Sports History," MLB.com, December 11, 2023, https://www.mlb.com/dodgers/news/shohei-ohtani-contract-with-dodgers.

10. Demos, Telis, "Ohtani's Deal Features Powell as MVP," *Wall Street Journal*, December 23, 2023.

CHAPTER FOUR

MADOFF'S PONZI SCHEME: TRUST, BUT VERIFY BEFORE INVESTING

I n late 2008, a decade-long ordeal that changed Harry Markopolos's life had finally ended. He no longer had to check underneath the chassis and wheel wells of his car for explosives before turning the key. He didn't mince words about his nemesis, Bernie Madoff. "He would show up at weddings, funerals. At funerals, he would put his arm round the grieving widow and say, 'I'll take care of you' and of course he did, he'd wipe her out. He was hunting at social occasions. Everybody thought of him as nice uncle Bernie. But he was a predator."[1] This is a story about perseverance, trust, investment returns that looked too good to be true, and the largest Ponzi scheme ever.

BERNIE MADOFF

Bernard (Bernie) Madoff[2] was born on April 29, 1938, and grew up in the middle-class town of Laurelton, near New York City. Madoff wasn't a standout in high school, but was remembered as a bright student who didn't work too hard. In 1956, a few months before graduating, Madoff met Ruth Alpern, class of 1958, and they got married three years later. Madoff went to the University of Alabama for one year, then to Hofstra University on Long Island. In 1960, he graduated with a degree in political science. By that time, Madoff had passed the Series 7 exam, obtaining a license that allowed all types of securities trading.

In November 1960, Madoff founded Bernard L. Madoff Investment Securities (BMIS), with a $50,000 loan from his father-in-law, Sol Alpern. BMIS was a broker-dealer firm registered with the Securities and Exchange Commission (SEC). Brokers act as agents, executing trades on behalf of clients. Dealers trade on their own account. Madoff wasn't the first family member in the business—his mother was. Shortly after he started his firm, the SEC forced the closure of a broker-dealer firm registered in his mother's name and listed at his parents' home address. While BMIS operated essentially as a broker executing trades for others, Madoff was building a separate, shadowy investment business. This one was hidden from the SEC. He developed a reputation as a savvy investor thanks in part to the bragging and promotion of his father-in-law.

In 1962, Sol Alpern hired Frank Avellino and Michael Bienes to work for his accounting firm, Alpern & Heller. They became major recruiters of clients for the BMIS side-business over the next three decades. They eventually brought in over $400 million from 3,200 people. Madoff paid

Avellino and Bienes for the referrals. Avellino and Bienes were acting as money managers and investment advisors but weren't licensed as such. Madoff's brother, Peter, a lawyer, joined BMIS in 1970. The 1970s saw an ascent in Madoff's social status. The social circle and the investors included friends such as the Wilpons, the future owners of the New York Mets.

HARRY MARKOPOLOS

Harry Markopolos[3] was born in Erie, Pennsylvania, in 1956, the year Madoff graduated from high school. Markopolos was the oldest of three children. His parent ran Greek-American restaurants.[4] In the seventh and eighth grades, he was having major problems in algebra and needed a tutor. And yet, later in life, Markopolos was to become a math whiz and a quantitative analyst. He later observed, "I speak the language of numbers. Numbers can tell an entire story. I can see the beauty, the humor, and sometimes the tragedy of numbers."[5]

Markopolos's father and two uncles owned a chain of 12 Arthur Treacher's Fish & Chips restaurants. Markopolos became the assistant controller, and eventually the manager of four of the units in Baltimore County.[6] He carefully tracked inventory relative to sales. One time he noticed a particularly high discrepancy between inventory and sales at one of the restaurants. His ability to understand numbers allowed him to catch the employee who was stealing food.

Markopolos graduated from Loyola College in Baltimore in 1981 with a bachelor of business administration. He worked as the district manager at ATFC Finance Corporation in Towson, Maryland, for seven years. He was also a part-time reservist for the Army National Guard.[7]

A former banker for Markopolos's father formed a brokerage firm, Makefield Securities. Markopolos's father bought a 25 percent interest in the firm and Markopolos went to work there in 1987.[8] His first day as a licensed broker was October 19, 1987. Known later as Black Monday (see Chapter 15), that day turned out to be the worst in U.S. stock market history. Stocks dropped by an average of 22 percent.

In early 1988, Markopolos was promoted to over-the-counter (OTC) trader, making a market in 18 Nasdaq stocks. At the time, the two major stock exchanges were the New York Stock Exchange (NYSE) and the American Stock Exchange. Trading on those two exchanges occurred in the traditional face-to-face manner on the floor of each exchange. In contrast, OTC markets were decentralized, with trading outside the traditional stock exchanges. In 1971, the National Association of Security Dealers formed the Nasdaq Stock Market, which brought traders together through an automated system. Stock quotes were originally provided through cathode-ray-tube video display terminals and primitive desktop computers.[9]

Markopolos traded regularly with Madoff Securities. This was the first time he ever heard the name Madoff. He knew the firm to be a large, well-respected stock dealer, a "market maker" that was prepared to buy or sell certain stocks at any time. While Markopolos encountered massive trading violations in the OTC market on an hourly basis, he never recalled a single incident in which Madoff brokers were dishonest.[10]

CLOSE CALL

In 1992, Madoff's Ponzi scheme almost came crashing down. The SEC received a tip from two customers of the accounting firm of Frank Avellino and Michael Bienes—Avellino & Bienes (A&B).[11] A&B was the successor accounting firm started by Madoff's father-in-law. In 1981, the firm had been sued for shoddy audit work. The current concern was that A&B was illegally selling unregistered securities. The firm was soliciting selected customers to provide loans to A&B. According to a letter received by a potential investor, A&B then invested "with one particular Wall Street Broker (the same company since we first started doing business over 25 years ago)."

According to the A&B promotional letter, this unnamed broker invested in blue-chip stocks and also protected the portfolio from losses. Those who provided loans would receive quarterly interest payments at a compound rate of 14.1 percent annually. (At the time, risk-free Treasury bills were yielding around 5 percent.) The loans were said to be 100 percent safe: "At no time is a trade made that puts your money at risk. In over 20 years there has never been a losing transaction."

The SEC contacted Avellino. He admitted he borrowed money from friends, relatives, and referrals and invested in real estate and "some securities." A Ponzi scheme takes in money by offering exceptional returns with little or no risk, and makes payouts to early investors from some of the money brought in from later investors, without making any actual investments. Although the A&B return promise had all the hallmarks of a Ponzi scheme, the SEC focused on the apparent violation of selling securities to the public without registration. A&B's lawyer, Ira (Ike) Sorkin, called the SEC to report "nothing inappropriate is going on here. [Avellino and Bienes] are former IRS [Internal Revenue Service] agents and I'll bring them in to testify."

Avellino and Bienes then went to the SEC office to give testimonies. According to Avellino, here's how things worked. After receiving the loan, "I now write a check from my checking account, send it to Bernard L. Madoff on behalf of Avellino & Bienes. Like any other brokerage account, he takes the cash, gives me credit for it, and goes out and executes whatever position he has to."[12] A&B had over $400 million of customer money invested through Madoff. According to Avellino, A&B and its predecessor firms had referred clients to invest in Madoff's fund since 1962. This admission suggests that, despite Madoff's later insistence that his Ponzi scheme started in the early 1990s, it might have lasted for 45 years before collapsing.

The SEC then conducted a brief examination of Madoff's business, including a one-day site visit, to verify certain security positions. Depository Trust Company (DTC) was a firm that processed and settled security transactions. Rather than gathering data directly from DTC, the inexperienced SEC agents sought the transaction information from Madoff. No surprise that Madoff's phony data perfectly matched information in client statements. The SEC inspectors walked out of the visit impressed with Madoff. One later concluded that Madoff was "a pioneer in the industry . . . wow."[13]

The SEC decided to shut down A&B for selling unregistered securities and return the money, by then $441 million, to investors. Price Waterhouse was sent in to audit A&B's financial statements. The auditors found records lacking. But Avellino and Bienes refused to cooperate further. Sorkin, their lawyer, later admitted to Price Waterhouse auditors that they were auditing phantom books. Avellino and Bienes were permanently barred from selling securities without registration and were fined a total of $350,000. The SEC was pleased with the outcome. Sorkin defended his clients by characterizing the infraction of the sale of unregistered securities as "technical violations." According to the *Wall Street Journal*, an SEC representative indicated that "the returns appeared to have been generated legitimately. 'Right now, there's nothing to indicate fraud.'"[14] It was definitely a close call for Madoff. Undeterred, over the next 16 years, the Ponzi scheme would grow by billions of dollars.

THE CHASE IS ON

In 1988, Markopolos went to work for a former client, Greg Hryb, who had started his own asset management firm, Darien Capital Management.[15] Markopolos started as an assistant portfolio manager. While a relatively small firm, by the early 1990s Darien was managing over a billion dollars.

After three years, Markopolos moved from Darien, Connecticut, to Boston, joining Rampart Investment Management Company, a firm with almost $9 billion in assets under management. Clients were institutional investors such as pension funds. His role was derivatives portfolio manager. (Derivatives are assets whose value was derived from another asset.)

In 1999, Frank Casey, a marketing representative at Rampart, was looking to expand the company's product offering. He was trying to build a low-risk fund that provided consistent returns. Markopolos referred him to an acquaintance at another firm, Access International Advisors. The acquaintance had heard of a hedge fund manager who was consistently providing clients with returns of between 1 and 2 percent per month. (Hedge funds are marketed toward wealthy clients and typically invested in more complex strategies compared with simply buying stocks.) Casey and Markopolos met with Access's CEO, René-Thierry de la Villehuchet, a French nobleman, to find out more about this manager. De la Villehuchet was at first reluctant to give them the manager's name: "If I do, he might not give me any capacity."[16] Eventually he relented. It was Bernie Madoff.

Madoff's strategy was marketed as a "split-strike conversion." That strategy essentially involved two parts. The first part was buying a basket of blue-chip stocks, like those that made up the Dow Jones Industrial Average. The second part involved guarding against losses or hedging by buying derivative securities. This part was like buying insurance for downside protection. The strategy was well known on Wall Street, but typically didn't provide the kind of returns Madoff was getting. Back at Rampart after their meeting, Casey and Markopolos met with the managing director, Dave Farley. Farley was impressed with the revenue stream Madoff was able to provide to Access. Could Rampart develop something similar to what Madoff was doing? It only took Markopolos five minutes to review the figures to determine Madoff's numbers were bogus. He would spend the next decade proving his case. "We weren't looking for a crime; we simply wanted to see how he made his numbers dance."[17]

SEC SUBMISSIONS

After almost six months of investigation, in May 2000, Markopolos, with the help of a small team of investigators he informally stitched together, had enough evidence to go to the SEC. Markopolos's eight-page report began, "In 25 minutes or less, I will prove one of three scenarios regarding Madoff's hedge fund operation: (1) They are incredibly talented and/or lucky and I'm an idiot for wasting your time; (2) the returns are real, but they are coming from some process other than the one being advertised, in which case an investigation is in order; or (3) the entire case is nothing more than a Ponzi scheme."[18]

Markopolos included six red flags that raised serious questions about the legitimacy of Madoff's hedge fund business. These included how the returns couldn't have come from the purported strategy; how there weren't enough derivative securities in existence to provide the purported hedging; and how it wasn't possible to obtain such consistent returns. He also pointed out that Madoff didn't allow outside auditors.

Shortly after sending his submission to the SEC, Markopolos met with two Boston SEC representatives to discuss his Madoff concerns. He left the meeting with the impression that they didn't understand. He "walked out of the meeting feeling dejected. . . . I didn't think [the SEC administrator] had a clue."[19]

Markopolos made a second SEC submission to the SEC Boston office in March 2001, and a third submission to the same office in October 2005.[20] Not mincing words, Markopolos titled the third submission "The World's Largest Hedge Fund Is a Fraud." In June 2007, he made yet another submission to the SEC, but by this time it appeared the SEC had effectively closed its investigation into Madoff.[21] Markopolos attempted to send a version of the 2005 submission to the SEC's Office of Risk Assessment in April 2008, but it wasn't received.[22]

THE WORD IS OUT

In the meantime, reporters were raising alarm bells in a more public fashion. Markopolos's co-worker Frank Casey was speaking at a hedge fund conference in Europe sponsored by a hedge fund industry publication, *MARHedge*.[23] That's where he met *MARHedge*'s editor-in-chief, Michael Ocrant. Casey won a dinner bet by claiming he could name a hedge fund manager running billions of dollars that Ocrant hadn't heard of. Of course, he was referring to Madoff. After Casey told Ocrant what they knew about Madoff, Ocrant agreed to investigate and write a story about Madoff's hedge fund business.

The story appeared in May 2001, with a provocative title: "Madoff Tops Charts; Skeptics Ask How."[24] Ocrant had interviewed more than a dozen industry experts, of course including Markopolos. Most were "baffled by the way the firm has obtained such consistent, nonvolatile returns month after month and year after year." They noted Madoff's "seemingly astonishing ability to time the market and move to cash in the underlying securities before market conditions turn negative; and the related ability to buy and sell the underlying stocks without noticeably affecting the market. In addition, experts ask why no one has been able to duplicate similar returns using the strategy." Ocrant may as well have been yelling, "Liar, liar, pants on fire!"

Six days later, the Madoff story got a major boost in the prestigious *Barron's* magazine.[25] Reporter Erin Arvedlund's article was titled "Don't Ask, Don't Tell: Bernie Madoff Attracts Skeptics in 2001." (She later wrote a book about the Madoff affair.[26]) Many of her observations were similar to Ocrant's. She quoted a satisfied investor who noted, "Even knowledgeable people can't really tell you what he's doing." She also quoted another fund manager who inherited a pool of assets that included an investment in Madoff's fund. "When [Madoff] couldn't explain how they were up or down in a particular month, I pulled the money out."

After Markopolos submitted his 2005 report to the Boston SEC office, he contacted the New York SEC office, identifying himself as the anonymous whistleblower.[27] There was still no apparent interest in the case. At this point, Markopolos began to fear for his safety since more people knew what he was trying to uncover, and there were billions of dollars at stake. He began looking over his shoulder and started carrying a Model 642 Smith and Wesson revolver.[28]

SWIMMING NAKED

Despite the public skepticism that started in 2001, Madoff continued to take in billions of dollars for a further seven years. Madoff's eventual downfall would have come as no surprise to John Kenneth Galbraith, one of the most influential economists of his time. He was an advisor to Democratic presidents from Franklin Delano Roosevelt to Lyndon Johnson. After Enron's collapse in 2001 and around the time of a tech-stock meltdown and economic downturn, Galbraith famously remarked, "Recessions catch what the auditors miss." The recession brought on by the 2007–2009 financial crisis is what brought down Madoff. This was in spite of all of Markopolos's detective work, which no one would listen to. And as Warren Buffett memorably quipped, "You don't find out who's been swimming naked until the tide goes out." Madoff swam naked for decades.

In the summer of 2007, a global financial crisis emerged that morphed into a global recession. The U.S. housing market "bubble" started to burst, with spillover effects like the breakdown of mortgage-related investment products. Storied investment institutions like Lehman Brothers were forced into bankruptcy, while Merrill Lynch barely avoided bankruptcy by agreeing to a takeover by Bank of America. As stock markets were crashing, investors—particularly those who had borrowed money to make investments—were liquidating positions. These investors included those who had money with Madoff. Ponzi schemes are fueled by money coming in. They unravel when more money goes out.

On December 10, 2008, Madoff supposedly confessed to his two sons that the hedge fund was a fraud. The following morning, after being tipped off by Madoff's sons, two FBI agents knocked on Madoff's door, asking if there was an innocent explanation. Shaking his head, he replied, "There is no innocent explanation."[29]

SENTENCING

On June 29, 2009, in the United States District Court for the Southern District of New York, the honorable Judge Denny Chin was about to speak. He was presiding over the *U.S. v. Madoff* case. He asked 71-year-old Madoff to stand. In March, Madoff had pled guilty to 11 counts of securities fraud, investment advisor fraud, wire and mail fraud, money laundering, making false statements, perjury, filing false documents with the SEC, and theft from employee benefits funds.[30] It was now the much-anticipated sentencing day. Would Madoff spend the rest of his life in prison?

The United States attorneys spoke first. They described the Government's Sentencing Memorandum that they had provided to Chin. The sentencing guideline was based on two factors: Madoff's criminal history, and the calculated offense level. Madoff was a Category I, first-time offender. That was the only bit of good news for him. Based on the financial losses, the number of victims, Madoff's role as organizer of the scheme, and other factors, the offense level was 52. It didn't get much higher than that.

Since no individual charge carried a maximum term of life imprisonment, the guideline calculation was the maximum sentences for all of the 11 counts added together. That total was 150 years in prison. Chin made it clear that he wasn't bound by the guideline. He noted that the probation department recommended a 50-year sentence. Before deciding, he asked to hear from other various parties: some of the victims, who had requested to speak; Madoff's lawyer, Ira Sorkin (this was the same Sorkin who in 1992 represented Madoff fund feeders Avellino and Bienes, and had told SEC investigators that "Nothing inappropriate is going on here"[31]); Madoff himself; and finally the government's assistant attorney, Lisa Baroni.

Some of the victims shared harrowing stories, like having their life savings "drop right out from under your nose." One victim, a prison guard, commented, "I'll know what Mr. Madoff's experience will be and will know he is in prison in much the same way he imprisoned us as well as others." One lamented the failure of the government, and the SEC in particular. Another observed that Madoff had shown no remorse. And finally, another victim cited the seriousness of Madoff's crimes by quoting Dante's *The Divine Comedy* and the eighth circle of hell: "[Dante] placed perpetrators of fraud in the lowest depths of hell, even below those who had committed violent acts."

Then it was Sorkin's turn. He conceded, "We represent a deeply flawed individual, but we represent, your Honor, a human being." He played up the legitimate trading business that Madoff had built, with 200 employees, and at one point accounting for almost 10 percent of all NYSE transactions. Madoff helped revolutionize the investments industry. Sorkin asked for a sentence of 12 years. His request was based on Madoff's health, family history, and life expectancy, "just short, based on the statistics that we have, of a life sentence."

Next, Madoff spoke. "I cannot offer you an excuse for my behavior . . . and I don't ask any forgiveness. Although I may not have intended any harm, I did a great deal of harm. I believed when I started this problem, this crime, that it was something I would be able to work my way out of, but that became impossible. As hard as I tried, the deeper I dug myself into a hole. I made a terrible mistake. . . . I made an error of judgment. . . . Nothing I can say will correct the things I have done. . . . I apologize to my victims. I will turn and face you. I am sorry. I know that doesn't help you."

On behalf of the government, Assistant Attorney Lisa Baroni spoke. "This defendant carried out a fraud of unprecedented proportion over the course of more than a generation. For more than 20 years, he stole ruthlessly and without remorse. . . . The defendant continued his fraud scheme until the very end, when he knew the scheme was days away from collapse. . . . And even at that point, rather than turning himself in, he tried to take the last of his victims' money. He prepared $173 million in checks that he planned to give to his family, his friends, and some preferred clients." She concluded with a call to ensure Madoff would spend the rest of his life in jail.

Then it was Chin's time to speak. He disagreed with Madoff's claim that the fraud only began in the 1990s. It was clear to Chin that it began earlier. Chin recognized that there was some dispute in terms of the actual dollar loss. However, for sentencing purposes, "the offense level 52 is calculated by using a chart for loss amount that only goes up to $400 million. By any measure, the loss figure here is many times that amount. It's off the chart by many fold."

Chin then considered mitigating factors, particularly common in white-collar fraud cases. "I would expect to see letters from family and friends and colleagues. But not a single letter has been submitted attesting to Mr. Madoff's good deeds or good character or civic or charitable activities. The absence of such support is telling."

Finally, Chin agreed with Sorkin's life expectancy analysis. Given that Madoff was 71 years old, he recognized that "any sentence above 20 or 25 years would be largely, if not entirely, symbolic." But Chin then contended that the symbolism of a long sentence was important, for three reasons. First, for retribution: "Mr. Madoff's crimes were extraordinarily evil." Second, for deterrence: "The strongest possible message must be sent to those who would engage in similar conduct." And third, for the victims. Chin was particularly struck by one story of a man who invested his family's life savings with Madoff, only to die two weeks later. "The widow went in to see Mr. Madoff. He put his arm around her, as she described it, and in a kindly manner told her not to worry, the money is safe with me." Uncle Bernie, indeed.

TOO GOOD TO BE TRUE

Is there a tell, like in poker, that can help us identify fraudsters? Madoff was well respected in the investment community, and a true technology innovator. He was also highly regarded among the Jewish community. He represented an exclusive club that everyone wanted to join. But there were tells. Madoff was a liar. While his brother, Peter, had a law degree, Bernie didn't. And yet he created a myth that he had a law degree. He even indicated on the company website that he founded the company "in 1960, soon after leaving law school."[32] There was Madoff's incessant penchant for secrecy. And of course, there were the incredible returns.

Madoff had to be a clever fraudster to get away with his Ponzi scheme for as long as he did. His purported returns weren't the highest among hedge funds. Unlike risk-free Treasury bill returns, there were occasional down months—although never any down quarters. But his fund's return-to-risk measure, commonly known as the Sharpe ratio, was off the charts. Imagine a graph of a fund's value over time that shows an upward line at an almost perfect 45-degree angle. This is the stuff of every investor's dreams. But it's not a real-life phenomenon. It's simply too good to be true.

Sometimes we overlook what risk *really* is. The conventional industry performance benchmark, the Sharpe ratio, measures risk as the volatility or standard deviation of returns. Think of that practically perfect 45-degree line, with almost no volatility. As part of a routine examination of a leading hedge fund in 2003, the SEC uncovered a revealing internal email. The hedge fund manager proposed that his firm should entirely divest from Madoff's fund: "Sure it's the best risk-adjusted fund in the portfolio," he noted. However, he then cautioned, "If one assumes that there's more risk than standard deviation would indicate, the investment loses its luster in a hurry."[33] How prophetic.

Sometimes it's like one side of our brain hopes to see something, and so the other side of our brain convinces us a fallacy is true. We want excellent, steady investment returns. We want to see a 45-degree angle on a risk-return chart. It's almost surely a fallacy, but if we don't ask any questions, then maybe it won't go away. We're hardwired with behavioral biases like overoptimism. It takes a lot of work and discipline to overcome these biases.

How can we do that? In 1986, when Ronald Reagan was preparing for talks with Mikhail Gorbachev, his Russian affairs advisor, Suzanne Massie, suggested Reagan learn a few Russian proverbs. Reagan's favorite was *Doveryai no preryai*—"trust, but verify." Gorbachev was annoyed that Reagan used it at every meeting.[34] Thousands of clients trusted Madoff. Some lost their life savings. Markopolos didn't trust Madoff, but he did try to verify. That's when he realized that Madoff was a fraud.

HISTORY RHYMES

We keep wanting to believe there are quick roads to riches, with no downside. But now that we know about Madoff's Ponzi scheme, we wouldn't succumb to fraudsters anymore, right? Mark Twain purportedly exclaimed, "History doesn't repeat itself, but it often rhymes." It's clear that Madoff was greedy. He and his family lived a lavish lifestyle. *Greed* happens to rhyme with *Sam Bankman-Fried*, also known simply as SBF.

SBF was lauded as a cryptocurrency visionary. He appeared in a cover story for *Forbes*. In January 2022, his crypto-exchange company, FTX Trading Ltd., was valued at $32 billion.[35] But by November that year, SBF's world came crashing down when FTX was forced to file for bankruptcy. Investigators uncovered a massive fraud between FTX and another company controlled by SBF, Alameda Research. In 2023, SBF was convicted of defrauding customers.

Back to the June 29, 2009, sentencing day. After asking Madoff to stand, Chin announced that Madoff was hereby sentenced to a term of imprisonment of 150 years. Under federal law, there was no chance for parole. That meant that if he served the full sentence, Madoff wouldn't be released until he was 221 years old. And to top it off, based on technical requirements, Chin imposed an additional supervised release term of three years. Sorkin's estimate of Madoff's life expectancy and request for a 12-year sentence was prescient. Madoff died in jail 12 years later.

NOTES

1. Clark, Andrew, "The Man Who Blew the Whistle on Bernard Madoff," *Guardian,* March 24, 2017, https://www.theguardian.com/business/2010/mar/24/bernard-madoff-whistleblower-harry-markopolos.
2. Unless otherwise noted, facts in this section are from Arvedlund, Erin, *Too Good to Be True: The Rise and Fall of Bernie Madoff* (New York: Portfolio, 2009).
3. Unless otherwise noted, facts in this section are from Markopolos, Harry, *No One Would Listen: A True Financial Thriller* (Hoboken, NJ: Wiley & Sons, 2010).
4. Reinicke, Carmen, "Who Is Harry Markopolos? The Famed Madoff Whistleblower Could Make Millions After Publishing a Report Accusing GE of Fraud," *Insider,* August 16, 2019.
5. Markopolos, *No One Would Listen,* 9.
6. Ibid., 8–10.
7. Prabook.com, "Harry Markopolos: Investigator, Company Executive."
8. Markopolos, *No One Would Listen,* 11.
9. Editorial staff, 1999, "The History: How Nasdaq Was Born," *Traders Magazine,* February 1.
10. Markopolos, *No One Would Listen,* 13–14.

11. Securities and Exchange Commission (SEC), "Investigation of Failure of the SEC to Uncover Bernard Madoff's Ponzi Scheme—Public Version," Report No. OIG-509, August 31, 2009 (Washington, DC: Government Printing Office), 42–61.

12. Ibid., 45.

13. Ibid., 50.

14. Smith, Randall, 1992, "SEC Breaks Up Investment Company That Paid Off Big but Didn't Register," *Wall Street Journal,* December 1, C25.

15. Markopolos, *No One Would Listen.*

16. Ibid., 25.

17. Ibid., 20.

18. Ibid., 59.

19. SEC, "Investigation of Failure of the SEC to Uncover Bernard Madoff's Ponzi Scheme," 63–64.

20. Ibid.

21. Markopolos, *No One Would Listen*, 192.

22. SEC, "Investigation of Failure of the SEC to Uncover Bernard Madoff's Ponzi Scheme."

23. Markopolos, *No One Would Listen*, 67–70.

24. Ocrant, Michael, "Madoff Tops Charts; Skeptics Ask How," *MAR/Hedge* 89, May 2001.

25. Arvedlund, Erin, "Don't Ask, Don't Tell: Bernie Madoff Attracts Skeptics in 2001," *Barron's,* May 7, 2001.

26. Arvedlund, Erin, *Too Good to Be True: The Rise and Fall of Bernie Madoff* (New York: Portfolio, 2009).

27. Markopolos, *No One Would Listen*, 138.

28. Markopolos, *No One Would Listen*, 142.

29. Markopolos, *No One Would Listen*, 202.

30. Chin, Denny, District Judge, *United States of America v. Bernard L. Madoff,* Sentence, June 29, 2009.

31. SEC, "Investigation of Failure of the SEC to Uncover Bernard Madoff's Ponzi Scheme," 45.

32. Arvedlund, *Too Good to Be True*, 20.

33. SEC, "Investigation of Failure of the SEC to Uncover Bernard Madoff's Ponzi Scheme—Public Version," Report No. OIG-509, August 31 (Washington, DC: Government), 147.

34. Swain, Barton, "'Trust, But Verify': An Untrustworthy Political Phrase," *Washington Post*, March 11, 2016, https://www.washingtonpost.com/opinions/trust-but-verify-an-untrustworthy-political-phrase/2016/03/11/da32fb08-db3b-11e5-891a-4ed04f4213e8_story.html.
35. Browne, Ryan, "Cryptocurrency Exchange FTX Hits $32 Billion Valuation Despite Bear Market Fears," CNBC, January 31, 2022, https://www.cnbc.com/2022/01/31/crypto-exchange-ftx-valued-at-32-billion-amid-bitcoin-price-plunge.html.

CHAPTER FIVE

HOW INVESTOR FOMO COST NEWTON A FORTUNE

W hen you think of Sir Isaac Newton, what comes to mind? Perhaps it's an image of Newton sitting under an apple tree, being hit in the head by falling fruit and suddenly coming up with the law of gravity. In fact, the concept of gravitation *did* come to Newton's mind when apples occasionally fell as he sat under an apple tree in a contemplative mood. That famous apple tree apparently still grows at his childhood home, Woolsthorpe Manor near Grantham, England. But there's no evidence suggesting an apple actually hit him on the head.[1] Less well known is the fact that Newton was an avid investor.

Newton had an incredible career as a mathematician, physicist, and astronomer. He developed the laws of motion, including his third law, stating that for every action there is an equal and opposite reaction. He also dabbled in alchemy. After he retired from his academic post at Cambridge University, he was Master of the Royal Mint. Yet his desire to invest cost him dearly. His losses in 1720 were estimated at up to $20 million in equivalent money today.[2]

Famously, Newton supposedly said, "I can calculate the motion of heavenly bodies, but not the madness of people" (although some historians think that he never actually made reference to heavenly bodies). This story is about a different Newton than we find in science textbooks, and how, emotionally, he's just like most investors today. And as brilliant as Newton was, records recently uncovered by a mathematics professor confirm a folktale that Newton suffered from FOMO (fear of missing out). According to Andrew Odlyzko, this is "a tale about perpetual folly of mankind in gullibly trusting the array of innovations that the finance industry concocts."[3] We will see this is as true today as it was three centuries ago.

NEWTON'S LIFE AND CAREER

Newton was born on Christmas Day, 1642 (the year Galileo Galilei died), to his recently widowed mother, Hannah. He was so weak and tiny that he could fit in a one-quart pot and wasn't expected to survive.[4] When Newton was three, a 63-year-old nearby rector, Barnabas Smith, married Hannah. While the marriage settlement resulted in a parcel of land for Newton (and he later inherited more land that his mother had purchased for him from the estate of her second husband), his stepfather had no intention of taking him with his mother. So Newton was left to be raised by his grandmother.[5]

A tormented child, Newton later confessed to a litany of sins, including "threatening my father and mother Smith to burne them and the house over them."[6] Fortunately, he didn't. After Smith died (presumably of natural causes), Hannah returned to live with 10-year-old Newton, along with his young half-brother and two half-sisters. At age 12 Newton was sent to grammar school in Grantham, where his genius was noted, along with "his strange inventions and extraordinary inclination for mechanical works."[7] Often lost in thought, he once dismounted a horse to lead it up a hill, then when he got to the top, he forgot to remount. At other times he forgot to eat.[8]

At age 18, Newton was admitted to Trinity College at Cambridge University, where he discovered a whole new world.[9] He entered Trinity as a subsizar, a poor student who had to perform menial tasks for affluent fellow students, acting as a valet and cleaning boots.[10] During his studies, he kept a list of "Quaestiones" that foreshadowed the scientific problems that he would address in his career. These included topics that he would expand into two of his greatest works, *Philosophiæ Naturalis Principia Mathematica* (which formulated the laws of motion and gravitation, and established classical mechanics) and *Opticks* (his work on light).[11] By 1664, Newton obtained a scholarship and marked the beginning of his scientific career.[12] By 1665, he had discovered the fundamental theorem of what we now call calculus,[13] thought to have also been independently invented by Gottfried Wilhelm Leibniz.

Around the time Newton was scheduled to commence with a bachelor of arts in the summer of 1665, the Great Plague descended on Cambridge, forcing a temporary closure. Newton returned to Woolsthorpe for two years, providing him with reflective time. That's where the famous apple story originated.[14] He returned to Cambridge in 1667, and beat the odds (as a former subsizar) to be elected as a fellow. This provided him with a permanent membership in the academic community, along with the freedom of studies.[15] In 1669, Newton was awarded the prestigious Lucasian professorship of mathematics, with a plum stipend of £100.[16] In 1672, he was elected a fellow of the Royal Society based on his excellent contributions to the field of science.[17] Later, in 1703, Newton was elected president of the Society.[18]

After an illustrious career with major contributions in calculus, optics, gravity, and other areas, Newton retired from his academic post at Cambridge University. He then spent over three decades at Britain's Royal Mint, first, at age 54, as warden (1696–1699), then as the highest-ranking master (1699–1727) until his death. The Royal Mint was located in the Tower of London, along with the Royal Prison, and had a mandate to produce a large number of coins with known and consistent properties, such as size and weight. During his tenure, Newton was able to stop the illegal practice of culling by goldsmiths and bankers who melted heavier coins and sent them back to the Mint as lighter pieces. A conservative estimate is that Newton saved the Mint over £41,000 during his time as master, around $40 million today,[19] by ensuring consistency in the sizing of gold and silver coins. This amount covered more than his entire career's salary at the Mint.[20]

While Newton was warden at the Mint, he took on an active role as a counterfeit detective, like a real-life Sherlock Holmes, and with a nemesis in William Chaloner.[21] At the time, counterfeiting was a capital crime. Chaloner sent a letter to the Lord Justices accusing the Mint of grave abuses, including counterfeiting, supplying coin dies to common criminals, and other illegalities. Newton was called in by the Lord Justices to investigate. Newton found that it was actually Chaloner himself who was a counterfeiter of foreign gold and a forger of bank notes. Newton concluded that Chaloner was attacking the Mint in order to gain employment there, to assist in his illegal activities. After much investigation, Newton indicted Chaloner, who was soon after sentenced to death and hanged.

With Newton spending half his adult life at the Mint, scholars have wondered whether Newton's contribution to Britain's currency was as great as it was to natural philosophy, what we now call physics, and mathematics.

Some argued that in his reports at the Mint "we see the fullest expression of expert official sense on the question of Mint laws and tariff, in steadying and safeguarding the internal currency," and that he "produced a complete revolution throughout the department which was under his direction." However, others argued "throughout his official career at the Mint, he was first and foremost a mathematician" who, in his spare time, even solved perplexing problems like "orthogonal trajectories of a series of curves represented by a single equation" in one evening.[22] The seeds of all of his great discoveries, such as calculus, the law of gravitation, and in optics, were all made before he turned 25. Nonetheless, his time at the Mint suggests he was not a neophyte when it came to investments. And in fact, he was a shrewd investor, albeit with a common weakness of many of today's investors: a FOMO affliction, when it came to his South Sea stock investments.

THE SOUTH SEA STOCK

Newton was a long-term investor who didn't make many portfolio changes, except in 1720, now known as the Bubble year.[23] Newton also acted as one of four executors of the estate of Thomas Hall, a civil servant who worked with Newton in the 1690s on England's great recoinage to replace silver coins. While Newton was only one of the Hall estate's executors, it is likely that he had a strong influence on the estate's investment decisions. Evidence suggests Newton was both a careful steward and knowledgeable about financial markets.[24] Both Newton and the estate were invested in South Sea stock.

The South Sea Company was a joint-stock company incorporated in 1711 by an act of Britain's Parliament. It planned to reduce the cost of the national debt in return for providing monopolistic trade with Spanish colonies in South America, Central America, and the Caribbean, and a few years later, exclusive rights to sell slaves in that region.[25] The stock rose from £128[26] in January 1720 to almost £1,000 in August of that year, despite dubious prospects of profitability. But there is more to the story.

Like two other major joint-stock companies, the Bank of England and the East India Company, the South Sea Company bought government securities to fund the national debt. As of the end of 1719, £6.6 million of national debt was owed to the Bank of England and the East India Company, £12 million to the South Sea Company, and the remaining £32 million to the public.[27] About half of the debt was in irredeemables (annuities that paid a fixed amount of money for a certain period of time—in this case, typically 99 years), with the remainder in redeemables (consol or perpetual bonds, like today's preferred dividends that provide regular payments forever but with no return of capital).

While the South Sea Company as a commercial enterprise was mainly just passing along to stockholders fund payments received from the government, it was the *prospect* of huge future profits through South America trade that justified to investors why they should pay higher prices for the stock. It was in the interest of many parties to have the South Sea Company stock price increase, first and foremost the government, but also the company itself, its shareholders, and annuitants. This was because part of the "scheme" was to entice holders of government annuities into converting their assets directly into South Sea stock.[28] For example, imagine today owning U.S. Treasurys with a 4 percent yield, and being enticed into trading those for Company XYZ units that combined a bond yield of 3 percent with shares that might pay huge dividends in the future—a lower guaranteed yield, but more upside potential.

It was up to the government to determine the price at which annuitants could covert to South Sea stock, and so a debate ensued in parliament. Some argued that a higher conversion price benefited all. On the other side, one member of parliament, Archibald Hutcheson, wrote in a pamphlet that anyone who bought South Sea stock, at its price in April 1720 at around £300, must be "deprived of all common Sense and Understanding."[29]

Sorting out the intrinsic value of South Sea stock wasn't easy—and that was precisely the intent of John Blunt, a founding director of the company and leader behind the conversion scheme. Blunt was driven by two maxims: first, "advancing by all means of the price of the stock," and second, "the more confusion the better."[30] In this spirit, in addition to enticing annuitants to convert to South Sea stock, he orchestrated four opportunities for new investors to subscribe to the stock, and he made it more attractive by only requiring 20 percent deposits. Conversions were extremely successful, with annuitants rushing in before even knowing the exact conversion terms. Savvy professionals who blindly rushed in included those at the Bank of England as well as at the Million Bank, which was like a modern investment trust.[31]

The mania in the summer of 1720 was neatly captured in a letter by investor Jonathan Swift, of *Gulliver's Travels* fame, in which he wrote, "I have enquired of some that have come from London, what is the religion there? They tell me it is South Sea stock; what is the policy of England? The answer is the same; what is the trade? South Sea still; and what is the business? Nothing but South Sea."[32]

BURSTING OF THE BUBBLE

With the price of South Sea stock dipping from its high of £1,050 in June to £850 in August, Blunt and other directors were trying to prop up the stock with a series of initiatives. A slew of "bubble companies" were increasingly joining the ranks of joint-stock companies, in areas as varied as financial services, eventual settlement and trade in Terra Australis, more than 50 years before Captain James Cook discovered Australia, and new technologies like the Puckle machine gun[33] (more on bubble companies Chapter 8).

Blunt persuaded his friends in government to pass the Bubble Act, which made it illegal for other companies to become established, and illegal for existing companies to operate outside of their charter. They further required the attorney general to start prosecution proceedings against companies that had diversified beyond their charters. They also announced a 30 percent South Sea dividend, and a guaranteed 50 percent dividend for the next 12 years. All of these measures backfired. The threat of prosecution caused market panic, and even one of the leading insurance companies saw its stock drop by over 75 percent. Speculators who bought South Sea stock on margin were forced to sell, further depressing the price. Foreigners also sold their stock. In September, the Sword Blade Bank, which acted as the banker to the South Sea Company, failed.

At the start of 1720, Newton held about 10,000 shares of South Sea stock, worth about £13,000. By mid-1721, he owned 16,300 shares, which represented his entire investments. In between, around April 1720, he liquidated most of his South Sea holdings, for a profit of £20,000.[34] In a matter of weeks, the stock price doubled. Feeling a sense of FOMO, Newton took all of his profits, cashed out other investments, and repurchased South Sea stock. He started buying again on May 23, then again on June 14 after selling Bank of England stocks. Then, as he was finishing liquidating most of his own holdings to buy South Sea stocks, he was purchasing South Sea stocks for Hall's estate. He continued to buy, both for himself and Hall's estate, well past the peak stock price, around mid-September.[35] The stock ended the year at a similar price to where it began.

According to Odlyzko, the researcher who uncovered new information about Newton and the South Sea stock, the most interesting transactions occurred in the middle of September, when South Sea stock was being purchased while the stock was in a free fall.[36] Odlyzko concluded that buyers such as Newton "could only have been motivated by deep conviction that the market's change of heart about the South Sea Company was *just a temporary irrational panic* [emphasis added], and there was real value in the venture."[37] Newton had apparently become a true believer, and he was all-in.

The in-then-out-then-in-again misadventure cost Newton £13,000. The South Sea debacle was said to have haunted him for the rest of his life, and he didn't want to talk about it. Had he put all his money in South Sea stock in June 1719 and sold near the peak in June 1720, he would have cashed out around £250,000.[38] Even a buy-and-hold investor who purchased South Sea stock as late as mid-1719 and did nothing for the next four years would have experienced a 50 percent capital gain in addition to dividends.[39] Records indicate Newton owned thousands of shares as early as 1712 and increased his holding several times over the next few years.

FOMO EXPLAINED

A 2013 study published in *Computers in Human Behavior*[40] was the first empirically and theoretically grounded examination of the FOMO phenomenon. It defined FOMO as "a pervasive apprehension that others might be having rewarding experiences from which one is absent." The researchers looked at FOMO in the context of social media, which provides a multitude of interactive opportunities, too many for anyone to pursue. They conducted surveys and found that those with higher FOMO scores tended to have higher levels of social media engagement but were less satisfied.

The term *FOMO* was added to *Oxford Dictionaries Online* in 2013.[41] It is often attributed to Patrick J. McGinnis, author *of Fear of Missing Out*, who popularized the term in an op-ed he wrote in 2004[42] while attending Harvard Business School (HBS). In the op-ed, he described the feelings of an HBS student who accepts numerous social invitations to the point of exhaustion for fear of missing out on networking opportunities. But the term goes back further, at least to marketing researcher Dan Herman, who used the term in a publication in 2000[43] to describe consumers who desired combinations of products such as "2-in-1" and "3-in-1" offerings, fearing missing out on some product attribute.

Investors also experience FOMO. Suppose you own an asset, perhaps a stock or cryptocurrency, and the price goes up, so you decide to sell it. You'd think you might be happy because you just made a profit. But your feelings often depend on what happens next in terms of the price of the asset you just sold. You may decide to continue to track it. If the price goes down, you'll attribute your good fortune to immaculate timing and knowing when to sell. But what if the price continues to rise? You'll probably think about all of the profits you're missing out on, and fear that you're missing the party that's still going on. That's precisely the situation in which Newton found himself.

FOMO AND CRYPTOCURRENCIES: THE DOGECOIN EXAMPLE

Which brings us back to recent times, and where we see that, like in 1720, conditions have been ripe for FOMO investing. In 2021, a number of so-called meme stocks like GameStop Corp., as well as cryptocurrencies, saw dramatic increases in the price of assets over a short period of time, before falling back to earth. A meme stock is one that has become popular with individual investors, has experienced price spikes and increased trading volume, and trades at a price that appears to be excessive based on traditional measures such as price-to-earnings.

As a cryptocurrency example, let's look at Dogecoin (pronounced "dohj coin"),[44] which was created in 2013 by Jackson Palmer and Billy Markus as a parody of bitcoin, with a Shiba Inu dog as its mascot. It was designed with no purpose except to get some laughs. It rose to prominence in part because of tweets by Elon Musk and other celebrities.

At the start of 2021, Dogecoin was trading at less than a cent. By May it was trading for more than 68 cents. By the end of the year it was trading at 17 cents. Six months later it was at 5 cents. What's amazing is the striking similarity of the price of Dogecoin in 2021 to South Sea stock in 1720, with its dramatic rise and fall. There are spikes in the volume of trading while Dogecoin's price is increasing—no surprise there—but also volume spikes at and past the price peak. Perhaps that volume in part reflects trading by FOMO investors. If Newton was alive today, would he have gotten in early, sold at around 30 cents, then reentered the market and invested all of his gains at a price of around 60 cents? Perhaps.

AVOIDING FOMO

There are a number of ways to avoid the fears and regrets that Newton experienced:

- By being disciplined, having a well-thought-out investing plan, and sticking to it
- By consistently investing a small amount of money every month, a strategy known as dollar-cost averaging
- By avoiding peer pressure and succumbing to hot tips, for example, from your social network
- By not tracking an asset's price once you sell it
- By thinking long-term, and not checking how your investments are doing several times a day

Newton died rich in 1727, with an estate valued at £30,000,[45] worth around $30 million today. But the primary reason he died rich is because he was already rich *prior to* his mishap in the South Sea Bubble. As the saying goes, the easiest way to make a small fortune is to invest a *large* fortune in [insert latest investing craze here]. If you resist FOMO, then your fortune may be bigger than if you had acted on FOMO, like Newton did. And to paraphrase Franklin D. Roosevelt, there's nothing to fear but FOMO itself.

NOTES

1. Nix, Elizabeth, "Did an Apple Really Fall in Isaac Newton's Head?" History .com, September 1, 2018, https://www.history.com/news/did-an-apple-really-fall-on-isaac-newtons-head.
2. Odlyzko, Andrew, "Newton's Financial Misadventures in the South Sea Bubble," Royal Society Publishing, *Notes and Records of the Royal Society Journal of the History of Science* 73, no. 1 (2019): 31, https://royalsocietypublishing.org/doi/10.1098/rsnr.2018.0018.
3. Ibid., 32.
4. Westfall, Richard, *Never at Rest: A Biography of Isaac Newton* (New York: Cambridge University Press, 1980), 47–49.
5. Ibid., 52–53.
6. Ibid., 53.
7. Ibid., 60.
8. Ibid., 64.
9. Ibid., 1.
10. Ibid., 71.
11. Ibid., 91, 96.
12. Ibid., 102.
13. Ibid., 123.
14. Ibid., 140–143.
15. Ibid., 176–179.
16. Ibid., 206.
17. Royal Society, "Fellows," https://web.archive.org/web/20150316060617/https://royalsociety.org/about-us/fellowship/fellows/.
18. Westfall, *Never at Rest*, 629.
19. This is a rough estimate. See Odlyzko, "Newton's Financial Misadventures," 31, footnote 9.
20. Belenkiy, Ari, "The Master of the Royal Mint: How Much Money Did Isaac Newton Save Britain?" *Journal of the Royal Statistical Society* 176, part 2 (2013): 481–498, https://rss.onlinelibrary.wiley.com/doi/full/10.1111/j.1467-985x.2012.01037.x.

21. Accounts in this section are from Craig, John, and Harold Brewer Hartley, "Isaac Newton and the counterfeiters," *Notes and Records of the Royal Society Journal of the History of Science* 18, no. 2 (1963): 136–145, https://royalsociety publishing.org/doi/pdf/10.1098%2Frsnr.1963.0017.

22. Shirras, Findlay, and J. Craig, "Sir Isaac Newton and the Currency," *Economic Journal* 55, no. 218–219 (1945): 217–241.

23. Odlyzko, "Newton's financial misadventures," 33.

24. Ibid., 36–37.

25. Chancellor, Edward, *Devil Take the Hindmost: A History of Financial Speculation* (New York: Plume, 1999), 59–60.

26. Odlyzko, "Newton's Financial Misadventures," 42.

27. Ibid., 41.

28. Chancellor, *Devil Take the Hindmost*, 59–62.

29. Ibid., 65.

30. Ibid., 66–67.

31. Ibid., 68.

32. Ibid., 77.

33. Ibid., 70.

34. Odlyzko, "Newton's Financial Misadventures," 35.

35. Ibid., 35–37.

36. Ibid., 37.

37. Ibid., 37–38.

38. Ibid., 35.

39. Ibid., 43.

40. Przybylskia, Andrew, Kou Murayama, Cody DeHaan, and Valerie Gladwell, "Motivational, Emotional, and Behavioral Correlates of Fear of Missing Out," *Computers in Human Behavior* 29, no. 4 (2013): 1841–1848, https://www .sciencedirect.com/science/article/abs/pii/S0747563213000800.

41. Dirda, Michel, "Oxford Dictionaries Adds 'Twerk,' 'FOMO,' 'Selfie,' and Other Words that Make Me Vom," *Washington Post,* August 28, 2013, https://www .washingtonpost.com/lifestyle/style/oxford-dictionaries-adds-twerk-fomo-selfie-and-other-words-that-make-me-vom/2013/08/28/678ddd48-102c-11e3-8cdd-bcdc09410972_story.html.

42. McGinnis, Patrick, "Social Theory at HBS: McGinnis' Two FOs," Harbus, May 10, 2004, https://patrickjmcginnis.wordpress.com/2010/01/03/social-theory-at-hbs-mcginnis-two-fos-may-2004/.

43. Herman, Dan, "Introducing Short-term Brands: A New Branding Tool for a New Consumer Reality," *Journal of Brand Management* 7, no. 5 (2000): 330–340, https://www.researchgate.net/publication/263327722_Introducing_Short-term_Brands_A_New_Branding_Tool_for_a_New_Consumer_Reality.

44. Ostroff, Caitlin, and Caitlin McCabe, "What Is Dogecoin, How to Say It, and Why It's No Longer a Joke," *Wall Street Journal,* June 2, 2021, https://www.wsj.com/articles/what-is-dogecoin-how-to-say-it-and-why-its-no-longer-a-joke-thanks-elon-11612820776.

45. Odlyzko, "Newton's Financial Misadventures," 31.

CHAPTER SIX

HETTY GREEN, THE QUEEN OF VALUE INVESTING

In late spring of 1907, at a boardinghouse on Madison Avenue in New York City, the gas failed and the lights went out.[1] A spinster living on the second floor heard the sound of someone fumbling along the dark hallway. With a lighted candle, she opened her door, to the relief of an old woman holding the banister. The old woman, an acquaintance, was invited in by the younger woman. After the door was closed, the old woman clasped her bosom, to the sound of crackling papers. "If you could see what I have in here you'd be surprised," the old woman exclaimed. "I've just taken everything I possess out of a shaky bank downtown."

Seizing the opening, the younger woman thought this might be an opportune time to ask the older woman for some financial advice. The younger woman had money in the Knickerbocker Trust Company, New York's second largest trust. What did the older woman think about that? With a sharp look, the old woman admonished her, "If you have any money in that place, get it out first thing tomorrow." The younger neighbor wanted to know why. The older woman playfully replied, "The men in that bank are too good-looking." Then her tone took a serious turn. "You mark my words," said Hetty Green.

The Knickerbocker Trust Company was originally located at the northwest corner of Fifth Avenue and Thirty-fourth Street, on the opposite corner of the grand Waldorf-Astoria hotel.[2] It was covered in Vermont marble and sported four 17-ton Corinthian columns. Inside was an elegant four-story structure with white Norwegian marble contrasting with bronze detailing and mahogany woodworking. The central banking room reached three stories. The second through fourth floors each boasted 5,000 square feet and four executive offices. A massive safety deposit vault in the basement featured an outer door that weighed almost nine tons and whose hinges alone weighed 3,700 pounds. The bank's appearance was one of strength and sobriety, as if calling out, "You're money is always safe here!"

And yet appearances can be deceptive, just like the good-looking men at the bank. As Green predicted, a few months later there was a run on Knickerbocker Trust. The Panic of 1907 was in full swing. The Panic devastated bank depositors, investors, financial institutions, and New York City itself. It took a concerted and coordinated effort to avoid total financial disaster. No surprise that rescue efforts were led by prominent financier John Pierpont (J. P.) Morgan, and included another pillar of the financial establishment, John D. Rockefeller. But another key rescuer was the shabbily dressed boardinghouse occupant who was so cheap that rather than pay for cab fare, she would pull a pair of heavy woolen stockings over her shoes and walk through snow to parties.[3] That summed up the life of Hetty

Green: purportedly both the world's richest woman[4] and also the most frugal. And arguably one of the greatest investors.

THE PRINCESS OF WHALES

Henrietta Howland Robinson (later Hetty Green; for simplicity as we will refer to her throughout as "Green," although that's the name she acquired later when she married) was born in New Bedford, Massachusetts, in 1834 to a Quaker family.[5] As an adolescent, Green learned about markets and investing from her successful and wealthy father, Edward Robinson, who came from a whaling family. He had been disappointed that his firstborn wasn't a boy, and devastated that his second child, a boy, died at a few weeks of age. But eventually Hetty and Edward became close. She often accompanied him to work, inspecting inventories and ships, watching him bargaining with merchants, and learning to read ledgers at the countinghouse. As Edward's eyesight began to fail, he had Hetty read the evening news from the *Boston Herald* and *New York Tribune*. She learned about stocks, bonds, commodities, and bulls and bears.

Green had little interest in academic subjects in school.[6] As she reached the typical age of marriage, she was sent to a finishing school. Her father wanted to improve her marriage prospects and ensure she didn't marry beneath herself. So in 1854, he sent 20-year-old Hetty to live in New York City. But while her friends thrived in the social scene and wore the latest fashions, Green was more interested in men's conversations about finances and enhancing her wealth. She wasn't looking for the luxuries that money could buy, but rather money itself. Finance excited her. "I have a head for numbers. They light up and tell me a story."[7]

In the fall of 1860, New York was abuzz with the news that the 19-year-old Prince of Wales was going to visit, and so a ball was organized in his honor.[8] Green was invited. For two hours, nearly three thousand admirers rushed to meet the prince. The crush was so intense that the specially built wooden dancefloor collapsed. Hours later, as planned, the prince invited the governor's wife for the first dance. Eager females waited their turn and eventually Green was tapped. After she was introduced to the Prince of Wales, she joked, "And I'm the Princess of Whales." The prince replied, "Ah, I've heard that all of Neptune's daughters are beautiful. You are proof of that."

SIGNATURE MOVE

In that same year, Green's mother, Abby Howland Robinson, died at age 51.[9] Abby Robinson came from a wealthy family, and was the daughter of her husband's partner in the whaling business. Hetty and her mother were never close and so she had nothing to mourn. Abby Robinson died without a will and so her entire estate, worth more than $100,000, went to her husband, much to the chagrin of Hetty, who felt hurt and angry. Her aunt, Sylvia Howland, urged her to appeal to her father for her share of the inheritance. She did, but to no avail. She felt alone and sought solace with her aunt, who was quite close to her. Yet their lifelong relationship was like a rollercoaster of ups-and-downs.

Howland had become frail.[10] Green was the sole heir to the Howland money and wanted to ensure she would receive what she felt she rightfully deserved. Howland had gifted her $20,000 in stocks, but her estate was worth hundreds of thousands of dollars. Howland employed a staff whose size Green thought was excessive, and she felt Howland was wasting money out of her eventual inheritance. Green became enraged when Howland announced she was building a wing to her house to accommodate the growing staff.

In the fall of 1861, Green sat down with her aunt to discuss their wills.[11] They concurred that if Green died first without children, her estate would go to her aunt's favorite charity. Papers were witnessed and signed. Howland's own will had been written earlier and stipulated that three-quarters of her estate would go to Green, half of which would be put in a trust. But now Green insisted that almost all of it be left to her directly. They argued for hours till dark, when Howland finally agreed. But Howland claimed she was too weak to sign then, and went to bed. It then turned into months of cajoling by Green before Howland signed the will, in the presence of witnesses. Later Green would claim that her aunt signed another piece of paper when they were alone.

In 1865, as the Civil War came to a close and the nation was shocked by the assassination of Abraham Lincoln, Green's life was changing.[12] She was being courted by millionaire international businessman Edward Green. Hetty's father, Edward Robinson, was bedridden and weak but enthusiastically agreed to give Edward Green permission to marry his daughter. A prenuptial agreement stipulated that Edward Green would have no claim to Hetty's inheritance. Shortly afterwards, Hetty's father died at the age of 65, with an estate of almost $6 million. He bequeathed his daughter $1 million in cash and the ownership of a San Francisco warehouse, with the remainder placed in a trust. Green was to have no control of the trust, and upon her death, the principal would go to her children. Green felt betrayed.

Weeks later, Green received more sad news: her aunt, Sylvia Howland, also passed away.[13] At the reading of the will at her aunt's house, Green discovered that Howland's estate was worth over $2 million. Of that amount, $1 million was to go to Green, but all of it in trust. The will had been signed and witnessed a year and a half after the wills written by Howland and Green. Again, Green was devastated that she hadn't inherited the vast bulk of her aunt's estate. Once guests left, Green demanded that a housekeeper give her the key to her aunt's private trunk. She retrieved a copy of the will she had helped her aunt to write, which also had a second page attached, and showed it to her fiancé, Edward Green. The second page invalidated future wills. She then met with her family's attorney. Hetty Green became desperate and even tried to bribe a probate judge to cancel Howland's final will. Months later, the latest will was approved in probate court.

Green was to spend much of her lifetime in courtrooms, relishing the chance to take down her adversaries, often for mundane reasons. But a case shortly afterwards, against Howland's trustees, turned out to be a landmark.[14] Green claimed she was the lawful heir, and her aunt had even told her lawyer that she didn't want to write a new will without notifying Green. The proof was in a letter that Howland had signed, and was attached to the Howland-Green will. But there was a major problem: the signature appeared to be identical to the one on the will.

The trustees' lawyers claimed the signature was forged and brought in experts. Green's own expert witnesses were convinced the signature was genuine. They included the chairman of Harvard's Department of Natural History; Harvard lawyer and doctor Oliver Wendell Holmes; and the grandson of John Quincy Adams, who argued that his grandfather often signed his name in an identical manner.

But the most memorable expert witnesses, for the defense, were Harvard mathematician Benjamin Pierce and his son. Using statistical analysis of pen strokes, they concluded the chance that the signatures were coincidentally identical to be "once in 2,666 millions of millions of millions of times." In other words, they concluded that the signature was a forgery. The judge ultimately side-stepped the forgery allegations and ruled against Green, arguing that even if the second page was legitimate, it didn't constitute a separate contract.[15]

Decades later, Green continued to plead her innocence. "I had the will and the other people had the property all laid out to suit themselves. There was nothing else for them to do but cry forgery, and they were all against me. . . . Why do you suppose my daughter was named Sylvia Ann Howland if I had forged my aunt's name? She would have been a living picture of forgery before me for all these past years. Absurd."[16]

VALUE INVESTING

Green started from a position of wealth but, through an astute investment approach unlike most at the time, was able to see her wealth snowball. She developed an investment philosophy very much akin to what is known today as value investing, as encapsulated by well-known investors Ben Graham and Warren Buffett (more on Buffett in our next story). Value investors look for investments that appear to be selling at prices below their true intrinsic value. These investors are often contrarian, and look not only to buy when market sentiment is for selling, but also to sell when the sentiment is for buying. Value investors park their emotions, gather information, and make rational investing decisions.

One major investing area for Green was in railroads. She had more access to information in this area than most other investors.[17] She had overseas connections, read constantly, performed in-depth research, and was able to navigate the complicated yet burgeoning industry. Consequently, she had accumulated a large stake in railroads—both stocks and bonds. She wasn't alone in her interest in railroads; well-known contemporary railroad investors included J. P. Morgan, Andrew Carnegie, and Commodore Vanderbilt. Green espoused her value investing approach: "I believe in getting in at the bottom and out at the top. . . . I like to buy railroad stock or mortgage bonds. When I see a good thing going cheap because nobody wants it, I buy a lot of it and tuck it away."[18]

Green's investments were much wider than just in railroads. She amassed a huge portfolio that provided a steady stream of both interest payments and dividends. By 1905, it was reported that she had an "octopus-like" array of mortgages that included "some of the safest and soundest properties in a chain of cities extending from Boston to San Francisco, and the income flows toward her from every national section and corner between Maine and Texas. Railroads and steamboats, mines of copper in Michigan, of gold in Nevada, and of iron in Missouri and Pennsylvania, telegraph and telephone securities, her wealth covers all sorts and conditions of gilt-edged dividend-paying investments."[19] At one point, she held the mortgages of 28 churches.[20]

Green was a big proponent of real estate investing in general, particularly if it represented good value. "I would advise any woman with five hundred dollars at her command to invest in real estate. She should buy at an auction on occasions when circumstances have forced sale. If she will look out for such opportunities they will surely come, and she will find that she can buy a parcel of land at one-third its appraised value. I regard real estate investments as the safest means of using idle money."[21]

Value investing is often associated with frugality. Why waste money on frivolous things when you could be spending that money on undervalued assets with a huge potential payoff? Green was certainly frugal, and was even recognized posthumously by the *Guinness Book of World Records* as the World's Greatest Miser.[22] Stories abounded that she bought sacks of broken graham crackers, asked the butcher for free bones for her dog, and bargained over the price of potatoes.[23] Later in life, she constantly moved from boardinghouses to hotels to flats not only for privacy, but to escape city and state taxes since she hadn't established a residence.[24] In 1899, by the time her wealth had grown to a reported $60 million, she was living in a cheap boardinghouse in Hoboken, New Jersey, paying about $5 a week.[25] She once faced a court summons because she had tried to evade paying a $2 license tax on a favorite dog.[26]

In one of Green's railroad investments, she was supporting a reorganization plan by Reading Railroad, which required exchanging old shares for new ones.[27] When she arrived at the office of a New York investments firm with a satchel filled with a million dollars of stock certificates, she enquired whether there would be a transfer fee. She was told that, yes, there was a $100 fee to transfer the certificates from New York to Philadelphia.

She was incensed. "A hundred dollars! Why, I can go to Philadelphia and return for four dollars." And so she did, to deliver her satchel of stock certificates in person, thereby saving $96.

Some rumors of her frugality were misplaced—somewhat. Her young son, Ned, hurt his knee while riding on a sled.[28] A few years later, he fell from a tree and reinjured his knee. The rumor was that Green was too cheap to call a doctor, but in fact she immediately called one. However, while waiting for the doctor to arrive, she applied a warm bandage to the wound, and she felt that had taken care of things. "I went outside and stood at the gate. When the doctor came, I waved him away and called that he wasn't needed. If he'd gotten out of his buggy, I'd have had to pay him, even if he didn't do anything, you know." (As an adult, Ned would reinjure his knee again, this time so severely that it required amputation.)

Green was an expert on bargaining, and proud of her skills. One time, she implored her husband to sell his fancy carriage because she had found a smaller one for sale.[29] She located a man who had a grudge against the carriage owner and convinced the man to tell her every fault of the carriage. Armed with this knowledge, she approached the seller. "I succeeded in depreciating the owner's opinion of his property." She was able to secure the carriage for less than half the initial asking price, even lower than she was willing to pay.

In the two decades following the deaths of her father and aunt, Green's reputation and money had grown immensely. In 1885, the *New York Times* wrote, "Mrs. E. H. Green is well-known, by reputation, at least, on Wall Street. She is believed to be the richest woman in America, a titled earned by her own business sagacity, energy and watchfulness. She has lived a frugal life, exercised extraordinary keenness in her investments, and by embracing every good opportunity that the stock market afforded her, she has more than quintupled her heritage."[30]

What's more remarkable is how Green thrived in spite of the prevailing 19th- and early-20th-century attitudes toward women in America.

As an example, in his 1888 memoir of his career on Wall Street, famed investment banker Henry Clews devoted a scathing chapter to "Women as Speculators."[31] Clews felt that Wall Street was no place for a woman. The chapter began with his observation that "as speculators, women hitherto have been utter failures. They do not thrive in the atmosphere of Wall Street, for they do not seem to have the mental qualities required to take in the varied points of the situation upon which success in speculation depends."[32] Furthermore, Clews asserted, "Women are too impulsive and impressionable" and "they don't reason in the way that is indispensable to a successful speculator."[33]

But according to Clews, the exception was Hetty Green, "whose unaided sagacity has placed her among the most successful of our millionaire speculators. She is, however, made up of a powerful masculine brain in an otherwise female constitution, and is one among a million of her sex."[34] So, in order to justify his thesis, Clews reckoned that Green's success was because she must have had a man's brain. Ironically, on numerous occasions she would have to bail out her husband—who presumably had a masculine brain—when his investments went sour.

Hetty Green was a devoted and protective mother to her son and daughter. She schooled Ned on business dealings and investments. One time, she sent Ned to Texas to bid on part of a defunct railroad.[35] Also bidding was one of her old enemies, Collis Huntington. Green won the auction, but Huntington claimed he had a $100,000 lien on the property, and that she owed him that money. She refused to pay, and the unresolved issue continued over the next three years. Huntington was angry and wanted to prosecute. He met with Green at her New York office, and made a threat against Ned. Green was livid. "Up to now, Huntington, you have dealt with Hetty Green, the business woman. Now you are fighting Hetty Green, the mother. Harm one hair of Ned's head and I'll put a bullet through your heart." She then reached for a gun that she kept on her desk. Huntington quickly departed.

IT'S UP TO YOU, NEW YORK

Green was a huge financial supporter of New York City. In June 1898, after the amalgamation of Brooklyn, the Bronx, Staten Island, Queens, and New York, the city needed funds. She provided a loan at 2 percent interest for four months, at a time when the usual rate was 3.5 percent.[36] In 1901 when the city needed money, she lent $1.5 million at an interest rate of 5.5 percent.[37] In November 1905, she provided $2.5 million in loans at 5 percent interest. That loan made her the largest lender to the city.[38]

Early in 1906, she provided yet another loan, $4.5 million, at well below the going interest rate.[39] This was at a time when banks were increasing their lending rates. It was reported that "she would have been ready to lend more if the city needed it." A city official reported, "We can always rely on her." With the death of financier Russell Sage in July 1906, a few months shy of his 90th birthday, referring to Green as the city's leading lender, a newspaper trumpeted, "The King Is Dead; Long Live the Queen."

A TREMBLING BEGINNING TO THE PANIC OF 1907

The Panic of 1907 can be traced to a precise moment and place, a year and a half before the run on Knickerbocker Trust, and more than 2,500 miles from New York. At 5:12 a.m. on Wednesday, April 18, 1906, there was a rupture on the northernmost 296 miles of the San Andreas Fault, running from Hollister to Cape Mendocino in California.[40] A 55-second earthquake, later estimated measuring up to 8.3 on the Richter scale, caused the eastern side of the fault to shift to the south-east by 24 feet.

The earthquake itself was devastating for San Francisco, but fires resulting from broken gas lines cause by the quake were even worse. Firefighters tried to fight flames but pumped sewers dry. An army battalion from Presidio, the nearby military fort, used dynamite to collapse buildings in the hope of creating firebreaks. Often the explosions started new fires. Almost none of the properties in San Francisco were insured against earthquakes but most were insured against fires. Over the next several days, many homeowners whose houses had been damaged by the quake set their own homes on fire in order to receive insurance payments.

At least 225,000 people were homeless, more than half of all San Franciscans. More than 27,500 buildings covering 500 square blocks were destroyed. Beyond the human tragedy, stock prices tumbled. The Dow dropped by more than 10 percent in the two weeks following the earthquake. British insurance companies were hit hard since they covered over half of all of the fire insurance policies in San Francisco, costing an estimated $200 million. At a time when major currencies were backed by gold, 14 percent of Britain's gold stockpile was sent to San Francisco to settle claims. To provide liquidity, every spare dollar and pound in London, New York, Boston, and elsewhere was sent to San Francisco since cash and gold there weren't available for weeks, until the vaults cooled.[41]

With gold flowing out of the country, the Bank of England responded as expected by raising interest rates to compensate those who left their gold on deposit. Thus began a worldwide increase in interest rates, which is never good news for stocks because it increases opportunity costs (as we discussed in Chapter 3). By the summer of 1907, credit conditions had tightened and businesses as well as municipalities had trouble getting loans. On June 28, New York City failed in a $39 million bond offering, having received only $2.1 million in bids.[42] Stock prices continued to weaken throughout the summer and into the fall. On November 11, 1907, a month after the Knickerbocker bank run, the Dow would bottom out at a level 45 percent below its pre-quake mark.

TRUST BUSTING

A stock market crash rarely has a single cause. So it was with the Panic of 1907. The first pillar was the earthquake. The second pillar was political. On September 15, 1901, Theodore Roosevelt was on a hunting trip in a remote stretch of the Adirondacks. He got word that President William McKinley had died from the two gunshots delivered by anarchist Leon Czolgosz on September 6. Roosevelt, the former governor of New York and branded a troublemaker and reformer, was now president of the United States.[43]

Just over two weeks after the San Francisco earthquake, on May 4, 1906, Roosevelt delivered an important speech in the House of Representatives. In it he resumed his battle against trust companies, networks of enterprises led by a board of trustees. In his cross-hairs was Standard Oil, co-founded by business magnate John D. Rockefeller. Roosevelt accused Standard Oil of benefiting from secret and unlawful deals with railroads. On June 22, the company was officially under investigation. On August 27, the U.S. government charged Standard Oil with 6,428 violations. Each was punishable by a fine of up to $20,000, for a potential fine of over $128 million. Another suit was filed on November 15 demanding the breakup of Standard Oil.[44] With Roosevelt's anti-business stance, coupled with rising interest rates, markets were getting more jittery.

The trial of *Standard Oil v. United States* commenced on March 4, 1907. A month later, a Chicago jury found Standard Oil guilty on every one of the 1,463 separate counts. In a speech on May 30, Roosevelt further fueled the anti-business flames, calling on the federal government to take action against interstate railways that were abusing property rights. On July 8, Roosevelt's new attorney general, Charles Bonaparte, the great-nephew of the French emperor, announced a new policy to effectively take down trusts. Then on August 3, the court reconvened, with the judge imposing the maximum fine of over $29 million against Standard Oil. He then shocked the court by calling for a special grand jury to consider criminal charges that could result in jail terms for executives of both the railroads and Standard Oil.[45] The Dow had now declined more than 20 percent since the April 1906 earthquake.

SELLING SHORT

The third pillar leading to the Panic of 1907 involved a number of shady characters and created a perfect storm around Knickerbocker Trust. The first was Fritz Heinze, born in Brooklyn and educated at the Columbia University of Mines before moving to Butte, Montana, the center of the country's copper mining.[46] With the introduction of electric lighting in 1882, starting with J. P. Morgan's home, demand for copper for electrical wiring was skyrocketing. Heinze was unscrupulous in business from the beginning. When he leased his first mine, the contract specified that the owner would get all the ore with at least 12.5 percent copper. So he instructed his miners to mix waste rock with the copper-bearing ore to get below the threshold.[47]

Heinze capitalized on another loophole, an obscure Montana law that allowed the owner of land to mine any vein wherever it surfaced, even on a neighboring property. This put him at odds with the Amalgamated Copper Company, which offered him $500,000 for his Butte properties to settle lawsuits. After stubbornly holding out for years, Heinze finally agreed to a $12 million buyout. That allowed him to return to New York in 1907 and open an office just southwest of Wall Street, to pursue his dream of creating a financial powerhouse.[48]

Heinze reconnected with an acquaintance, Charles Moore, who was described as a "scumbag." While branch banking wasn't yet legal, Morse used a work-around known as chain banking. It involved acquiring a series of banks with just enough cash to buy stock to gain control. Morse had complete control of three banks, investments in 31 others, and was on the board of directors of seven more. Heinze and Morse began working together. Morse took a stake in United Copper that Heinze controlled, while Heinze exchanged shares to take a stake in Morse's American Ice Company. Then in February 1907, Morse convinced Heinze to buy a controlling interest in Mercantile National Bank, in which Morse already had a stake.[49]

Before returning to New York, Fritz Heinze helped establish his brothers Otto and Arthur in the stock brokerage business. Now Heinze got his brothers involved in his scheme. United Copper shares had dropped from $70 at the start of 1907 to $40 by October. There were sound fundamental reasons for the drop as demand for copper was down by a similar amount along with the price of copper. Nonetheless, Heinze wanted to reverse the downward stock trend. He also believed the cause was aggressive short-sellers. Short-selling is a risky process by which one borrows and sells a stock in the hopes of buying it back at a much lower price later. Fritz Heinze directed his brother Otto to start a stock pool to buy United Copper shares, hoping to prop up the price, using borrowed money as well as Heinze's own wealth. But the stock price continued to fall.[50]

What to do now? Fritz and Otto Heinze, along with Morse and one of his friends, Charles Barney, the president of the Knickerbocker Trust Company, concocted a "short squeeze" plan. The plan involved paying off the loan from Heinze used to buy United Copper shares for the pool and demanding back all the stock certificates on deposits that had been lent to short-sellers. The idea was to force short-sellers to buy back the stock at a much higher price, and one they couldn't afford. They needed an estimated $3 million. Mercantile National Bank, controlled by Heinze, was a possible source of capital, but had incurred substantial withdrawals when Heinze gained control and fearful depositors fled. This was in the era before deposit insurance became available in 1934. It didn't look like they'd be able to implement the plan.[51]

Otto took matters into his own hands and ordered a brokerage firm to start buying United Copper shares anyway. He also began to demand back some of the shares on deposit. That helped push up the price from around $37 to $60. Otto finally informed his brother Fritz Heinze what he had done. Fritz was angry at first, but also quite impressed that the scheme seemed to be working. He reluctantly agreed to allow Otto to borrow from Mercantile National to cover checks he was writing.[52]

But then the plan backfired. Otto expected the short-sellers to default but instead they were able to deliver the requested stock certificates. Otto hadn't expected the overwhelming response and stopped accepting stocks. Brokers were stuck in the middle with unwanted stock and so they sold in a panic. That caused the stock price to plummet to $36. The next day, United Copper opened at $30 and after a day of frenzied selling, closed at $10. Fritz Heinze, who still had major loans outstanding, was broke. When word got out of his self-dealing loans, Heinze was forced to resign from the Mercantile National Bank on October 16. Soon after, Morse was forced to resign from all leadership positions in any bank. On October 18, rumors were now focused on Barney as the speculation was that Knickerbocker Trust had been involved.[53]

BANK RUN

By this time, with all of the jitters, in some cases short-term interest rates had briefly soared from 25 percent to 125 percent and the stock market kept tanking.[54] Hearing the news about the Heinze-Morse-Barney fiasco and the Knickerbocker Trust rumors, J. P. Morgan, who had been attending an Episcopal convention in Richmond, Virginia, decided to return to New York on October 20. Despite a reassuring front page article in the *New York Times* on the morning of Monday, October 21, that banks were sound, panic was about to set in. National Bank of Commerce, the clearinghouse for Knickerbocker Trust, announced it would no longer clear Knickerbocker checks.[55] It was also announced that, after a board meeting, Barney was asked to tender his resignation as president of Knickerbocker Trust.[56]

As Green had predicted months earlier, on October 22, 1907, there was a run on Knickerbocker Trust. It was a fair and mild day.[57] By 9 a.m. about a hundred people lined up on the sidewalk by the bank, waiting for the 10 a.m. opening to withdraw their deposits. They were ushered in, in an orderly fashion, as the line extended outside. With stacks of money piled high on the counters beside them, tellers dispensed the currency. Clerks made frequent trips to the vault to retrieve more cash. As word spread of the bank run, a line of automobiles and carriages formed in front of the bank. Knickerbocker's vice president told depositors that they would keep paying out deposits until the bank's official close at 3 p.m.

But at around 12:30 p.m., a bank officer announced that no more payments would be made that day, although payments would probably resume the next morning. Some of the people gathered in the banking room couldn't hear him and asked him to speak louder. He simply shouted, "The company is solvent," and then retreated to his office. Tellers closed their windows. For an hour after doors were closed, most of the depositors who had been outside remained in line, not understanding what was happening. In two and a half hours that morning, more than $8 million had been returned to depositors. Knickerbocker Trust was no longer solvent.

Three weeks later, a gunshot rang out in Charles Barney's home. Lily Barney ran to find her husband Charles lying on the floor with a bullet wound though his abdomen and a revolver beside him. He died shortly afterwards.[58]

THE MYSTERIOUS WOMAN IN A BLACK VEIL

Behind the scenes, J. P. Morgan had supervised a group of bankers to consider a bailout of the Knickerbocker Trust, but he concluded it was beyond saving.[59] Within weeks, two other trusts were in trouble: the Trust Company of America and Lincoln Trust. On November 5, Morgan convened another meeting. Clusters of men descended to the meeting on 36th Street, including bank heads, directors of trusts, and prominent business leaders. At around 6 p.m., a mysterious woman in a black veil entered the building to join them. Morgan later claimed it was Russell Sage's widow, who had inherited her husband's $100 million fortune just over a year prior.[60] But rumors persisted, and some reporters were convinced that it was the veil-wearing Hetty Green. Finally, at 3 a.m., an agreement was reached to save the two trusts.[61]

While this was happening, another storm was brewing. J. P. Morgan, his trusted partner George Perkins, and a few others were privy to information that showed New York City was on the verge of financial collapse.[62] A city official came to Perkins privately indicating that unless the municipal government was able to raise $20 to $30 million by November 1, the city would be insolvent. It couldn't pay its employees or contractors. After the failed bond attempt in the summer, the city was only successful in a bond issue in September after Morgan's intervention. According to Perkins, "To raise even one million dollars seemed about as possible at that moment as to move a mountain."[63]

Mayor McClennan announced that the city needed to reduce its budget as much as possible. The city was in dire shape. It was only when Morgan led a group to buy $30 million of the city's bonds that New York was saved. Green's contribution was over $1 million.[64] She also lent money to

New York Central Railroad. She commented, "Those to whom I loaned my money got it at 6 percent. I might just as easily have secured 40 percent."[65]

On July 3, 1916, Green passed away. Her estate was estimated at more than $100 million. It was evenly distributed between her son, Ned, and daughter, Sylvia. Neither of them had heirs, so upon their passing Hetty Green's wealth was scattered in the wind, distributed to 63 different charities.[66]

PANIC REDUX

The Panic of 1907 wouldn't be the last financial crisis. In October 1929, U.S. stocks tumbled and ushered in the Great Depression that lasted for years and spread globally. On October 19, 1987, stocks suffered their worst one-day decline (as we'll see in Chapter 15). In 2007, what started as defaults on subprime mortgages in the U.S. led to the Global Financial Crisis and a global recession. In March 2023, unintended consequences of tight monetary policy and the hiking of interest rates by the Federal Reserve, combined with poor risk management practices, led to a bank run and the demise of Silicon Valley Bank and other banks as well.

BUY THINGS WHEN NO ONE WANTS THEM

Benjamin Graham was a well-known economist and professional trader. He is often considered the first proponent of value investing, an approach that he began teaching at Columbia Business School in 1928. In 1949, he wrote his classic book, *The Intelligent Investor: A Book of Practical Counsel*. In one of many famous quotes from the book, he distinguishes between investments and speculation. "An investment operation is one which, upon thorough analysis, promises safety of principal and an adequate return. Operations not meeting these requirements are speculative."[67] His most famous student, and protégé, was Warren Buffett.

Buffett, Berkshire Hathaway's chairman, had a lot in common with Green. Both were known for their frugality. Green had an office at New York's Chemical National Bank. Including her walnut desk, it was estimated that "all the furniture would not bring $15 at auction. . . . There is little sign of comfort or luxury about this little office."[68] At a time when Berkshire Hathaway's headquarters boasted only 20 employees—exceedingly small for a company its size—Buffett once joked that Green wouldn't approve of Berkshire's "lavish headquarters."[69]

Buffett's teacher, Graham, wasn't the first person to distinguish between investments and speculation. Nor was he the first value investor in America, although he was most certainly the first to codify the approach through his teaching and writing. Green's value investing approach clearly predated Graham's. In 1897 (when Graham was only three years old), a reporter commented to Green, "You are said to speculate a great deal in Wall Street and to make money there." She corrected him: "That is a mistake. I never speculate. I sometimes buy stocks but I buy them as investments and not as speculations. I never buy on a margin [by borrowing]."[70]

That same reporter asked her to describe her investment principles. She reflected, "I only use common sense. I buy when things are low and no one wants them. I keep them until they go up and people go crazy to get them. That is, I believe, the secret of all successful business."[71] As we saw in our last story, emotions got the best of Sir Isaac Newton. He's the type of person that Green viewed as going crazy and buying something when everyone else also wanted it. It's not easy to go against the grain. But doing so in a disciplined fashion can be rewarding. That means doing your homework and not taking anything for granted—like leaving your money in Knickerbocker Trust, where the men were too good-looking.

In February 1908, after the Panic of 1907 had subsided, Green reflected on lessons learned.[72] "I saw the situation developing three years ago, and I am on record as predicting it. I said that the rich were approaching the brink, and a 'panic' was inevitable. There were signs I couldn't ignore. Some of the solidest men of the 'street' came to me and wanted to unload all sorts of things, from palatial residences to automobiles. . . . There had been an enormous inflation of values, and when the unloading process was begun the holders of securities found great difficulty in getting real money from the public."

She continued, "I saw the handwriting on the wall and began quietly to call in my money, making few new transactions and getting into my hands every available dollar of my fortune against the day I knew was coming. . . . When the crash came I had my money, and I was one of the very few who really had it. The others had 'securities' and their 'values.' I had the cash, and they came to me. They did come to me in droves." Liquidity matters, particularly in times of distress. That's when cash is king. Or rather, in the case of Hetty Green, when cash is queen.

NOTES

1. Sparkes, Boyden, and Samuel Taylor Moore, *The Witch of Wall Street: Hetty Green* (Garden City, NY: Doubleday, Doran & Company, 1935), 280–281.
2. Bruner, Robert, and Sean Carr, *The Panic of 1907: Lessons Learned from the Market's Perfect Storm* (Hoboken, NJ: John Wiley & Sons, 2007), 65–66.
3. "Richest Woman, Mrs. Green, Dies," *El Paso Herald*, July 3, 1916.
4. Carpenter, Frank, "A Chat with Hetty Green: The World's Richest Business Woman Talks About Herself," *Saint Paul Globe*, July 18, 1897.
5. Wallach, Janet, *The Richest Woman in America: Hetty Green in the Gilded Age* (New York: Doubleday), 8–18.
6. Ibid., 18–30.
7. Ibid., 121.
8. Ibid., 47–49.
9. Ibid., 44.

10. Ibid., 53.

11. Ibid., 54–55.

12. Ibid., 63–65.

13. Ibid., 65–68.

14. Ibid., 68–70.

15. *Robinson v. Mandell et al.*, Circuit Court, D. Massachusetts, Case No. 11,959, October 1868, https://law.resource.org/pub/us/case/reporter/F.Cas/0020.f.cas /0020.f.cas.1027.3.pdf.

16. "The Richest Woman in America," *New York Times*, November 1, 1905.

17. Wallach, *The Richest Woman in America*, 80.

18. Ibid., 94.

19. "The Richest Woman in America," *New York Times*.

20. Ford, Carol, "Hetty Green: A Character Study," *National Magazine*, April 1905, 630.

21. Ibid., 632.

22. Slack, Charles, *Hetty: The Genius and Madness of America's First Female Tycoon* (New York: Ecco, Harper Perennial, 2005).

23. Wallach, *The Richest Woman in America*, 99.

24. Ibid., 125.

25. Weyde, Vander, "Hetty Green, the Richest Woman in America," *San Francisco Call*, March 26, 1899, 18.

26. "The Richest Woman in America," *New York Times*.

27. Wallach, *The Richest Woman in America*, 128.

28. Ibid., 103.

29. Ibid., 100.

30. Ibid., 116.

31. Clews, Lewis, *Twenty-Eight Years in Wall Street* (New York: Irving Publishing Co., 1888), 437–446.

32. Ibid., 437.

33. Ibid., 444.

34. Ibid., 441.

35. Wallach, *The Richest Woman in America*, 149–150.

36. Ibid., 179.

37. Ibid., 187.

38. Ibid., 198.

39. Ibid., 201.

40. Nations, Scott, *A History of the United States in Five Crashes* (New York: William Morrow, 2017), 16.

41. Ibid., 17–18.
42. Bruner and Carr, *The Panic of 1907*, 31.
43. Nations, *A History of the United States in Five Crashes*, 1–3.
44. Ibid., 19–20.
45. Ibid., 22–26.
46. Ibid., 27.
47. Ibid., 28.
48. Ibid., 30.
49. Ibid., 31–32.
50. Ibid., 32–33.
51. Ibid., 34–36.
52. Ibid., 36–37.
53. Ibid., 37–40.
54. Wallach, *The Richest Woman in America*, 202–205.
55. Nations, *A History of the United States in Five Crashes*, 41–46.
56. Bruner and Carr, *The Panic of 1907*, 71.
57. Ibid., 77–81.
58. Ibid., ix–x.
59. Wallach, *The Richest Woman in America*, 202–205.
60. Sparkes and Moore, *The Witch of Wall Street*, 278.
61. Wallach, *The Richest Woman in America*, 202–205.
62. Bruner and Carr, *The Panic of 1907*, 111.
63. Ibid.
64. Wallach, *The Richest Woman in America*, 205.
65. Sparkes and Moore, *The Witch of Wall Street*, 282.
66. Higgins, Mark, "The Story of Hetty Green, America's First Value Investor and Financial Grandmaster," *Financial History,* Fall 2022, 11–15.
67. Graham, Benjamin, *The Intelligent Investor: A Book of Practical Counsel* (New York: Harper & Brothers, 1949).
68. Carpenter, "A Chat with Hetty Green."
69. Laneri, Raquel, "Why Wall Street's 'Witch' Was Actually a Woman to Be Admired," *New York Post,* August 8, 2018, https://nypost.com/2018/08/08/why-wall-streets-witch-was-a-actually-woman-to-be-admired/.
70. Carpenter, "A Chat with Hetty Green."
71. Ibid.
72. Sparkes and Moore, *The Witch of Wall Street*, 281–282.

CHAPTER SEVEN

GREED AND FEAR: BUFFETT AND THE GREAT SALAD OIL SWINDLE

This story brings together a tipster, a villain, a visionary, and arguably the greatest investor of all time. And it's mixed with salad oil. The Great Salad Oil Swindle can be traced back to June 1960. That's when an anonymous tipster, known as "the Voice," raised concerns with American Express Company about what was *really* in tank number 6006 in a warehouse in Bayonne, New Jersey—and it wasn't just soybean oil. The villain was a shady character, Anthony (Tino) DeAngelis, who wore black-rimmed glasses and crumpled clothes. He was described as having a girth that appeared to be as wide as his height, and was possibly tied to organized crime.[1] The visionary was Howard Clark, who transformed American Express, a company with an emerging iconic brand. It was also a company whose shareholders faced unlimited losses from the Great Salad Oil Swindle as the only major U.S. company without limited liability protection. And it propelled Warren Buffett as the Oracle of Omaha, who had to fight fellow shareholders with his vision of the importance of long-term value versus short-term profits.

THE VILLAIN

Tino DeAngelis was born in 1915 in the Bronx, where his parents had immigrated from Italy. His early business start was in the meat industry. As a major supplier of pork to the army during World War II, he was able to avoid the draft. According to credit reports that called into question his character, it was alleged that he was involved in black market sales during the war. He was accused of exporting substandard cooking fat to Yugoslavia, resulting in his eventual payment of $100,000 in damages.[2]

DeAngelis acquired control of the publicly traded Adolf Gobel Company, a meatpacking business. After allegations of inferior products, he was required to pay new damages of $100,000, which were followed by SEC investigations. Shortly afterwards, another one of his companies was accused of exporting inferior lard to Germany, resulting in "the usual" $100,000 in damages paid.[3]

DeAngelis later created Allied Crude Vegetable Oil Refining Corporation with $500,000 in capital. He formed the company in order to partake in a U.S. government program known as Food for Peace. The program subsidized the export of crop surpluses, including edible oils, by private U.S. companies.[4] It was both political and humanitarian: it helped to keep crop prices high when there was excess supply, and also distributed surplus oil to countries with starving populations.[5] DeAngelis took 22 employees with him from Adolf Gobel. They became known as the 22 Club. One of their tasks was to convert old petroleum tanks into edible oil storage tanks.[6] Members of the 22 Club were paid the generous salary of $400 per week (over $200,000 annually today), some with no obvious roles. Most drove company-provided Cadillacs.[7]

Allegations of fraud and underworld connections followed DeAngelis. He was accused of falsifying documents for the Food for Peace program. He was accused of $1.5 million in personal tax evasion. Both charges resulted in out-of-court settlements. He was also accused of falsifying inventories at Adolf Gobel. That charge was dropped when, mysteriously, the key prosecution witness changed his mind about evidence he had previously presented.[8]

Mafia members were said to have direct connections with one of DeAngelis's business partners, including Leo "The Mouse" Rugendorf and John "Donkey Ears" Wolek.[9] DeAngelis's businesses had huge sales volumes, but they bought commodities at really high prices, and sold at really low prices. According to author Norman Miller, "It was a mystery to orthodox business[people] how he could make money at the game."[10] Such a business model made sense in one context: underworld connections looking for a business front to launder money.

THE VISIONARY

American Express Company (Amex) was dominant in travel and financial services. It traced its roots to the New York stagecoaches and the express parcel delivery business started by Henry Wells in 1841.[11] In 1960, Howard Clark succeeded Ralph Reed as chief executive.

Clark was born in 1916 in South Pasadena, California. He loved sports and excelled in both golf and tennis.[12] He was Southern California junior golf champion in 1933 and later in life served on the executive committee of the United States Golf Association, helping to establish the World Cup of Golf. Clark was also a top amateur tennis player who defeated the legendary Bobby Riggs five times. (Riggs was later the world's number-one professional, and at age 53 famously lost the "Battle of the Sexes" tennis match to the women's champion, Billie Jean King.)

Clark graduated from Stanford University, and later attended business school at Columbia University and law school at Harvard University. After serving as a lieutenant in the navy in World War II, Clark joined Amex as an assistant in the executive office before working his way up to chief executive.

Clark's initial priority as chief executive was focusing on the viability of the American Express credit card, which was losing money. He considered selling the card or merging it with Diner's Club, the first independent general-purpose payment card. Eventually Clark decided to stick with the card.[13]

One of the most visible changes that Clark made soon after taking the top job was to make the Amex brand more visible. He personally decided to adopt a new logo that was first a simple blue stripe but later became a blue box. He also changed advertising agencies and boosted the advertising budget.[14] The new agency, Ogilvy, Benson & Mather, created the slogan "The company for people who travel." The public began to identify with the brand.

Clark then focused on four Amex subsidiaries that were marginally profitable. One was the separately incorporated American Express Field Warehousing Company (AEFW), whose chief executive was Donald Miller. The parent company had set a target of $500,000 in profits for each subsidiary.[15] But between 1944 and 1962, AEFW made money in only 10 of 19 years and had a cumulative loss.[16]

In the late 1950s, AEFW had around 500 client accounts, but all the profits were from two companies that happened to have the same owner: Tino DeAngelis. One company was Freeze House Corp. and the other, Allied Crude Vegetable Oil Refining Corporation (Allied), was an account AEFW acquired in 1957. Amex officials were delighted with the Allied account in particular. In 1959, one Amex official commented that it "turned in $12,000 in February, with damn little expenses. That's what we need more of."[17]

BIRTH OF THE ORACLE

On May 1, 1956, at the age of 25, Warren Buffett started his first partnership, Buffett Associates Ltd.[18] On January 1, 1962, Buffett dissolved all eleven partnerships he had accumulated and brought them into one new entity, Buffett Partnership Ltd. (BPL). Net assets were $7.2 million. Buffett had already become a millionaire.[19] Over the next few years, BPL had strong performance. Buffett's 1964 investment in Amex would be the start of an entirely different approach of investing, launching him into the realm of all-time greatest investors.

What would be different with the Amex investment, compared to Buffett's previous investments, was the *way* he invested in it. It's well known how much of Buffett's value-investing style was inherited from Benjamin Graham, co-author with David Dodd of the 1934 classic *Security Analysis*. Buffett viewed stock investing akin to owning a business. But he felt that it was only worthwhile acquiring that business at a reasonable price. To ensure he didn't overpay, he looked for a margin of safety, or the difference between what he felt a stock was worth compared with what it was selling for. Buffett wasn't concerned with diversification and was prepared to go all-in when he saw a bargain. But his investment style was about to evolve.

Prior to his Amex stock acquisition, when Buffett bought what he considered to be an undervalued stock, he pushed for board representation or even control. That was the case with his Dempster Mill Manufacturing Company investment.[20] He invested in that stock because the shares were trading for less than half the value of Dempster's cash, inventory, and accounts receivable less all liabilities. He first bought stock in 1956, got board representation in 1958, and achieved control of the firm with more than 50 percent ownership in 1961.

Buffett pushed management to increase profits but was unsuccessful. So he installed a new manager who turned things around, but at a reputational cost to Buffett. For example, Buffett's new management team laid off one hundred workers from the only factory in tiny Beatrice, Nebraska. Buffett was subsequently vilified in the local newspaper—an experience he never wanted to go through again. Starting with Amex, Buffett's approach was first to uncover undervalued firms that were fundamentally good businesses and had capable managers. He then let the managers do their jobs, resulting in cash flowing into Buffett's partnership.

THE VOICE

In June 1960, Donald Miller, chief executive of Amex's warehousing subsidiary AEFW, received a phone call from a tipster who said his name was Taylor; Amex employees later referred to him simply as "the Voice."[21] He claimed to work on the night shift at Allied in Bayonne, New Jersey. The Voice warned Miller, "The biggest hoax ever pulled is being pulled on American Express because there is in fact water in the tanks, and we are counting it as oil." At first he demanded $5,000 (about $50,000 today) to provide more information.[22] He eventually provided more information anyway, specifically about tank 6006. "Whenever we went to take inventory at the tank, we would be dropping the weight into this metal chamber, which was filled with soybean oil, but the balance of the tank had water in it."[23]

Allied was in the commodities business, particularly salad oils such as soybean. Borrowing was important for a growing business. Banks would lend to these types of companies using the commodities as collateral. But they first insisted that independent specialist storage companies guarantee the quantity and quality of the commodity. That's where AEFW came in. The warehouse company needed to ensure the goods were being safely stored, and then it issued receipts to banks, validating the storage of the commodities, which in turn acted as security for loans.

A variation on the practice was for the storage company like AEFW to establish a "field warehouse" right on the borrower's property. This was the case in Allied's Bayonne, New Jersey, facility. Effectively, Amex's subsidiary AEFW was just putting their name on Allied's storage facility. Further blurring the lines, AEFW hired guards who were previously on Allied's payroll. So, while technically being employed by AEFW, for all intents and purposes, they were Allied employees. As you can imagine, such an arrangement was ripe for fraud.

After his conversation with the Voice, AEFW chief executive Donald Miller ordered a surprise inspection at Allied of tank 6006, as well as other tanks. Amex inspectors first found that all of the tank openings were welded shut except for the measuring hatch. They then found water in the five tanks they were able to check that Friday. However, when they returned after the weekend, there was nothing suspicious in the other tanks. A report on the reliability of inventory in tank 6006 was inconclusive and water in the first five tanks was attributed to "broken steam pipes." Despite the Voice's warning and the eyebrow-raising initial findings, business between Allied and AEFW continued as usual.

Unbeknownst to investigators, DeAngelis had created an elaborate network of pipes with false compartments and special sampling tubes that contained actual oil. More than three years later, when the fraud was finally detected, the main tap on tank 6006 was finally opened. Instead of containing almost $4 million of soybean oil, seawater poured out for 12 days.[24]

SCAMS AND
THE DOWNFALL

Undeterred by the close call, DeAngelis created another scam field warehousing operation, this one with the Harbor Tank Storage Company. Harbor Tank subleased 41 tanks at Bayonne, but Allied legally owned only 10 of them. Seven of the tanks were condemned and not in use, and 23 were legally leased to other firms. Four tanks had been continuously used for petroleum.[25]

In the fall of 1961, Allied started buying heavily in the oil futures market. Futures contracts are agreements between two parties to exchange physical assets or their cash equivalents at an agreed-upon price and future date. Allied had secured a large export order to Spain for 275 million pounds,[26] but only had about 20 percent of that amount of physical oil. Allied continued investing heavily in futures, through respectable brokers, including Haupt & Co., that were able to trade on the New York Produce Exchange.

By 1963, DeAngelis was pushing up the prices of oil futures in anticipation of heavy demand by countries such as Poland, Yugoslavia, Pakistan, and Egypt as part of the Food for Peace program. Rumors also swirled around the commodity exchanges that a large number of Russia's crops had failed, and the country would soon be buying U.S. vegetable oil.[27] In fact, there were actually bumper foreign crops, and as such, high futures prices weren't sustainable.

Futures trading requires setting aside margins (a percent of the contract value) with brokerage firms as a cushion against price drops. So with each price decline, Allied needed to provide more money in the margin accounts. By November 1963, the exchanges and government commodities agencies finally realized that Allied trading was driving up the futures prices. When a commodities exchange investigator demanded to see Allied's records, the jig was up, and the company filed for bankruptcy. Futures prices plummeted.[28] Soybean oil futures went from $9.875 on November 15 to $7.75 on November 19, a drop of over 20 percent.[29]

An examination of publicly available information would have easily exposed the fraud. According to Census Bureau statistical reports, AEFW's warehouse receipts totaled twice as much vegetable oil as all of the oil in the U.S. By the end of 1963, warehouse receipts had been issued for 937 million pounds of oil worth $87.5 million, while actual quantities were less than 100 million pounds.[30]

Meanwhile, in the fall of 1963, Amex chief executive Howard Clark had finally decided to sell AEFW. The transaction, with Lawrence Warehousing Company, was to be effective December 1963. The tipping point for the sale was Clark's belief that senior warehousing officials had been compromised. He also found out that Miller, AEFW's chief executive, owned shares in one of DeAngelis's companies, a violation of the Amex's conflict-of-interest rules. Miller offered to resign, and Clark accepted his resignation.[31] Unfortunately for Amex, the timing of the planned sale came too late.

THE BRAND

At the time of the Great Salad Oil Swindle, Amex was unique in its corporate structure. It was a joint stock company, the last large U.S. public company with unlimited liability.[32] Its shares were traded in the over-the-counter (OTC) market, the predecessor to the Nasdaq market. By 1963, there were over 4 million Amex shares and over 24,000 shareholders. Around this time, Amex was looking to incorporate, becoming a limited liability company like almost all other listed companies (which it eventually did in 1965).

Soon after DeAngelis's firm went bankrupt in November 1963, claims against AEFW were reported to be $150 million or more. This was close to the year-end value of Amex's stock, which was around $162 million.[33] Since AEFW was a separately incorporated subsidiary, that meant Amex probably wasn't responsible for its liabilities. But there were also legal rules that might have overridden the separation. For example, if it could be successfully argued that AEFW wasn't healthy when it was first organized, or wasn't really independent, then Amex might have been responsible for AEFW's liabilities. All of this created uncertainty regarding Amex's potential liability.

Regardless of technical legalities, Clark pondered whether Amex *should* compensate for any losses at AEFW. He needed to consider important stakeholders with different perspectives. If Amex denied liability for its subsidiary, many banks would then be on the hook for losses. Given the huge role that banks played in Amex's travelers cheques business, that might kill all of the business that the banks brought to Amex.

On the other hand, satisfying bankers might risk upsetting shareholders. Clark also had to consider how the swindle would impact customers, and whether they would stop using Amex products. With permission of the board of directors, on November 27, 1963, Clark issued the following press statement: "If our subsidiary should be liable for amounts in excess of its insurance coverage and other assets, American Express Company feels morally bound to do everything it can, consistent with its overall responsibilities, to see that such excess liabilities are satisfied."[34]

BUFFETT INVESTS

The swindle started featuring in the press on November 20, 1963. Initially there were few details. Then for the next while almost no one paid attention because all eyes were focused elsewhere on one of the biggest stories of the century. On November 22, while riding in a Dallas motorcade,

President John F. Kennedy was assassinated. Buffett was having lunch in the Kiewit Plaza in Omaha, downstairs from his office, when he heard that Kennedy had been shot. He went back to the office and checked what was happening in the financial world. That's when Buffett found out about the carnage on the stock exchanges. Stock prices were dropping rapidly. On the New York Stock Exchange (NYSE), $11 billion in shareholder value was destroyed in the half hour before an emergency closure of the exchange. It was the first such emergency closure since 1933. (That's when tear-gas bombs, apparently tossed into the ventilating apparatus, had closed the exchange.)

Not surprisingly, Kennedy's death relegated the Great Salad Oil Swindle to the back pages. Intrigued by the possibility of buying the stock cheaply, Buffett tracked Amex's stock price. Even after markets reopened, the stock never recovered and continued to drop. Based on the market's reaction, the survival of Amex was in doubt.[35]

Here's what was happening with Amex's stock price. On November 21, 1963, it dropped by more than 1.6 percent as the scandal emerged. That day, commodities exporter Bunge Corporation filed a suit against AEFW for $15 million of lost oil. Amex chief executive Clark responded that if there was some error, losses would be covered by insurance. Clark was confident that the missing oil problem would be cleared up in a few days.[36] On November 22, the stock dropped by 4.6 percent. Also that day, the well-known stock market barometer, the Dow Jones Industrial Average (the Dow), dropped by 2.9 percent. That was by the time the NYSE halted trading due to Kennedy's assassination.

The next trading day, November 26, Amex's stock dropped by 11.5 percent, while the market rebounded with a gain of 4.5 percent. Over the next three days, when the market was up cumulatively by more than 1 percent, Amex's stock dropped by 6.9 percent, 6.4 percent, and 10.5 percent, respectively. Between the close on November 20, before the scandal broke, and December 2, when Amex's stock temporarily stabilized, its price dropped from $61.81 to $40.00, a decline of over 35 percent. The stock would reach a low on June 2, 1964, at a price of $35.31, for a drop of almost 43 percent in less than eight months since the scandal broke. By then it was 45 percent below the recent highest price of $63.88 on October 29, 1963.

When news of the swindle broke, Buffett wondered what impact it would have on Amex's reputation. He felt its reputation was what propelled the stock's value. It was all about trust in the travelers cheques and credit card. Rather than just speculate, Buffett needed facts. So to test this conjecture, Buffett visited restaurants and other places that accepted Amex credit cards and travelers cheques.[37] He also put one of his acquaintances on the case, a stockbroker named Henry Brandt. The top graduate from his class at Harvard Business School, Brandt looked like a scruffy Jerry Lewis.[38] He worked at Woods, Struthers & Winthrop, enjoyed sleuthing, and was being paid (through trading commissions) by Buffett's partnership, BPL, to do part-time research.[39] Both Brandt and Buffett were detail oriented and relished this kind of investigating.

Brandt talked to bank tellers, bank officers, credit card users, hotel employees, and restaurant workers in order to get a feel for whether usage of Amex credit cards and travelers cheques had fallen off because of the swindle. Brandt came back with stacks of research. Based on that research and his own, Buffett concluded that while Wall Street had punished Amex by battering the stock price, Amex's reputation hadn't been tarnished on Main Street.[40]

By early 1964, Buffett's father, Howard, was stricken with cancer. Warren assumed the role of family leader, organizing his father's estate. At that time, BPL was flush with cash from both profits and new money rolling in, with capital of $17.5 million. It takes both strong conviction and nerves of steel for a fund manager to risk a large amount of capital on one stock. But that's what Buffett did. In the last few weeks before Howard passed away on April 29, 1964, Warren invested in Amex at a frantic pace, as he had never before invested. By the end of June 1964, he had invested almost $3 million in Amex, making it BPL's largest single holding, at more than 17 percent.[41]

SHAREHOLDER VERSUS SHAREHOLDERS

Buffett's Amex investment was different compared to his previous ones. He wasn't looking to make a quick buck and get out. He wasn't simply buying a discounted business that had lots of assets like property, plant, and equipment. Buffett recognized that Amex's value depended on its reputation. Later, in 1969, he would tell *Forbes*, "Look, the name American Express is one of the greatest franchises in the world. Even with terrible management it was bound to make money. American Express was last in the travelers cheque market and had to compete with the two largest banks in the country. Yet after a short time it had over 80 percent of the business, and no one has been able to shake this position."[42]

Nevertheless, by the time Buffett was investing heavily, Amex's shareholders had lost a considerable amount of value. Before an eventual resolution with creditors, a small group of shareholders took legal action against the firm, arguing the firm had no legal obligation to settle liabilities of a separate subsidiary.[43] They felt any settlement would hurt Amex's shareholder value. They were particularly concerned that holders of a large number of forged warehouse receipts that DeAngelis had created would not receive any money.

Unlike his perspective in earlier investments such as Dempster Mill, where Buffett was looking to extract cash from the firm as quickly as possible, he viewed Amex in a different light. Buffett felt management was doing the right thing in protecting the Amex brand. He was concerned that attempting to derail any settlement would damage the brand. On June 16,

1964, Buffett sent a letter to Clark, praising management, and imploring them to settle for the sake of reputation. "While I am certain that management must feel at times like it is in the midst of a bottomless pit regarding the field warehouse activities, it is our feeling that three or four years from now the problem may well have added to the stature of the company in establishing standards for financial integrity and responsibility which are far beyond those of normal commercial enterprise."[44]

Buffett likened the situation to a typhoon that would soon pass, and even offered to testify, at his own expense, as a shareholder supporting management's actions. This was another pivotal moment for Buffett, taking a long-term perspective and being willing to sacrifice short-term profitability. Buffett's assessment of Amex's future was spot-on. Six decades later, Buffett still owned Amex stock.

According to Buffett's biography, *The Snowball*, the period when Buffett was buying Amex's stock was between mid-April and June 1964. Price records show that during that time, its average price was around $41.22. Two and a half years later, at the end of 1966, Amex's stock was at $92.50, a gain of over 124 percent. The Dow lost almost 6 percent over that time period. Given the amount of capital Buffett risked, his ability to buy near the bottom, and the huge gains in such a short period of time, a case can be made that this was one of the best investments ever, certainly for Buffett and his partnership.

GREED AND FEAR

By 1967, Amex was able to negotiate a settlement of $60 million with creditors involved with the Great Salad Oil Swindle. On an after-tax basis, that worked out to $31.6 million. Profits between the time the scandal broke and the settlement exceeded that amount. Amex was largely able to leave the scandal behind by the fall of 1964.[45]

Amex executives later realized the swindle was actually the greatest public-relations event in the firm's history. The press coverage of Amex was generally favorable during the scandal, and the public saw that the company stood behind its obligations. In 1964 alone, travelers cheques sales increased by almost 12 percent. When the storm had passed, Clark was later asked if perhaps a salad oil swindle every few years might be a good idea. He replied, "I don't think I have enough good years of my life to give away for another swindle."[46]

The Great Salad Oil Swindle showed why character and reputation matter. A leopard can't change its spots. DeAngelis had a long track record of unscrupulous behavior and never really changed. To him, paying fines seemed to be just a cost of doing business. And yet it didn't deter other companies from dealing with him, until his empire came crashing down. Even then, he didn't take responsibility for his actions.

So why did banks and commodity exporters lend to DeAngelis's businesses, and in increasing amounts? Before his downfall, rumors had swirled for years that a swindle was going on at Allied. Partly, it was through tunnel vision. As the president of a commodity export company that made large loans to Allied later said, "We didn't deal with this Tino character. We dealt with American Express."[47] It's easy to rely on someone else in place of your own due diligence, but there's no substitute for your own analysis. Investing requires hard work and analysis. Buffett and Brandt did a lot of legwork before investing in Amex. Buffett didn't simply rely on a hunch that Amex's reputation would survive, or because someone else was investing in the company.

Clark made a bold decision by pronouncing that Amex was "morally bound" to cover AEFW's liability. He's still remembered as one of Amex's great leaders. He recognized the importance of trust and a brand's reputation. To paraphrase from a quote attributed to Winston Churchill, he also didn't let a good crisis go to waste—the crisis enormously increased his prestige in Amex. He was even referred to as "a demigod."[48] It also made it easier for him to restructure Amex. Both Clark and Buffett recognized that long-term value trumped short-term profit.

How can we sum up the root cause of the scandal? Incentives and motives matter. In order to survive, AEFW needed to show consistent profits. This may have caused AEFW's chief executive Donald Miller to overlook DeAngelis's character flaws, since his dealings with Allied were profitable. As author Norman Miller concluded, "Tino succeeded because bankers, brokers and business [people], despite the glaring indications that they were dealing with a crook, could not resist the bait of big profits. . . . The reason they were convinced that Tino's deals were good can be stated in one word—greed."[49]

Those bankers, brokers, and businesspeople were all greedy until they feared they would lose it all. Buffett turned that premise on its head when he famously proclaimed his investing goal: "We simply attempt to be fearful when others are greedy and to be greedy only when others are fearful."[50] Stocks may become overvalued when everyone wants to invest in them, and undervalued when no one wants them.

NOTES

1. Woolf, Emile, and Moira Hindson, *Audit and Accountancy Pitfalls: A Casebook for Practising Accountants, Lawyers and Insurers* (Hoboken, NJ: John Wiley & Sons, 2011), https://onlinelibrary.wiley.com/doi/pdf/10.1002/9781119209287.app1.
2. Ibid.
3. Ibid.
4. Ibid.
5. Miller, Norman, *The Great Salad Oil Swindle* (New York: Coward McCann, 1965), 48–49.
6. Woolf and Hindson, *Audit and Accountancy Pitfalls*.
7. Miller, *The Great Salad Oil Swindle*, 35.
8. Woolf and Hindson, *Audit and Accountancy Pitfalls*.

9. Miller, *The Great Salad Oil Swindle*, 27.
10. Ibid., 26.
11. "American Express Company," Encyclopedia.com, June 8, 2018, https://www
    .encyclopedia.com/social-sciences-and-law/economics-business-and-labor/
    businesses-and-occupations/american-express-company.
12. Zuckerman, Laurence, "Howard L. Clark Dead at 84; Ex-Chief at American
    Express," *New York Times,* February 7, 2001.
13. Grossman, Peter, *American Express, The Unofficial History of the People Who
    Built the Great Financial Empire* (New York: Crown Publishers, 1987), 299–304.
14. Ibid., 297.
15. Weinstein, Mark, "Don't Buy Shares without It: Limited Liability Comes to
    American Express," *Journal of Legal Studies* 37, no. 1 (2008): 189–227.
16. Grossman, *American Express,* 306.
17. Ibid., 308.
18. Schroeder, Alice, *The Snowball: Warren Buffett and the Business of Life*
    (New York: Bantam Books, 2008), 201.
19. Ibid., 240.
20. Gramm, Jeff, "Warren Buffett and American Express: The Great Salad Oil
    Swindle," in *Dear Chairman: Boardroom Battles and the Rise of Shareholder
    Activism* (New York: Harper Business, 2016), 48–49.
21. Unless otherwise noted, descriptions of events in this section are from Woolf
    and Hindson, *Audit and Accountancy Pitfalls*; and Gramm, "Warren Buffett
    and American Express," 50–55.
22. Ibid.
23. Ibid.
24. Woolf and Hindson, *Audit and Accountancy Pitfalls*.
25. "Lost Tank Adds to Oil Mystery; Turn in Commodities Case Confirmed at a
    Hearing Held in New Jersey; Some Leases Invalid; Storage Facility Subleased
    from Allied Not Shown on Map of Bayonne Farm," *New York Times*, January 4,
    1964, https://www.nytimes.com/1964/01/04/archives/lost-tank-adds-to-oil-
    mystery-turn-in-commodities-case-confirmed-at.html.
26. Miller, *The Great Salad Oil Swindle*, 107.
27. Ibid., 137.
28. Woolf and Hindson, *Audit and Accountancy Pitfalls*.
29. Taylor, Bryan, "Warren Buffett vs the Salad Oil Swindler, November 1963,"
    Reformed Broker, November 20, 2013, https://thereformedbroker.com/2013/
    11/20/warren-buffett-vs-the-salad-oil-swindler-november-1963/.

30. Woolf and Hindson, *Audit and Accountancy Pitfalls*.

31. Grossman, *American Express*, 316.

32. Weinstein, "Don't Buy Shares without It."

33. Ibid.

34. Grossman, *American Express*, 321.

35. Schroeder, *The Snowball*, 259–260.

36. Miller, *The Great Salad Oil Swindle*, 165–166.

37. Schroeder, *The Snowball*, 260.

38. Ibid., 187.

39. Ibid., 257.

40. Ibid., 260.

41. Ibid., 261–262.

42. "How Omaha Beats Wall Street," *Forbes,* November 1, 1969, https://klse .i3investor.com/web/blog/detail/JTYeo/2014-07-01-story55217-Forbes_on_ Warren_Buffett_How_Omaha_Beats_Wall_Street_1969.

43. Gramm, "Warren Buffett and American Express," 58–60.

44. Ibid., 218–219.

45. Grossman, *American Express*, 327.

46. Ibid., 328.

47. Miller, *The Great Salad Oil Swindle*, 89.

48. Grossman, *American Express*, 328.

49. Miller, *The Great Salad Oil Swindle*, 246, 249.

50. Buffett, Warren, "To the Shareholders of Berkshire Hathaway Inc.," 1986, https://www.berkshirehathaway.com/letters/1986.html.

CHAPTER EIGHT

THE BLANK-CHECK COMPANY SCAM

D o you like new and exciting opportunities? Well, if you're a stock
investor, then there's nothing newer or more exciting than an initial public offering (IPO). That's when a company is first listed
on an organized exchange, like the New York Stock Exchange (NYSE) or
Nasdaq. If you're a major client of an investment bank that is facilitat-
ing or underwriting the IPO, you may have special access to buying the
stock at its IPO issuing price. This matters because, on average, U.S. stocks
increase by about 20 percent on their first day of trading.[1] That's a fabulous
one-day return. Much of that bounce comes right at the opening trade, so
if you don't have IPO access, you've already missed out.

But there are also risks involved in buying an IPO stock compared with stocks that are already public companies. IPO stocks tend to have a shorter track record and the companies are often not yet profitable. They might be in an emerging industry, like the internet industry was in the mid-1990s. That's when Netscape Communications Corporation (originally Mosaic Communications Corporation) had the most popular web browser, before Microsoft's Internet Explorer, Alphabet's Chrome, and others came along. It was one of the first internet-related companies to go public, on March 9, 1995.

Netscape's stock had a wild ride. The price jumped on the first day from $28.00 to $58.25. By December, the stock had skyrocketed to $171. But by early 1998, the stock had plummeted to $32.13. After a resurgence in late 1998 and early 1999, the company was acquired by AOL for over $195 per share (the total value of all shares was $4.2 billion). That was just before the bursting of the so-called dot-com bubble. Many other internet-related companies didn't fare nearly as well. For example, Pets.com filed for bankruptcy nine months after its February 2000 IPO. Its lasting legacy was a doglike sock puppet carrying a microphone, which even appeared on ABC's *Good Morning America*.

Now suppose you weren't a major client of an underwriting firm and yet you wanted to get access to those up-and-comers that are still private companies, but on the cusp of becoming public companies. What could you do? Special-purpose acquisition companies (SPACs) were all the rage in the early 2020s. Invented by investment bankers David Nussbaum and David Miller in 1993, their popularity exploded in 2020 and 2021. That's when more than 860 SPACs raised $246 billion.[2] But then the SPAC market took a dive in 2022, with proposed Securities and Exchange Commission (SEC) regulations that were anticipated to effectively kill the SPAC market.

Compared with IPOs, there was a big catch with SPACs: you really didn't know what you might be investing in, because SPACs were shell companies formed for the purpose of seeking out a private firm in order to take it public. You can see why they were also known as blank-check companies.

It was like handing a signed blank check to someone you trust to go out and buy something that they thought would make a good investment. More on SPACs later, but first let's take a look at a cautionary tale from 18th-century England, in what may have been the world's first blank-check company. We'll see why it sometimes looks like everything old is new again, and we have to painfully relearn old lessons.

THE SOUTH SEA COMPANY

To set the stage, let's take a look at the emerging stock market in the early 18th century. The precursor to today's publicly traded company was known as a joint-stock company. Investors owned a share in the company, but unlike today, they faced unlimited liability for the company's debts. One early joint-stock company in Britain was the South Sea Company.

In 1711, the South Sea Company was incorporated by an act of Britain's Parliament to reduce the cost of the national debt in return for providing monopoly trade in and around South America. Despite dubious prospects of profitability, the stock rose from £128 per share in January 1720 to over £1,000 in August of that year, before retreating to around £100 later that year—not unlike stock gyrations in so-called meme stocks like GameStop in 2021. As our story in Chapter 5 recounted, Sir Isaac Newton got caught up in the South Sea frenzy and lost much of his wealth due to a bad case of FOMO, or fear of missing out.

THE BUBBLE ACT

Partly in response to the hype at the time, the so-called Bubble Act, as it became known, was passed in 1720. Many contemporary accounts tend to refer to its main purpose as containing stock market speculation and reining in joint-stock companies' excesses. But the reality was quite different. Let's start with the Act's actual title: "An Act for better securing certain Powers and Privileges, intended to be granted by His Majesty by Two Charters, for Assurance of Ships and Merchandize at Sea, and for lending Money upon Bottomry; and for restraining several extravagant and unwarrantable Practices therein mentioned."[3] It was a hodgepodge omnibus bill. Only the last part of the title referred to stock market excesses.

The genesis of the bill was a House of Commons committee formed on February 22, 1720.[4] The original intent was to protect the interests of the South Sea Company, which was already in the process of refinancing the national debt by converting government-backed annuities into South Sea stock (more on annuities, in 18th-century France, in Chapter 10). By April 27, 1720, the Act that authorized the scheme had received royal assent. Not coincidentally, South Sea Company stock was held by many members of Parliament. On May 27, 1720, the committee amended the bill to include the incorporation of two marine insurance companies, the Royal Exchange and London Assurance. This was somewhat surprising because these companies had recently been under investigation for their stock subscription practices. The final version of the Act was rushed through and received royal assent on June 11, 1720.

Nineteen of the 29 clauses in the Act referred to the insurance companies. Six of the clauses referred to protections for the South Sea Company and a few other companies. Only a few of the clauses were directed at the so-called Bubble Companies—that's the last part in the title of the Act, "for restraining several extravagant and unwarrantable Practices." The Act deemed such companies "illegal and void" unless authorized by Parliament. Perhaps those clauses were aimed at protecting investors. But a cynical view is that they were trying to protect the interests of the South Sea Company by preventing the diversion of capital to these Bubble Companies. And recall that South Sea Company stock was held by many members of Parliament.

THE BUBBLE COMPANIES

Around the time of the South Sea frenzy, nearly 200 other joint-stock companies were formed, collectively denoted as Bubble Companies. The term wasn't referring to the inflated asset price "bubble" connotation commonly used today, but rather to con artists. Most Bubble Companies that made it to the market flamed out in short order, just like Pets.com in 2000. However, a few emerged as successful firms, including the two marine insurance companies: the Royal Exchange and London Assurance.[5]

According to John Caswell in *The South Sea Bubble*, in late 1719, "The rising whirlwind of speculation was catching up innumerable projects, old and new, possible and visionary, sound and unsound."[6] That depiction has a modern-day parallel to U.S. technology stocks in the mid- to late 1990s. That's when former Federal Reserve chairman Alan Greenspan famously referred to possible "irrational exuberance" in the markets. While it's difficult to get a precise number because companies were advertised in different coffeehouses and taverns under different names, Caswell estimates that about five were promoted in December 1719, over 20 by February 1720, and almost 30 by April 1720.

Initially, genuine joint-stock companies were coming to market in conventional industries such as insurance, fisheries, and finance. But then came a second wave of companies related to services, inventions, and new trading opportunities. These included improving the coal trade from Newcastle, large-scale funeral furnishings, and pawnbroker chains. There was one company for carrying on the patent for heat-resistant paint, trading in wool, and "preserving our countrymen from being carried into slavery." There was also a company that made a patent sword, described as "worth a victory to the army first has it."[7]

Between May and mid-June 1720, more than a hundred new companies were advertised, causing some newspapers to double in size to accommodate the notices. On June 9 alone, there were 24 advertisements. These new listings included trading in hair, trading in "the true national commodity of woad," purchasing the disputed titles of land, importing broomsticks from Germany, and extracting silver from lead.[8] While this last company's mission sounds outlandish today, around that time alchemy was a serious endeavor; even Sir Isaac Newton was a dedicated alchemist.

Among the genuine companies that did go to market was one by Sir Richard Steele, an English essayist, dramatist, journalist, and politician. Steele was elected to Parliament as a Whig in 1713.[9] The company was 18th-century new tech. His Fish-Pool company had received a patent in 1718 and was designed for boats to carry live fish to London markets. As the patent stated, it was a "New way or Method of making Shipp . . . for ye Conveying and Preserving of Fish (tho' caught in parts ever so remote) alive and in as healthy and thriving a Condition as they would be were they to be still in the Sea."[10] Sounded like a great idea: catch fish remotely and keep them alive and fresh. Steele's Fish-Pool company's share price quickly increased from £100 to £160. While the idea of fresh fish brought directly to a nearby market sounds great in theory, the problem was that the new technology didn't work. When the seas were stormy, the fish smashed against one another and perished.

THE BLANK-CHECK SWINDLE OF 1720

Charles Mackay's 1841 classic, *Memories of Extraordinary Popular Delusions* (which later became *Extraordinary Popular Delusions and the Madness of Crowds*), detailed some of the companies that would eventually be declared to be illegal by the Bubble Act and abolished. They included ones for insuring horses, encouraging the breeding of horses in England, improving the land in the county of Flint, paving the streets of London, furnishing funerals, improving the art of making soap, improving gardens, importing walnut trees from Virginia, increasing children's fortunes, importing beaver fur, improving malt liquors, drying malt by hot air, insuring all masters and mistresses against the losses they may sustain by servants, a hospital for taking in and maintaining illegitimate children, and fitting ships to suppress pirates. There was even a company that claimed it made a wheel for perpetual motion.[11]

Mackay also documented the most celebrated—or perhaps infamous— prospective company of the era. It's a candidate for consideration as the world's first blank-check company, described in 18th-century lingo as "A company for carrying on an undertaking of great advantage, but nobody to know what it is."[12] When you think about it, that's just what a SPAC is.

The prospectus stated that the required capital was £500,000, issued in 5,000 shares of £100 each. There was a required deposit of £2 for each share. For each share owned, the subscriber would then receive £100 per year. So, in one year, investors would get their capital back, and then enjoy similar amazing returns in future years. The promoter promised that in one month the full details of how the company would make that money would be revealed.

According to Mackay, the next morning at nine o'clock, the (unnamed) promoter opened his office in Cornhill to crowds of people at his door. By the time he closed at three o'clock in the afternoon, he had more than 1,000 subscribers. He had collected over £2,000 in five hours, around $2 million[13] in today's money. He was philosophical enough to be content with that amount and set off for continental Europe that evening, never to be heard from again. Sounds far-fetched? Mackay anticipated a skeptical reaction from his readers. So Mackay added, "Were not the facts stated by scores of credible witnesses, it would be impossible to believe that any person could have been duped by such a project."[14]

SPACs: THE NEW BLANK-CHECK COMPANIES

Fast-forward three centuries to the new blank-check companies: SPACs. They were formed through IPOs, for the sole purpose of combining with private companies, typically start-ups.[15] SPACs had no assets beyond the cash they took in and no specific business plan. The SPAC companies generally had two years to merge with or acquire another company—otherwise they needed to return the money to investors. If 20 percent or more of investors disapproved of a proposed acquisition, it wouldn't go forward.

Perhaps it's unfair to compare SPACs with the infamous 1720 swindle. But there were some parallels. The major similarity was that for both the 1720 swindle and SPACs, investors provided the upfront capital without knowing how that capital was going to be deployed. Another similarity was the optimism and leap of faith of investors. SPACs might have been the only type of investment where you didn't really know what you were getting at the time of the investment. But of course, there were major differences. First and foremost, SPACs certainly weren't outright swindles, and there were some rules in place to protect investors. Nonetheless, just like the eager investors in 1720, SPAC expectations were excessive and actual returns often didn't meet expectations.

SPAC investing was essentially betting on the jockey, the sponsors who formed the company, because there wasn't any horse. The sponsors often included high-profile names to attract investors, such as tennis star Serena Williams, basketball star Shaquille O'Neil, legendary skateboarder Tony Hawk, former football quarterback Colin Kaepernick, and former *Cosmopolitan* editor Joanna Coles. Some well-known SPAC mergers included Richard Branson's space-tourism Virgin Galactic Holdings Inc., sports-betting firm DraftKings Inc., electric-car battery company QuantumScape Corp., and flexible workspace company WeWork Inc.

It's true that with a SPAC there was initially relatively little downside, as most money was returned if no suitable acquisition was identified in two years. Of course, that's after initial costs, which include paying the sponsors. That was a huge issue because they tended to get a 20 percent stake in any merged company at a deep discount.[16]

There was also an opportunity cost. Based on history, a low-cost index fund might easily return 10 to 20 percent cumulatively over two years. According to a critical reporter from the *Wall Street Journal*, "SPACs appeal to those with short attention spans, offering immediate gratification."[17] Perhaps that's too harsh. But if you were considering a SPAC or any type of investment, it was useful to take a hard look in the mirror first. Are you tired of boring long-term buy-and-hold index investing (not that there's anything wrong with that!) and just looking for a quick gain? Be clear as to what your motivations and expectations are.

DEVIL TAKE
THE HINDMOST

Would you have been duped by "A company for carrying on an undertaking of great advantage, but nobody to know what it is?" Even before the astounding rise (and fall) in the South Sea Company stock price, 13 new joint-stock companies were launched in 1719, and each had eager investors.[18] With great foresight, a contemporary newspaper, the *Daily Post*, tried to warn its readers of the hype that might be coming. It did that by creating a ruse. And it's possible that this stunt might have been the origin of the cautionary tale that Mackay famously described. On December 18, 1719, the *Daily Post* started carrying a series of ads for an "extraordinary scheme for a new insurance company to be proposed, (whereof publick notice will speedily be given in this paper)," and offered "permits to subscribe" for £0.05, around $50 today.

No details of the scheme were presented, and the permit sales took place on December 24. Several hundred people eagerly bought the permits, from a person who was unknown to anyone in the crowd. The promoter signed the receipts with a clearly fictitious name, made up from the initials of the six individuals who fabricated the scheme. On December 26, the *Daily Post* ran another ad, explaining that the whole incident was a hoax designed with the sole purpose to show how easy it was to "impose upon a credulous multitude," and offered refunds to all.

The 18th-century equivalent to today's bloggers, YouTubers, and social media influencers were pamphleteers. They were particularly popular during the South Sea Bubble. One such anonymous pamphleteer summed up the mood prophetically in May 1720, noting about South Sea stock, "The additional rise of this stock above the true capital will be only imaginary; one added to one, by any rules of vulgar arithmetic, will never make three and a half; consequently, all the fictitious value must be a loss to some persons or other, first or last. The only way to prevent it to oneself must be to sell out betimes, and so let the Devil take the hindmost."[19]

In other words, the pamphleteer accurately envisioned that South Sea stock was like a game of musical chairs and the music was about to stop. Making an investment on the basis that prices of an asset like stocks, real estate, or even cryptocurrency will continue on an upward trend without any consideration of the asset's true underlying value is fraught with danger. If you assume there's always a greater fool out there who will buy your asset at a higher price, that just may end up making you the fool.

So how did some of those well-known SPACs turn out? Virgin Galactic Holdings Inc. was listed in 2019 and its price increased by almost 500 percent before dropping by 96 percent by the end of 2023, to one-fifth of its initial SPAC price. Sports-betting firm DraftKings Inc. started as a SPAC in 2019 and was listed on Nasdaq in 2020 after its business combination. It increased from its $10 SPAC price by over 600 percent before dropping by over 50 percent. By the end of 2023, it was still more than 3.5 times above its initial SPAC price. Electric-car battery company QuantumScape Corp. was listed in 2020, and increased from its $10 SPAC price by over 1,200 percent before dropping by 95 percent. By the end of 2023, it was about one-third below its initial SPAC price. Of the 401 SPACs listed since 2021 that acquired other companies, only 27—less than 7 percent—had increased in price by early 2024.[20]

Perhaps one of the most infamous SPACs was flexible workspace company WeWork Inc. It was listed in 2020 and its stock price increased by 32 percent before a major price drop. On November 6, 2023, WeWork filed for bankruptcy protection. After restructuring that month, by the end of 2023 its stock price was down 99.996 percent from its initial price. There's an interesting backstory about the person who was the face of WeWork, who at one time was about as charismatic and clever as that 1720 Cornhill promoter was. But this modern-day promoter wasn't a crook. He didn't commit fraud, although he did end up with a lot of other people's money.

WeWork was co-founded in 2010 by then 30-year-old Adam Neumann. He became its captivating and somewhat quirky CEO. Besides his official corporate title, Neumann was colorfully described by the *Guardian* as "the tall, long-haired, barefoot, meat-banning, weed-smoking, tequila-drinking, Kabbalah-studying, experimental school–opening Paltrow-cousin-in-law."[21] In August 2019, WeWork was a darling and had just filed documents for its traditional initial public offering. But then the bottom fell out.

What came out in the filing really wasn't new information, but caused potential investors to pause as they reviewed the information in a new light.[22] The company was losing a lot of money; its projection for the size of the shared office space market was wildly optimistic; and its entire corporate culture and strategy were completely tied to Neumann's whims and somewhat wild ideas. The IPO was pulled and Neumann exited from his position. But the price for the exit that Neumann negotiated was a testament to his negotiating skills.

Around the time of the failed IPO, Neumann received $185 million from a noncompete agreement, a $106 million settlement payment, and $578 million for shares he sold to Softbank Group Corp. He also obtained a loan from a Japanese firm for $432 million, secured by some of his WeWork shares that he kept.[23] Once those shares became virtually worthless, that meant that if he chose not to repay the loan, the bank would get the virtually worthless shares in return. After WeWork's bankruptcy filing in November 2023, according to the Bloomberg Billionaires Index, Neumann was still worth $1.7 billion.[24]

With such a spectacular flame-out like WeWork, you would think that Neumann's business reputation would be in tatters. Who would ever invest in another company he founded? Well, in 2022, Neumann created a new start-up called Flow. It planned to operate multifamily residential properties with an aim to give a feeling of community and ownership. Neumann received a $350 million investment from Andreesen Horowitz, a venture capital firm. Before the business had even commenced operations, it was already valued at $1 billion.[25]

While it seemed like a good idea for that 1720 Cornhill promoter to quietly slip away to continental Europe and never be seen again, perhaps, for his sake, he should have come back a few years later and started another blank-check company.

NOTES

1. Ritter, Jay, "Initial Public Offerings: Updated Statistics," University of Florida, June 20, 2022, https://site.warrington.ufl.edu/ritter/files/IPO-Statistics.pdf.
2. Kiernan, Paul, "SPAC Mania Is Dead: The SEC Wants to Keep It That Way," *Wall Street Journal*, January 24, 2024.
3. Harris, Ron, "The Bubble Act: Its Passage and Its Effect on Business Organization," *Journal of Economic History* 54, no. 3 (1994): 610–627.
4. Ibid.

5. Chancellor, Edward, *Devil Take the Hindmost: A History of Financial Speculation* (New York: Plume, 2000), 72.

6. Caswell, John, *The South Sea Bubble* (Stanford, CA: Stanford University Press, 1960), 141.

7. Ibid., 142.

8. Caswell, *The South Sea Bubble*, 155–156.

9. Mutter, Reginald, "Sir Richard Steele, British Author and Politician," *Britannica*, https://www.britannica.com/biography/Richard-Steele.

10. Chancellor, *Devil Take the Hindmost*, 70.

11. Mackay, Charles, *Extraordinary Popular Delusions and the Madness of Crowds* (Petersfield, UK: Harriman House Classics, 2003), 71–74.

12. Ibid., 65–66.

13. Estimate according to Odlyzko, Andrew, "Bubbles and Gullibility," *Financial History*, Winter 2020, 16–19, http://www.dtc.umn.edu/~odlyzko/doc/mania17.pdf.

14. Mackay, *Extraordinary Popular Delusions*, 65. Authors in the 20th and 21st centuries are divided on the legitimacy of the event. According to Caswell, "I have found no evidence from the most celebrated of all [Bubble Companies]—the company for a project which shall hereafter be revealed; but perhaps its prototype is the 'Proposal for raising the sum of Six Millions sterling to carry on a design of more general advantage . . . and of more certain profit . . . than any undertaking yet set on foot' advertised in the *Daily Post* for 21 May [1720]" (Caswell, *The South Sea Bubble*, 156). According to Chancellor, "This legendary company may relate to a spoof promotion recorded in *Mist's Journal* in early January 1720. J. P. Malcolm in *Anecdotes of the Manners and Customs of London during the Eighteenth Century* (London, 1808, p. 67) records a similar scheme." (Chancellor, *Devil Take the Hindmost*, 72.) And yet, according to Andrew Odlyzko, "It is possible that there was even a project that did advertise itself literally as "an undertaking of great advantage, but nobody to know what it is," since *Mercurius Politicus* for June 1720 listed it, and *Political State of Great Britain* for July 1720 reprinted that listing" (Odlyzko, "Bubbles and Gullibility").

15. A similar vehicle is a "blind pool" offering that raises funds to purchase assets that haven't yet been identified. However, blind pools are limited partnerships, and tend to have a specific plan, such as a real estate limited partnership that plans to invest in apartment buildings that haven't yet been selected. See Heyman, Derek, "From Blank Check to SPAC: The Regulator's Response to

the Market, and the Market's Response to the Regulation," *Entrepreneurial Business Law Journal* 2, no. 1 (2007): 532–552.

16. Kiernan, "SPAC Mania Is Dead."
17. Forman, Laura, "Sports Stars Think They Got Game in SPAC Arena," *Wall Street Journal*, April 5, 2021, https://www.wsj.com/articles/sports-stars-think-they-got-game-in-spac-arena-11617622201.
18. This account is from Odlyzko, "Bubbles and Gullibility."
19. Chancellor, *Devil Take the Hindmost*, 69.
20. Kiernan, "SPAC Mania Is Dead."
21. Zeitlin, Matthew, "Why WeWork Went Wrong," *Guardian*, December 20, 2019.
22. Ibid.
23. Maloney, Tom, and Bloomberg, "WeWork Founder Adam Neumann Is Still Worth $1.7 Billion Even After the Company's Stunning Bankruptcy," *Fortune*, November 8, 2023.
24. Ibid.
25. Ibid.

CHAPTER NINE

A TENNIS BOOK AND THE INDEX REVOLUTION

On the surface, two best-selling authors don't appear to have anything in common. Simon (Si) Ramo wrote *Extraordinary Tennis for the Ordinary Player*. Charles (Charley) Ellis wrote *Winning the Loser's Game*. Ramo was the co-founder of a major aerospace company and the oldest person to receive a patent. Ellis was the founder of a major financial services consulting company, and was dubbed by *Money* magazine the Wisest Man on Wall Street.

The connection is that reading Ramo's book inspired Ellis to think about how the tennis strategies that Ramo promoted could be applied successfully to investing.[1] Ellis not only wrote his own best-seller about the strategy, but he was instrumental in changing the mindset on Wall Street. In this story, you'll get to know the colorful Ramo, understand Ellis's key investing insights, and gain a fresh perspective on improving your own investment performance. And as an added bonus, you might improve your tennis game. But even if you don't play tennis, there are some important life lessons everyone can take away.

SI RAMO

Si Ramo was born in Salt Lake City, Utah, on May 7, 1913.[2] He aspired to be a concert violinist until age 12. That's when he heard the legendary Russian-born American violinist Jascha Heifetz play. Thinking he could never become a famous violinist like Heifetz, Ramo decided his better career path would be in science. Ramo and Heifetz subsequently became friends and, years later, after playing a duet together at a dinner party, Ramo was even more convinced he had chosen the correct career path.

In elementary school, Ramo skipped four half-grades. At the young age of 23, he earned a doctorate in electrical engineering and physics from Caltech. He was able to finish his degree in three years even with having to pass both French and German language proficiency exams. As Ramo recounted in an oral history,[3] he didn't bother to take either the French or German courses. He decided to take the German exam first because he felt it would be more difficult. He arrived at the three-hour exam, was asked his field of studies, and was given some readings in German related to his field of electricity.

After 90 minutes, Ramo completed the German translations. He figured there was no point in staying around, so he left. As he walked down the hall, he noticed a sign for the French exam, and figured, "Why not?" since there were still 90 minutes left. The French instructor pointed out that Ramo was late and wouldn't be given any extra time. He was given a

French book about vacuum tubes and radio tubes, and away he went. A week later he found out he had passed both exams. That caused quite a stir among the faculty, and later the rules were changed so that Ramo's clever show couldn't be repeated.

After World War II, Ramo worked at reclusive billionaire Howard Hughes's aircraft company. He chose to work for Hughes in part because he knew that one of the richest men in the world was an absentee owner and so would rarely be around. In 1953, Ramo co-founded his own aerospace firm, the predecessor to TRW Inc. Ramo was the "R" in TRW. The company was acquired in 2002 by Northrop Grumman Corporation for $6 billion.

Ramo was known as the chief architect of America's intercontinental ballistic missile (ICBM) system, the weapon most closely associated with the Cold War. The weapon had a range of 6,000 miles and could deliver a nuclear warhead capable of destroying a city while avoiding any defensive system. The U.S. and its Cold War rival, the Soviet Union, built so many intercontinental ballistic missiles that it was estimated they could destroy the world 10 times over.

At age 100 Ramo became the oldest person at the time to receive a patent, for a computer-based learning invention. He wrote 62 books on a wide range of subjects. His 1965 textbook, *Fields and Waves in Communication Electronics*, sold over a million copies.

Ramo also had a sharp sense of humor. In the 1950s, when the ICBM was in the development stage, test rockets were regularly blowing up on their launch pads. He was watching a test launch and sitting next to a U.S. Air Force general, Bernard Schriever. They saw one missile rise about six inches off the ground before toppling over. Undaunted, Ramo turned to the general and said, "Well, Benny, now that we know the thing can fly, all we have to do is improve its range a bit."[4]

EXTRAORDINARY TENNIS FOR THE ORDINARY PLAYER

Ramo wrote his first book about tennis, *Extraordinary Tennis for the Ordinary Player*, in 1970.[5] He wrote a follow-up book in 1984, *Tennis by Machiavelli*,[6] in which—tongue firmly in cheek—he claimed to have uncovered a 1517 manuscript about tennis written by Niccolò Machiavelli. Rather than claim authorship, Ramo referred to himself as the translator.

The premise of *Extraordinary Tennis for the Ordinary Player* was the importance of appreciating that there were actually two very different games of tennis. One game was played by professionals, and the other played by amateurs or ordinary players. According to Ramo, "The reason why it is worth recognizing that there are two games and not just one is that most players have no business playing one of them. They cannot do well, and they lose some of their happiness by trying. But it is worse than this. What they actually do is play one game while thinking they are playing the other. It is like being a cat and thinking you are a dog."[7]

According to Ramo, outstanding execution accounted for winning about 80 percent of the points made by professionals. In contrast, about 80 percent of the points were lost by amateurs on unforced errors.[8]

Ramo referred to the two games as "pro tennis" versus "ordinary tennis." He described ordinary tennis as "not to say that the players are necessarily terrible or inexperienced, awkward, slow, sloppy, incapable of hitting a backhand or getting anything but a gentle, high floating serve in. It just means, as the dictionary suggests, that they are undistinguished, of average capacity, a little dull to watch, more commonplace than inspired."[9]

According to Ramo, professionals played an entirely different game than ordinary players. They played a winner's game, by making brilliant and precise shots to win the match. In pro tennis, the players warmed up for a while before they started their game. The players had hard serves, the first faster than the second. The players rushed to the net after they served. The receivers often had a difficult time returning the serve, but sometimes hit the ball well, past the server, and scored a point. Occasionally, there was a rally with each player at the back lines, hitting hard drives to the corners, bouncing the ball barely in. The point was usually scored when the ball was placed well away from the opponent or hit extremely hard. The players had equally strong forehands and backhands.[10] In pro tennis, the audience might have to wait more than an hour for a serve to be broken.[11]

In ordinary tennis, players rarely warmed up. After impatiently chasing balls, they eventually determined who would start serving by "first ball in." The first few games acted like a warmup. After eventually getting a serve in, the server would start to rush to the net but invariably got caught halfway, missing the return serve. Low returns usually ended up in the net. Most often, the dominating plays ended up with errors. Players often hit shots off the graphite of the racket (or wood, when Ramo was writing in 1970) and often held their racket too loosely.[12]

Ordinary tennis players generally didn't win matches by their wonderful play. Rather, their opponent made a lot of mistakes, such as double faulting, hitting the ball into the net, or hitting the ball far out of the court. Ramo described the typical scoring. "In ordinary tennis, points are made as a result of your opponents' errors. The idea of the game is to make fewer errors than your opponent. . . . The only contribution made by the opponent is to keep the ball in play, thus offering to the ordinary player an irresistible attraction to the making of errors, most of them unnecessary, many of them stupid, all somewhat embarrassing, and none of them intended to be the way in which victory is to be achieved in tennis, as written in the official description of the game."[13]

Ordinary players botched shots. Ramo defined a botch as "a type of error, a mess, in which you cannot blame the performance of your opponent or your partner. A botch has to be an act that you do entirely on your own. Furthermore, it has to be something that is unnecessary. . . . You have to lose the point in an inexcusable way to create a botch,"[14] such as directing an easy serve into the net. Ramo continued, "In addition to the botch, there is the S.O.B., the 'son of a botch.' This, as the name implies, is a second-generation botch, the consequence of an earlier botch." There tended to be numerous S.O.B.s for every botch.[15]

What should the ordinary player do to succeed at tennis? According to Ramo, the key to winning in amateur tennis was to let your opponent make mistakes. All you needed to do was to try to not lose. In other words, don't try to play like a professional. "The principle was easy. If you wanted to improve your score in ordinary tennis, you would need to start giving attention to stopping these errors, particularly the large fraction of imbecilic ones."[16] For example, ordinary players should forget the attempted ace on their first serve. "The side with the fewest silly errors will win the game."[17] Ordinary players needed to recognize their limitations. Ramo concluded: "What we have been after is cutting down the errors around which ordinary tennis built—your errors, that is."[18]

CHARLEY ELLIS

Perhaps the most thoughtful person to read Ramo's *Extraordinary Tennis for the Ordinary Player* was Charley Ellis. Ellis was born in 1937 in Boston in the municipality of Roxbury, one of the first towns of the Massachusetts Bay Colony, originally settled in 1630. The most powerful educator in Ellis's early life was his sixth-grade teacher and school principal, Miss Nellie Walsh at the Elbridge Gerry School in Marblehead, Massachusetts. One day Ellis was surprised to be called into Walsh's office.[19] She told him, "Charles, I'm very disappointed with you. Am I right that you were found fighting with Peter on the school playground during recess?" The young

Ellis admitted that was the case, but he explained that Peter was picking on younger children and throwing snowballs at little kids, and he was trying to make Peter stop. Walsh replied, "Charles, I expect more of you than you would bring yourself to the likes of Peter. That will be all." Ellis would later say that that was the best lesson he had learned from anyone—to maintain a high personal standard.

For grades 9 through 12, Ellis attended Phillips Exeter Academy, the famous boarding school in Exeter, New Hampshire, and one of the oldest secondary schools in the United States. He then entered Yale College, the undergraduate liberal arts college at Yale University, to study art history. That's where he became involved in Yale's talk radio station, WYBC. After graduating from Yale, Ellis was briefly employed at WGBH, an FM radio station in Boston that eventually became a charter member of National Public Radio. A woman he dated there encouraged him to get an MBA from the Harvard Business School (HBS), so he did. It was a transformative experience for Ellis, helping him to think creatively.

Nearing graduation, a classmate who had some connections said that there was a job opening for an MBA graduate at Rockefeller. He encouraged Ellis to apply. Thinking his classmate meant the Rockefeller Foundation, the global philanthropic private foundation, Ellis immediately expressed interest. He soon had an interview. However, it quickly became clear that the position was for Rockefeller Brothers, Inc., the Rockefeller family office that managed investments and endowed the philanthropies. Although investing was a field that Ellis knew nothing about, he was offered a job and readily agreed.

Ellis's initial job involved writing research reports on various stocks. After reviewing Ellis's first report on textile stocks, his supervisor wasn't impressed. He arranged for Ellis to join a training program at the Wall Street firm Wertheim & Company, join the New York Society of Security Analysts, and enroll in night courses on investment basics at New York University.

Ellis learned an important lesson while in the training program. He recalled, "One day the firm's senior partner, J. K. Klingenstein, was our guest speaker. As he was about to leave, one of the trainees blurted out, 'Mr. Klingenstein, you're rich. How can we become rich like you?' Everyone else was mortified, and J. K. was clearly not amused. But then his face softened, and you could see that he was taking the question very seriously and trying to sum up everything he'd learned in a lifetime on Wall Street. The room was silent as a tomb, and finally Mr. Klingenstein said firmly, 'Don't lose.' Then he stood up and left. I've never forgotten that moment."[20]

In 1966, one of Ellis's classmates at HBS called him and suggested he visit his employer, the investment bank Donaldson, Lufkin & Jenrette (DLJ). The firm's business model was to provide quality independent corporate research to national investors. Ellis joined DLJ. While working there, he was also studying to earn his Chartered Financial Analyst (CFA) designation, the gold standard of credentials in the investment industry. To obtain the designation, candidates needed to pass three rigorous exams assessing a candidate's financial analysis and portfolio management skills. At that time, the exam was only offered once per year, on the first Saturday in June.

By 1968, Ellis had successfully passed the first two levels. But he was considered too young to take level III and had to wait another year. In June 1969, he finally had his chance at the final level. Ellis was shocked and delighted to see that the entire afternoon session was devoted to commenting on a recently published article in *Institutional Investing*. It was one that he himself had written! Prophetically enough, it was titled "To Get Performance, You Have to Be Organized for It." Not surprisingly, Ellis passed the exam and obtained his CFA designation that year.

In 1972, Ellis founded Greenwich Associates with $3,000 and an idea for a new kind of business research firm. It was based on consulting to banks, large fund managers, and Wall Street firms. His idea was to provide timely, unbiased, effective managerial information based on high-quality proprietary research, maintaining the relationship at a senior level. The primary added value of his company was providing good advice based on listening to a firm's clients, since those clients rarely provided feedback directly to their firms. Its business model was based on conducting thoughtful interviews with clients and analyzing the results. His customer base would eventually grow from 28 clients in North America in its first year of business to over 250 clients in 130 financial markets across the globe.

WINNING THE LOSER'S GAME

When Ellis read Ramo's *Extraordinary Tennis for the Ordinary Player*, it immediately struck him that Ramo's concept could be applied to investments. Certain investment professionals were playing the investment "game" brilliantly and were being rewarded for their efforts. But many amateur investors who were trying to play the professional game were falling short. They were buying high and selling low, or getting in or out of the market at precisely the wrong times.

According to Ellis, "There are people who are playing a winner's game. And they are doing something that is so beautifully done that you and I would be very confident they'll keep it up. Then there are a lot of people who are in there competing as best they can, but candidly, they make mistakes. They buy high and sell low, and they have their portfolio arranged the wrong way. And sooner or later they fall short of what they're trying to do."[21] Ellis was fond of the saying that there are *old* pilots and *bold* pilots but no old, bold pilots. Similarly, almost no experienced or "old" investors were consistently good at "bold" strategies such as market timing.

Ellis came to a profound realization: investors needed to realize that mistakes are extremely important. Therefore, the key to success was to avoid making mistakes. The new premise was that investment managers couldn't beat the market, so the message should become not to do anything by way of active management. That meant not trying to select individual securities and not trying to time the market, because when you try to take action, it will most likely be a mistake. According to Ellis, if you can't beat the market, then you should consider joining it. How? Today, there's an easy answer: by buying an index fund. But not so in the mid-1970s.

This idea inspired Ellis to write a seminal and award-winning article in 1975 called "The Loser's Game."[22] He followed-up and expanded the concept in his 1998 best-selling book, *Winning the Loser's Game*.[23] When Ellis wrote the original article, index funds were a radical concept. Inspired in part by reading Ellis's article, Jack Bogle (described in Chapter 2) created the first index mutual fund the following year. The premise of winning the loser's game was to avoid investing actively like professional managers and instead to take a passive investing approach, like investing in index funds.

LOSING BY EXCESSIVE TRADING

Here's an example of the potential harm caused by active investing. In a classic study, academics Brad Barber and Terrence Odean from the University of California, Davis, examined the discount broker accounts for over 66,000 households between 1991 and 1996.[24] While the overall market annual returns were 17.9 percent, those investors who traded the most underperformed by 6.5 percent annually. Trading costs played a big part, yet even examining returns before trading costs, investors underperformed on average after adjusting for risk. Barber and Odean attributed these results to individual investor overconfidence and concluded that "trading is hazardous to your wealth." Another way to frame their results is that investors were trying to win through active trading—playing the professional game—but ended up losing.

DON'T LOSE

The premise behind index investing is that it's extremely difficult for amateur investors to consistently outperform the market, like the S&P 500 index. So instead of futilely trying to beat the market by investing in "hot" individual stocks—think GameStop Corp. or AMC Entertainment Holdings, Inc. in early 2021, or a multitude of other so-called meme stocks—simply join the market. Instead of trying to time the market by getting out when you think prospects don't look good, and then jumping back in when you think prospects look great, invest in stocks for the long run.

There are a few other ways that you can follow the "don't lose" mantra. Start with a plan that includes your long-term investing goals and make sure the goals are realistic—just as you wouldn't expect to beat Serena Williams as your tennis goal. Avoid excessive trading. Consider passive index mutual funds or exchange-traded funds (ETFs) that replicate traditional indices like the S&P 500. Take a long-horizon view and avoid frequent market exits and reentries. Don't speculate on "hot tips" that everyone seems to be talking about. Don't invest based on emotions. When the ball is hit to you, just concentrate on returning it in the court. And don't fool yourself into thinking that you can make a spectacular cross-court shot to the baseline, the way the professionals do.

If you follow these steps, your journey may not be quite as exhilarating—or nerve-racking—as it otherwise might be. But your chances of reaching your financial goals may improve. And if you apply these concepts to tennis, other sports, and life in general, then by not losing you may actually end up winning.

NOTES

1. Lo, Andrew, and Stephen Foerster, *In Pursuit of the Perfect Portfolio: The Stories, Voices, and Key Insights of the Pioneers Who Shaped the Way We Invest* (Princeton, NJ: Princeton University Press, 2021).
2. Unless otherwise noted, biographical information in this section is from Pae, Peter, and W. J. Hennigan, "Simon Ramo Dies at 103; TRW Co-founder Shaped California Aerospace," *Los Angeles Times,* June 28, 2016, https://www.latimes.com/business/la-fi-simon-ramo-20160628-snap-story.html.
3. Ramo, Simon, and Frederik Nebeker, "Simon Ramo, An Oral History Conducted in 1996 by Frederik Nebeker," Institute of Electrical and Electronics Engineers, Inc., February 27, 1996, IEEE History Center, Piscataway, New Jersey, https://ethw.org/Oral-History:Simon_Ramo.
4. Berges, Michael, "Simon Ramo's Guide to Playing 'Smart Up' Tennis," *Los Angeles Times,* April 28, 1985, https://www.latimes.com/archives/la-xpm-1985-04-28-vw-21588-story.html.
5. Ramo, Simon, *Extraordinary Tennis for the Ordinary Player* (New York: Crown, 1970).
6. Ramo, Simon, *Tennis by Machiavelli* (New York: Rawson Associates, 1984).
7. Ramo, *Extraordinary Tennis,* 13.
8. Becher, Jonathan, "An Aerospace Engineer's Guide to Winning Tennis," JonathanBecher.com, August 17, 2014, https://jonathanbecher.com/2014/08/17/aerospace-engineers-guide-winning-tennis/.
9. Ramo, *Extraordinary Tennis,* 14.
10. Ibid., 14–15.
11. Ibid., 31.
12. Ibid., 15–21.
13. Ibid., 22–23.
14. Ibid., 132.
15. Ibid.
16. Ibid., 26.
17. Ibid., 25.
18. Ibid., 158.
19. Lo and Foerster, *In Pursuit of the Perfect Portfolio*, 255–256. Biographical details in this section are from the book as well as chapter 10, "Charles Ellis and Winning at the Loser's Game," 255–280.
20. Ibid., 259.

21. Ibid., 265.
22. Ellis, Charles, "The Loser's Game," *Financial Analysts Journal* 31, no. 4 (1975): 19–26.
23. Ellis, Charles, *Winning The Loser's Game, Timeless Strategies for Successful Investing,* 8th ed. (New York: McGraw-Hill Education, 2021).
24. Barber, Brad, and Terrance Odean, "Trading Is Hazardous to Your Wealth: The Common Stock Investment Performance of Individual Investors," *Journal of Finance* 60, no. 2 (2000): 773–806.

CHAPTER TEN

WHY SWISS BANKERS BET ON YOUNG LIVES

We don't know much about little Jeanne Pictet's short life, but she lives on as one of "the immortals." She was born in Geneva in the late 1770s. Geneva's wealthy bourgeoisie followed reports of her health in local newspapers.[1] She died tragically at the age of four. No doubt her passing was mourned by her aristocratic parents. Any parents would be devastated by such a loss. Who wouldn't be shattered by the death of an innocent child? Well, as it turns out, King Louis XVI of France, who must have been secretly rejoicing. With young Pictet's passing, the royal government had just saved a bundle of money.

FINANCING FRANCE'S ANCIEN RÉGIME

What could possibly have connected Pictet with government funding? Let's take a look at France's royal government finances from the beginning of the 17th century through the mid-18th century. This was during the *Ancien Régime,* or Old Regime, prior to the onset of the French Revolution in 1789. In Europe, France was a standout country, but not in a good way. It was a serial defaulter. Within a 120-year period, France experienced seven sovereign defaults.[2] That's about one every couple of decades. This was during a time when France was the leading powerhouse on the continent and was vying with England for naval supremacy.

France's defaults were typically triggered by wartime spending.[3] Once the fighting was over, it would usually convert high-interest short-term debt into lower-interest long-term debt. It also resorted to debasement and recoinage during wartime. This lowered the value of its currency and effectively reduced what it owed. (Maybe that's where today's loyalty programs learned the art of debasement.) However, a change took place in the first quarter of the 18th century. That's when there were four *peacetime* recoinages.

In the 1700s, France's expenditures persistently grew faster than its revenues.[4] Compared with England, France's fiscal system was much less effective in balancing budgets, and tax revenues kept falling behind spending. Tax revenues as a percentage of output declined from one peace era to the next. After the onset of the Seven Years' War (1756–1763), among most of Europe's great powers and their colonies, interest rates on France's borrowing became much higher than England's. Two more defaults occurred in the Old Regime in the second half of the 18th century, in 1759 and 1770. The 1770 default was initially billed as an eight-year suspension of interest payments, but became permanent.[5] Since the French government was constantly at risk of default, and because of constraints on raising taxes, France's royal government effectively paid a "default premium" on its debt throughout much of the 18th century.[6]

Government debt had evolved to become like today: dispersed and anonymously held.[7] But the structural flaw in France was a separation between government expenditures and revenue. Spending decisions were made by the king along with officeholders who purchased the right to help manage the administration in return for an exemption from paying most direct taxes. (Selling these rights was a clever source of revenue for the crown.) The major components of spending were related to the military and debt servicing. However, there were constitutional limits to taxation. New taxes or loans had to be registered by regional *parlements*. Often there was an impasse between the crown and the regional parliaments. And even tax collection was complex, with roughly half of the task farmed out to quasi-private collection agencies.

TONTINES

Necessity is the mother of invention. When it came to funding, France's royal government learned to be creative. That's where a fascinating funding mechanism came into play. It combined public financing with a form of life insurance, but in a gamification way. Known as a *tontine*,[8] it originated in France in the 17th century and was popular for over a hundred years. It then became virtually extinct for centuries, but the concept has been revived recently.[9] A tontine is an insurance contract that provides the purchaser or annuitant with income for life. As such, it is similar to a life annuity, a common insurance product readily available today.

But what makes a tontine distinct from a life annuity is how the payment stream is determined. For life annuities, the payment stream is fixed. For tontines, payments depended on what happened to the "heads" or nominees of a designated pool of investors or annuitants. (An annuitant receiving income payments could also be the nominee on whose life the income depended, or the nominee could be someone else.)

When nominees within the pool died, tontine payments were redistributed to annuitants of the surviving nominees. Eventually, the annuitant of the sole survivor received all of the payments. When that sole survivor died, payments ceased. Think you have exceptionally strong genes? Why not bet on your longevity and be part of a tontine pool? You could end up winning an amazing stream of income! That was the general pitch.

The tontine was devised by an Italian, Lorenzo Tonti,[10] a banker and a political adviser. He was also a self-promoting hustler. He once promoted the idea of a silkworm culture that would be nothing less than a "gold mine." Another time, he promoted a plan to keep the plague from London entering French cities. In the event it did enter, he had another plan to eliminate it.

Tonti himself came up with the name, the tontine. (Imagine if Elon had called his electric vehicle the Musky instead of Tesla.) He had the ear of Cardinal Mazarin Jules, a fellow Italian. Mazarin was the chief minister of Louis XIV who effectively governed France on behalf of the young king. Mazarin was facing the pressures of balancing France's books. Around 1650, Tonti proposed a solution for raising new funds, through his innovative scheme. In a series of royal orders in 1652 and 1653, the tontine was endorsed.

Tonti made some bold predictions about how overwhelmingly favorably the tontine would be received. He envisaged that anyone who examined tontines seriously would not only "joyfully" participate, but also encourage their friends to do so. Tontines were for everybody. Parents would buy shares in their children's names. And through tontines, daughters would accumulate "enough income to marry advantageously."[11] Married couples would have a strong incentive to take care of one another. Older investors would have enough income to garner respect and care.

The royal decrees promised Tonti untold wealth if the plan went through. He'd receive one-tenth of all of the income raised for the crown. He and his heirs would also receive the privileges of nobility. But nothing came of the idea in France for almost 40 years, until after Tonti's death. Tonti eventually fell out of favor with the crown, and for a mysterious reason lost to history, he was imprisoned in the Bastille for seven years. However, the idea caught on elsewhere. In 1653, the year of France's endorsement of the tontine, the first tontine was launched in Denmark. It was introduced by the postmaster-general, Paul Klingenberg, most likely after he learned of Tonti's plan in France.

Tontines eventually became a huge source of financing for France's Old Regime. The first royal tontine was issued in 1689, although it failed to raise its intended £20 million (the French currency at the time was the livre tournois, expressed as £). The last royal tontine was issued in 1759 and raised a record £46 million.[12] Around that time, the crown's annual revenue was about £500 million,[13] so tontines represented about one-tenth of government financing. To put those amounts in perspective, at the time of the French Revolution, many workers were earning just one or two livre tournois per day.[14]

Tontines spread beyond France and Denmark. During the 1770s, the Irish government issued three tontines.[15] Tontines were eventually issued in England, Germany, and the Dutch Netherlands. In 1790, Alexander Hamilton, the U.S. secretary of the treasury, proposed the issuance of a tontine. Congress rejected the plan. However, in the 19th century, the tontine was in vogue in the private sector, as a popular life insurance product.

In the 18th century, gambling in Europe was all the rage. While tontines were often viewed as a form of gambling on their own, in 1714 the French royal government made it more so with a new plan.[16] The new scheme offered investors a type of tontine that was also part lottery. The crown's plan was to sell 10,000 tickets, each costing £1,000, thus raising £10 million.

Chances of winning were one in seven. The winning black ticketholders were awarded either cash prizes or attractive life annuities. The losing white ticketholders still received consolation prizes of tontines.

LIFE ANNUITIES

Before 1750, France relied heavily on short-term borrowing. After that time, France's major source of new financing was through *rente viagères,* or life annuities.[17] By 1789, life annuities would become the largest component of France's debt. As countries today are sensitive to the stigma of a heavy debt burden and borrowing costs, this was particularly true in the 18th century. So, as a side benefit, financing through life annuities allowed the government to obscure its borrowing costs since the effective interest rate on life annuities isn't explicit, compared with, say, a loan.

A life annuity makes a predetermined periodic payment for as long as the nominee is alive. So the ultimate cost of issuing a life annuity depends on the life expectancy of the nominee. In the 17th century, various scholars had started to consider the relationship between mortalities and annuities.[18] In 1662, John Graunt published a rudimentary mortality table, which showed that out of 100 people born in his sample, 36 would perish by the age of 6, and all would die by the age of 87. Thirty years later, a more precise table was published by a well-known astronomer and mathematician, Edmond Halley. His was based on a sample of almost 6,000 births and deaths. Halley is better known for the comet that is associated with his name (actually discovered centuries earlier by Chinese astronomers[19]) than for the mortality table he created—except among life insurance actuaries.

Life annuities were used by the French government as early as 1693, during the Nine Years' War between France and a European coalition.[20] For the first half of the 18th century, French life annuities were structured based on age grading. This made sense, because younger nominees who were expected to live longer generated more lifetime payments than older nominees. And this wasn't a surprise to the French crown. In 1746, the royal government sponsored Antoine Deparcieux to analyze the emerging mortality tables to help fine-tune the pricing of upcoming life annuity offerings.

However, age grading of life annuities was dropped in 1757 when Jean de Boullogne became the controller-general of finance. (Ironically, Deparcieux's masterpiece on life annuities was dedicated to the same Boullogne, for his support in creating the work.[21]) This was just after the start of what would become the Seven Years' War between France and Britain. Instead of age grading, more costly flat rates were paid regardless of the age of the nominee. Until this time, the main market for the government had been 40- to 60-year-olds looking for pension income. Those annuitants were also the nominees themselves. The effective borrowing costs were reasonable, generally around 6 to 7 percent. But the cost of the most recent war and desperation for finding new funding sources caused a policy rethink.

The new life annuities were issued at an effective flat rate cost of 10 percent. From the perspective of raising more funds, the new issues were a huge success. They brought in twice as much as any previous issue. And not surprisingly, most annuities were placed on the lives of children. In 1794 French statesman Joseph Cambon later examined these flat-rate life annuities and harshly concluded, *"C'est ainsi qu'on se jouait de l'imbécillité de notre ancient gouvernement"* ("This is how we played with the imbecility of our former government.").[22] And no doubt, cumulative heavy borrowing was a contributing factor to the onset of the French Revolution. But in the short term, the need for capital was paramount.

A conservative estimate was that by the eve of the French Revolution, life annuities issued between 1765 and 1787 brought in over £113 million to the royal government, with annual annuity payments reaching over £10.3 million.[23] Based on how long it would take a worker to earn one livre tournois and converting to modern-day U.S. wages, the amount raised was equivalent to about $25 billion, with annual annuity payments of about $2.2 billion.[24] For some of the issues, three-quarters were purchased by foreigners. But records showed that subscribers also included the French from all walks of life: artisans, pastors, shoemakers, bailiffs, wigmakers, booksellers, and widows.[25]

THE SWISS INNOVATORS

At the end of the Seven Years' War in 1763, the French crown enacted a number of initiatives to shore up its dire financial state.[26] First, it issued an edict that tontines, costly to the royal government, would no longer be issued. The next year, the crown arbitrarily demanded a *dixième* (one-tenth) reduction of tontine payments. Then in 1770, the crown saved even more money by nullifying all tontines and converting them to life annuities. Many disenchanted shareholders chose to sell their former tontines rather than hold on to them. This is where Swiss innovators entered the picture, as life annuity buyers.

Geneva had a rich banking history. In the 12th century, Geneva was a city-state, part of the Holy Roman Empire.[27] It issued its own currency. By the 15th century, Geneva was famous for its fairs that brought together merchants from many parts of Europe, who exchanged both commodities and currencies. Over the next few centuries, banks played an increasingly important role, including deposit creation and lending, while maintaining a certain amount of currency reserves. Money changers became central to the entire monetary system.

Geneva had an advantageous geographic position as a center for trade. Geneva also played an important role in financing foreign wars, particularly by the French. The banks secured funds from Swiss depositors at lower rates than they lent to France. To a large extent, the deposits came from an unusual export: Swiss mercenaries. Requests from foreign governments were made to various Swiss regions for a quota of soldiers. Regions were paid in hard currency, part of which went to soldiers, but part of which was also retained by local governments. The result was a buildup of investable funds.

Like noticing the obvious holes in Swiss cheese, the Genevan bankers knew loopholes when they saw them.[28] The French crown order converting tontines to life annuities also allowed for the appointment of a new nominee. The tontine was familiar to many Genevans because a Swiss banker named Jacob Bouthillier Beaumont had first organized a subscription of tontines in 1759. The Genevan bankers were also apparently more familiar with insurance theory than French government officials were, and homed in on an exploitable and profitable opportunity. This lucrative scheme became known as *Les Trente Demoiselles de Geneve* ("The Thirty Maidens of Geneva").

The purchaser of a life annuity would clearly like to have their nominee live as long as possible. Instead of purchasing an annuity on, say a 50-year-old like yourself, why not on a much younger nominee? This was a potential arbitrage opportunity—buying something cheap and engineering it into something more profitable, without taking on more risk. This weak point in the French life annuity design, which cost the crown money, was later acknowledged by Jacques Necker, the Swiss banker and director general of finance under Louis XVI. Writing in 1780, he belatedly conceded that in order to have prevented speculation, it would have been necessary to establish effective life annuity interest rates by gradation of age.[29] Necker's stellar reputation died when he did. Historians later claimed that Necker's public finance skills were dubious and he had been overpraised in his lifetime.[30]

It was immediately obvious to Beaumont that there was a terrific opportunity. He could buy life annuities at a discount from the unhappy French owners who had originally invested in tontines and not life annuities. He could then appoint much younger nominees, and receive a much longer stream of income.

But Beaumont also came up with other novel twists. He decided to form a syndicate of investors with a number of life annuities and nominees, to pool risk. Why should one investor depend solely on the life of only one nominee? Instead, the death of one nominee, perhaps every few years among a group of nominees, would be both expected and somewhat predictable. Furthermore, there were ways to manage the risk by extending the life expectancy of the nominees. (Today, we call this process of pooling and creating new products *securitization*. It developed a bad reputation during the Financial Crisis of 2007–2009, with the implosion of securitized subprime mortgage loans.)

Beaumont also solved another problem with life annuities: the difficulty in selling them.[31] Beaumont made it easy to buy and sell shares in his syndicate. (Today, this is what we would describe as creating liquidity, like with stock exchanges and public equity, as opposed to illiquid private equity.) As a sign of his success, Beaumont's syndicate spawned numerous imitators both within and outside of Switzerland.

There was also a custom that facilitated the purchase of life annuities. They could be bought on credit. Members of a syndicate would enter into an agreement to reimburse the Genevan bankers with annual installments. Members would continue to use money from annuity payments to make their annual installments until they had fully repaid the bankers.[32] (Here's yet another modern-day parallel. The process of purchasing securities on credit is known as purchasing of shares "on margin." This involves paying only a portion of the value of the security and borrowing the remainder through a stock brokerage firm.)

Beaumont did his homework in the design of the scheme, to manage risk and tilt the odds of a desirable outcome in his favor, through statistics and healthcare management. For example, he was also able to leverage the work of fellow countryman Nicolaus Bernoulli, the mathematician, scientist, and statistician known for the Bernoulli principle in fluid dynamics.[33] Bernoulli had recently collected data to prove how effective the new smallpox vaccine was. So Beaumont chose nominees who had either survived smallpox or had been vaccinated.

THE IMMORTALS

Here's how Beaumont chose the nominees. Women live longer than men, on average, so why not a young female? But how young? Infant mortality was a concern, particularly from smallpox. The Genevan bankers concluded that a sweet spot was young girls between the ages of four and seven who had survived smallpox and other infant health issues. And not just any young girls, but the pampered ones with access to good care— daughters of aristocrats.[34] One such girl was Amelie Odier, whose father, Louis, a Genevan physician, was a major promoter of the smallpox vaccine. The girls were known as "the immortals," and were stars in their communities because so much wealth was riding on their lives.

In some exceptional cases, young boys were chosen as annuitants. In those cases, the boys were provided with a regular stipend in return for a commitment to stay in Switzerland. They also had to promise not to pursue any dangerous careers, such as the foreign service.[35]

The Genevan bankers looked for other ways to mitigate risk. It was clear to them that diversification was key. Rather than bet on the lives of just one girl who might die prematurely, they chose a larger number of girls to pool the risk. The number of "heads" varied from 22 to 60, but most commonly was 30. Hence the name *Les Trente Demoiselles de Geneve*.[36] Pooling also provided greater accessibility for investors, who could buy in to the scheme for as little as £30.

At first, the annuitants were chosen with great care. Life expectancy for French girls born around 1765 was about 28.[37] In the first series, a cohort of 22, the first to die was Colombine Diodati, at age 20. For the series issued in 1778, out of 22 girls, 15 were still alive 42 years later, and two lived to be over 80. However, the cohorts in series issued between 1780 and 1782 weren't as lucky. That's when Jeanne Pictet died prematurely at the age of four, and Pernette Elizabeth Martin at age eight.[38]

ANCIENT PORTFOLIO THEORY

Through diversification, Beaumont's syndicate was able to increase its expected return for a given level of risk compared with earlier investors. Ironically, it would be more than two centuries later when Harry Markowitz would be awarded the 1990 Nobel Memorial Prize in Economic Sciences for this same insight. In 1952, Markowitz published his seminal work in the area of portfolio diversification, in a paper called "Portfolio Selection."[39] It was the first finance paper to use rigorous mathematics and equations to show important risk-return trade-offs in an investing context.

Markowitz's framework became known as Modern Portfolio Theory. Even Markowitz knew he didn't discover the concept of diversification. He had in mind Antonio's speech near the beginning of Shakespeare's *The Merchant of Venice*: "My ventures are not in one bottom trusted." Markowitz commented, "Shakespeare knew you diversify; everybody knows you diversify."[40] Perhaps Beaumont should be credited with putting Ancient Portfolio Theory into practice.

Diversification matters. It's the one and only true "free lunch" for investors, in a risk-return sense. There's a lot of risk to holding only one asset, and that risk can be reduced by holding a number of assets, so long as those assets don't move in lockstep (in statistical terms, meaning as long as they aren't perfectly positively correlated). Buying a share in a pool of life annuities is much less risky than buying just one life annuity.

APRÈS MOI LE DÉLUGE

The year 1757 wasn't a good one for King Louis XV, the grandfather of Louis XVI. There was an assassination attempt on his life, and the French faced a disastrous defeat by the Prussians in the Battle of Rossbach. In that year, he purportedly commented to his mistress, Madame de Pompadour, "*Après moi le déluge*" ("After me, the flood."). The phrase has become an idiom for foreshadowing approaching disasters, like the impending French Revolution. However, the *déluge* or flood Louis XV was referring to was actually Halley's comet[41] (that's the same Halley of mortality table fame). Louis was an amateur astronomer, and this was around the time when Halley's comet was expected to pass by the earth, which it did in April 1759. Since biblical times, comets had been associated with disasters like floods.

Just prior to the start of the French Revolution in 1789, it was estimated that debt service, or interest payments, accounted for almost two-thirds of the state budget.[42] In an attempt to avoid default, annuity payments were redenominated into money that was increasingly worthless. Subsequently, scheduled payments were missed. In 1794, the life annuity debt was restructured, relying on actuarial techniques rather than flat rates. Then in 1797, the French state canceled two-thirds of its debt.

Some historians have viewed the high interest rates that the French government paid as "prepaid repudiation." In other words, investors anticipated likely eventual default and were compensated in advance for the increased risk.[43]

DON'T LOSE YOUR HEAD

For the 18th-century French life annuities, the nominees had to report to authorities twice a year to confirm they were still alive. This was inconvenient, but there was a work-around. Investors could simply purchase a life annuity on a famous person. It was easy to confirm that these celebrities were alive. And so it became quite popular to purchase life annuities on the "heads" of famous people. Like the royals.

By 1789, £400,000 in annual life annuity payments (about $88 million today[44]) was placed on the head of King Louis XVI; £247,000 ($54 million) on the king's cousin, Philippe Égalité; and £200,000 ($44 million) on the king's wife, Marie Antoinette.[45] Early in the French Revolution, in 1789, each of them met the same fate. They were beheaded by guillotine. And each time the guillotine came crashing down, a considerable French government debt obligation was extinguished. It's doubtful that little Jeanne Pictet's family shed a tear. Karma perhaps?

NOTES

1. MacDonald, James, *A Free Nation Deep in Debt: The Financial Roots of Democracy* (Princeton, NJ: Princeton University Press, 2006), 247.
2. Burdekin, Richard, and Richard Sweeney, "The Evolution of Sovereign Debt Default: From the Thirteenth Century to the Modern Era," *Journal of Economic History* 52, no. 2 (2021): 9–56.
3. Ibid.
4. Ibid.
5. Velde, Francois, and David Weir, "The Financial Market and Government Debt Policy in France, 1746–1793," *Journal of Economic History* 52, vol. 1 (1992): 1–39.
6. Ibid.
7. Ibid.
8. Jennings, Robert, and Andrew Trout, *The Tontine: From the Reign of Louis XIV to the French Revolution Era*, Huebner Foundation Monograph 12 (Philadelphia: Wharton School, University of Pennsylvania, 1982).
9. Guo, Jeff, "It's Sleazy, It's Totally Illegal, and Yet It Could Become the Future of Retirement," *Washington Post*, September 28, 2015, https://www.washingtonpost.com/news/wonk/wp/2015/09/28/this-sleazy-and-totally-illegal-savings-scheme-may-be-the-future-of-retirement/.
10. Jennings and Trout, *The Tontine*, 4–25.

11. Ibid.
12. Ibid., 2–3.
13. In 1758, government revenues were around £492 million excluding short-term borrowing, according to Riley, James, "French Finances, 1727–1768," *Journal of Modern History* 59, no. 2 (1987): 209–243.
14. Jennings and Trout, *The Tontine*, 2.
15. Ibid., 61–68.
16. Ibid., 26–50.
17. Velde and Weir, "The Financial Market."
18. Jennings and Trout, *The Tontine*, 47–50.
19. Matthews, Robert, "Who Really Discovered Halley's Comet?" BBC Science Focus, https://www.sciencefocus.com/space/who-really-discovered-halleys-comet/.
20. Jennings and Trout, *The Tontine*, 41.
21. Velde and Weir, "The Financial Market."
22. Ibid.
23. Cramer, Marc, "Le Trente Demoiselles, de Genève er Les Billets Solidaires," *Swiss Journal of Economics and Statistics* 82 (1946): 113.
24. Source: historicalstatistics.org.
25. Cramer, "Le Trente Demoiselles," 113.
26. Jennings and Trout, *The Tontine*, 56–61.
27. Bauer, Hans, and Warren Blackman, *Swiss Banking: An Analytical History* (London: Palgrave Macmillan, 1998), 10–18, 51–52.
28. Jennings and Trout, *The Tontine*, 56–61.
29. Cramer, "Le Trente Demoiselles," 114.
30. Britannica, "Jacques Necker: French Government Official," https://www.britannica.com/biography/Jacques-Necker.
31. MacDonald, *A Free Nation Deep in Debt*, 247.
32. Jennings and Trout, *The Tontine*, 60.
33. Dematos, Daniel, "Thirty Maidens of Geneva," Tontine Coffee-House, August 5, 2019, https://tontinecoffeehouse.com/2019/08/05/thirty-maidens-of-geneva/.
34. Cramer, "Le Trente Demoiselles," 115.
35. Ibid., 116.
36. Ibid.
37. French Institute for Demographic Studies, "Life expectancy in France," https://www.ined.fr/en/everything_about_population/graphs-maps/interpreted-graphs/life-expectancy-france/.
38. Cramer, "Le Trente Demoiselles," 116.

39. Markowitz, Harry, "Portfolio Selection," *Journal of Finance* 7 (1952): 77–91.
40. Lo, Andrew, and Stephen Foerster, *In Pursuit of the Perfect Portfolio: The Stories, Voices, and Key Insights of the Pioneers Who Shaped the Way We Invest* (Princeton, NJ: Princeton University Press, 2021).
41. Antoine, Michael, Louis XV (Paris, France: Fayard, 1989), 740–741.
42. Demantos, "Thirty Maidens of Geneva."
43. MacDonald, *A Free Nation Deep in Debt*, 250.
44. Source: historicalstatistics.org.
45. Cramer, "Le Trente Demoiselles," 116–117.

CHAPTER ELEVEN

BRE-X: ALL THAT GLITTERS ISN'T GOLD

On the morning of March 19, 1997, the Alouette III helicopter was all set to fly from the Samarinda airport in Indonesia to Busang in East Kalimantan, a hundred miles northwest on the Island of Borneo.[1] On board was geologist Michael (Mike) de Guzman. He was in high spirits that day. He had recently bought a new suit, and he had just spent the previous night at a small karaoke bar, drinking local Bintang beer and belting out Frank Sinatra's signature song, "My Way."[2] Perhaps that night he was simply having fun, unwinding after a long day. Or maybe he was revealing his fate. The end is near. The final curtain.

At the Samarinda airport, there was the usual preflight routine: ensuring that passengers were strapped in and the doors securely shut. The helicopter took off, flying 800 feet over the dense Borneo jungle, and would land safely a while later. But when it landed, de Guzman wouldn't be on board.

Seventeen minutes into the flight, the pilot, Edi Tursono, a lieutenant in the Indonesian air force, reported feeling a sudden gust of wind. He looked around to the passenger section. The door was open and de Guzman gone.[3] An apparent suicide note was later found in the back seat of the helicopter. Imagine the shock that de Guzman's wife, Genie, must have felt when she heard the news. And his second wife, Tess. And his third wife, Susani. And also his fourth wife, Lilis.[4] Likewise, it would be a double shock to each when they found that de Guzman had more than one wife.

But was de Guzman really dead? Stories began to surface almost immediately, and would persist for years. On March 22, 1997, internet speculation claimed he was spotted in Alabama, of all places.[5] A more credible-sounding story involved an elderly maid of one of de Guzman's wives, Genie. That story went that, in April 1997, the maid answered the phone. She was shocked when she recognized de Guzman's voice. The man on the line apparently asked her to tell Genie to look for a wire transfer of $200,000 into her bank account.[6]

Then there was a report of a geologist who, also in April 1997, was having dinner with colleagues in the New World Hotel in the City of Makati, Philippines. According to the geologist's story, he noticed another man walking out of the restaurant. His geologist colleagues at the table stood up and clapped for the man. Before leaving the restaurant, the man turned around and gave them a smile. The geologist at the table asked his colleagues who the smiling man was. They said it was de Guzman.[7]

There was also a story of a Filipino who had settled in Seattle. The man claimed to have had lunch with de Guzman in Manila, in 2004. Apparently, de Guzman had undergone extensive plastic surgery.[8] Finally, one more story. On Valentine's Day in 2005, there was an apparent $25,000 wire transfer from a Citibank branch in Brazil. Genie de Guzman, so the story went, claimed that the wire transfer included a fax with de Guzman's handwriting.[9]

Were these just tall tales? It's not clear, as most of these stories weren't first-person accounts. And there's yet another scenario of what happened to de Guzman. A forensic scientist, known as the Philippine Sherlock Holmes, had a different take. After reviewing the case for one of de Guzman's wives, he believed de Guzman was tortured and murdered, most likely for information about the site of the major gold find that de Guzman had apparently uncovered.[10] But what is certain, once the word got out about de Guzman's final helicopter ride, is that C$5.8 billion ($4.3 billion) of Bre-X Minerals Ltd. shareholder value quickly vanished. What was thought to be the world's largest gold reserve ever was a mirage. And that lost money wasn't coming back from the dead.

A VERY BRIEF HISTORY OF GOLD

Gold usage[11] can be traced back to 4000 BCE, to cultures in modern-day Eastern Europe. For several thousand years, gold was used to make decorative objects, jewelry, and idols. Around 1500 BCE, Egyptians were the first to use gold as a medium of exchange for international trade. Around 560 BCE in Lydia in Asia Minor, gold coins were minted. A thousand years later, in 1066, William the Conqueror of Normandy introduced to England a metallic coin–based currency that included gold. In 1787, the first U.S. gold coins were struck. Starting in 1792, the U.S. was the first country on a bimetallic standard, with both gold and silver used to define monetary units. From then until 1976, the U.S. went through various forms of a gold standard, whereby paper currency was convertible into gold. Subsequently, the gold standard was abandoned, with fiat or paper money prevailing.

Throughout time, gold, like many other metals such as silver, had been considered an investment vehicle as a store of value.[12] Unlike dividend-paying stocks that rewarded shareholders as the company's business generated profits, gold didn't offer any income-earning opportunity. However, it was often viewed as a portfolio diversifier, a hedge against inflation, and a safe haven in uncertain economic and political times.[13] Given its long history, gold had held an allure. But ultimately, it only had any real value because enough people believed it had value. By buying gold, they felt they'd be able to eventually sell it to another like-minded person. The same logic could be applied to cryptocurrencies like bitcoin, although no cryptocurrency had come close to matching gold's long history and charm.

Publicly traded gold-mining companies tended to be a riskier way to invest in gold because their stock prices weren't perfectly correlated with the price of gold itself. That's because there was uncertainty in determining the amount of gold resources that a company actually had in the ground, as well as the cost for a particular company to extract the gold.

BRE-X HISTORY

Bre-X Minerals Ltd.[14] was incorporated in Alberta in 1988 by David Walsh. He was born in Montreal and grew up in the affluent Westmount area.[15] He quit high school in grade 10 and joined a trust company that did business with his father. Walsh was typically seen with a cigarette in his hand, accompanied by a hacking cough. His appearance was likened to that of Norm on the long-running television show *Cheers*.[16] In 1989, Bre-X filed a prospectus with the Alberta Securities Corporation. It began trading as a penny stock on the Alberta Stock Exchange in July 1989. The company name prefix was derived from the name of Walsh's son, Brett. The firm's main assets were some small mining claims in northern Canada.

In March 1993, Walsh contacted geologist John Felderhof to arrange a meeting. Walsh and Felderhof had known one another since the 1980s, and had spent many hours together in bars, scheming and dreaming of making it big together.[17] Felderhof was born in the Netherlands and grew up in Nova Scotia. His nickname was Locomotive because he was a chain-smoker, and if anyone wanted to find him, they would just follow his trail of smoke.[18] In the late 1960s, he helped discover a major copper deposit in Papua New Guinea, and boasted about it for decades.[19] More recently, Felderhof had worked for a Canadian mining consultancy firm stationed in the Australian office, which later opened a branch in Jakarta.

After some other jobs in Indonesia, Felderhof was hired to dispose of a property in Indonesia known as Busang. Felderhof had recently worked with his devoted sidekick, the Filipino geologist Michael de Guzman, surveying the Busang property in the northeastern part of Borneo. De Guzman seemed to thrive in the harsh jungle.[20] In April, Walsh met Felderhof in Jakarta. After discussions, Bre-X agreed to pay $80,000 for rights to explore the site known as Busang I for one year, with the option to acquire a majority interest in a firm that held Busang exploration rights. Felderhof was the project's general manager, and de Guzman was the chief geologist.

Drilling for samples began in September 1993. The drill cores were assayed primarily at a laboratory in Balikpapan, many miles from the Busang site. The initial holes didn't indicate any significant gold deposits. But by December, after further drilling, there were indications of viable deposits. As drilling continued, in May 1994, less than a mile from Busang I, Bre-X appeared to discover a geological formation related to volcanic activity. Such formations tend to indicate mineral deposits. The area, which became known as Busang II, was outside the area of Bre-X's exploration rights.

In September 1994, Bre-X entered into a licensing agreement with PT Askatindo Karya Mineral to explore Busang II. Bre-X then obtained an exploratory work permit from the Indonesian government and applied for a contract of work. The CoW, as it was known, was critical because, if it was granted, it would give Bre-X the authority to complete exploration and eventually bring a mine into production.

Throughout 1995 and 1996, Bre-X continued drilling at the Busang II site. As the drill cores were assayed, Bre-X revised estimates of its gold reserves upward. In April 1996, the company's shares started to trade on the Toronto Stock Exchange. Since it had previously been listed on the Alberta Stock Exchange, no new prospectus was required. By July 1996, Bre-X's estimates of gold reserves were 47 million ounces. How they arrived at that number was somewhat opaque, but Felderhof backed it with a good story. The amount of gold reserves was almost three-quarters the size of the world's largest known gold deposit.

BUSINESS INDONESIA STYLE

By 1996, President Suharto had ruled Indonesia for almost 30 years. To get a sense of the political environment, imagine arriving at the Sukarno Hatta airport and traveling to downtown Jakarta. Here's what you would probably have experienced. You'd walk through the airport, which was managed by companies owned by two of President Suharto's children. You'd get in a rental car or a taxi and drive on the road to the city that was built by a construction company controlled by Suharto's eldest daughter. You'd pass through a toll booth also controlled by her company. You would probably pass several Timor sedans, manufactured by a company controlled by one of Suharto's sons, who won the manufacturing contract by beating his own brother.[21]

The key to success for foreign mining companies doing business in Indonesia was to secure a CoW to develop a mine. That's where Walsh made a number of potentially fatal missteps. He hadn't secured a CoW for the main areas of Busang that purportedly had most of the gold.

He approved Bre-X's aggressive drilling program with only a provisional drilling license. His control of Busang was challenged by a billionaire Indonesian partner. And there were questions about the initial offshore corporate transfer that had secured the Busang property.[22] So in order to get the Indonesian government onside, in October 1996, Walsh struck a sweetheart deal with Suharto's oldest son, Sigit Harjoyudanto. Walsh agreed to give him a 10 percent stake in Busang, along with a consulting fee of $1 million per month for 40 months.[23]

THE BATTLE FOR BUSANG

However, it appeared that by dealing with Harjoyudanto, Walsh had backed the wrong horse. It turned out that Harjoyudanto wasn't the most influential child of Suharto. That opened the door for Canadian gold-mining giant Barrick Gold Corp. to step in. Barrick was led by Peter Munk, its charismatic CEO.

Munk had put together a gold-plated international advisory board that included former U.S. president George H. W. Bush, as well as former Canadian prime minister Brian Mulroney. Munk relied on their global expertise and connections. In September 1996, Bush sent a letter to President Suharto, recommending he support Munk and Barrick in their Indonesian gold-mining aspirations.[24] Unlike Walsh, Munk found the right entrée: Suharto's eldest daughter, Siti Hardiyanti Rukmana, or Tutut, as she was known. Barrick agreed to award all road construction contracts to her company.[25]

By November 1996, the Indonesian government was giving "guidance" to Bre-X and Barrick to create a joint venture. They were given a deadline of December 4 to formalize the agreement. It was shaping up for the proposed joint venture to be split to give Barrick a 75 percent stake and Bre-X 25 percent.[26] But then it looked like the joint venture partners together would only own 80 percent of the Busang project. Bre-X's existing

Indonesian partner would own a 10 percent stake, while the Indonesian government would have the remaining 10 percent.[27]

A day before the deadline, other competitive bidders emerged. Since October, Placer Dome Inc., a Canadian mining company, had been negotiating behind the scenes, and was now urging the government to institute a normal auction process.[28] The government was considering Placer Dome's request to make a bid. Other companies that had prior discussions with Bre-X included Canadian mining company Teck Corp., as well as U.S. mining company Newmont Mining Corp.[29]

While all of this was happening, investors were trying to figure out what to do with Bre-X shares. One reporter, Stephen Northfield, noted, "This is no longer mining story. Calgary-based Bre-X has become bogged down in a swamp of disinformation, political intrigue and backroom maneuvering that makes it all but impossible to predict precisely what the outcome will be."[30] One analyst, Rick Cohen, joked, "The thing I'm telling guys is that the only way to hedge yourselves in Bre-X is to buy shares of Pepto Bismol."[31] At this point, it looked like there were three possible scenarios: Bre-X getting squeezed out entirely, an open auction, or the forced marriage between Bre-X and Barrick.

While the fight for control was going on, the Toronto Stock Exchange (TSE) was grappling with whether or not it should add Bre-X to its flagship TSE 300 index (the Canadian equivalent of the S&P 500 index). The index generally included the largest 300 Canadian companies on the basis of size as measured by market capitalization. One company in the index had recently merged with another company, and so a slot opened up for inclusion in the index. Given its large market capitalization, Bre-X was being considered by the TSE index committee that made the decision.

In the span of a couple of days around December 10, 1996, the TSE first announced that Bre-X would be joining the index, only to reverse the decision. The TSE cited "continuing uncertainty" regarding Bre-X's Busang deposit as well as "the need to maintain the integrity of the TSE indices."[32]

Then the TSE reversed itself again, claiming it had received additional information from Bre-X, and its inclusion in the index would occur on December 16.[33] This decision mattered because investors were increasingly turning to index funds for their investments.

Around this time, it looked like the Barrick and Bre-X marriage was about to proceed. The two companies presented a joint submission to Suharto, who had extended the deadline until the end of December. The new proposal would see ownership of Busang at 67.5 percent for Barrick, 22.5 percent for Bre-X, and 10 percent for the government. It was unclear what would happen with the 10 percent owned by Bre-X's Indonesian partner, PT Askatindo Karya Mineral. Nonetheless, a mining industry source commented, "The deal is done, done, done."[34]

But it wasn't a done deal. The tentative agreement proved challenging to finalize. In January 1997, the Indonesian Minster of Mines and Energy, Ida Bagus Sudjana, announced that if Bre-X and Barrick didn't finalize a deal by February 15, 1997, the government would expropriate Bre-X's interest in Busang.[35] While the deal-making was occurring, on January 23, 1997, there was a major fire at a Busang site where important records were stored. It was so severe that it wasn't possible to determine the cause of the fire. But it sounded suspicious.

THE DEAL

On February 17, 1997, Bre-X finally announced a joint-venture deal. Surprisingly, it didn't include Barrick. Instead, Bre-X would have a 45 percent stake. Two Indonesian companies—both controlled by Mohamad (Bob) Hasan, an old friend of Suharto, with whom he played golf twice a week[36]— would collectively own 30 percent. The Indonesian government would own 10 percent. Finally, American mining company Freeport-McMoRan Copper and Gold Inc. would own 15 percent.[37]

And there was more news that day. Bre-X announced results from an updated consulting report with resource calculations by Kilborn SNC Lavalin. Busang was now estimated to have almost 71 million ounces of gold, making it "the largest and richest gold mine in the world."[38] What wasn't clear at the time was that the Kilborn estimates were totally based on samples that Bre-X had provided, and so it wasn't a truly independent assessment.

Two days later, more good news from Bre-X. After a conference call to talk about the joint venture, Bre-X issued a press release that summarized the call. "Commenting on the total potential of the deposit, John B. Felderhof indicated that he would feel very comfortable with a potential of 200 million ounces . . . [But this statement was] not to be interpreted as an increased resource calculation."[39] What did he mean by "comfortable"? That certainly wasn't a technical term. Yet if taken at face value, what did this imply for Bre-X?

With gold trading at $350 per ounce, and even with Bre-X's Busang ownership stake at 45 percent, down from 90 percent, Bre-X estimated that its "gross economic value in this property is $11.2 billion . . . [Bre-X was] confident that this figure could be substantially higher."[40] And why was it "confident" of this? What seemed to get little attention was how the gold-reserve estimates could increase by more than fourfold in seven months without new drilling results. A site with 200 million ounces of gold reserves was not only the largest discovery in history, but equivalent to the gold reserves of Canada's four largest mining companies combined.[41]

BEGINNING OF THE END

On March 10, 1997, Walsh, Felderhof, and de Guzman were in Toronto, attending the annual convention of the Prospectors and Developers Association of Canada. Felderhof was being honored as the Explorationist of the Year.[42] Both Felderhof and Walsh were also receiving awards, from the weekly industry tabloid the *Northern Miner*. In Felderhof's acceptance speech, he took a shot at those who tried to get a piece of the gold action that Bre-X had discovered, without naming Barrick. He mused that there should be an award for tree-shakers, especially those who had never prospected in the jungles. "And all I say to them is, Go find your own."[43]

That's also the day when Walsh got a frantic call from Freeport's CEO, Jim Bob Moffett. In this call, Walsh was advised of the status of Freeport's due diligence. Moffett said that Freeport's assay results didn't appear to support Bre-X's previously announced results. There were only insignificant amounts of gold. Where were the alleged millions of ounces? David Potter, Freeport's chief geologist, followed up with a call to Felderhof.[44] De Guzman was asked to return immediately to Indonesia to meet with Freeport representatives, to clear up the apparent contradictions.[45]

On March 18, 1997, de Guzman was back in Indonesia. That's the day he embarked on his fateful and final helicopter journey. Once Felderhof heard of de Guzman's death, he returned to Indonesia to assist Freeport in its investigation. Bre-X hired geological consulting firm Strathcona Mineral Services Limited to review the assay work of both Freeport and Bre-X. In a March 23 press release, Walsh indicated that the Bre-X board "has absolute confidence in the integrity and accuracy of assay results and resource calculations reported by the company."[46] He then poohpoohed naysayers who doubted Bre-X.

THE COLLAPSE AND AFTERMATH

But the tune soon changed. Two days after Strathcona consultants arrived in Indonesia, in a March 26 press release, Bre-X announced that it had been advised by the consultants that "there appears to be a strong possibility that the potential gold reserves on the Busang project in East Kalimantan, Indonesia have been overstated because of invalid samples and assaying of those samples."[47] In the coming days, there were some trading-system halts and shutdowns due to the overwhelming trading in Bre-X stock. When the dust settled, on March 27, Bre-X's share price plummeted by 83 percent.

On May 3, 1997, Strathcona presented their findings in a confidential letter to Walsh.[48] The letter didn't pull any punches and got right to the bad news. "We very much regret to express the firm opinion that an economic gold deposit had not been identified in the Southeast Zone of the Busang property, and it is unlikely to be. . . . [T]he magnitude of the tampering with core samples that we believe has occurred and resulting falsification of assay values at Busang is of a scale and over a period of time with a precision that, to our knowledge, is without precedent in the history of mining anywhere in the world."[49] On May 7, Bre-X shares were delisted from the Toronto Stock Exchange. Felderhof resigned.[50] The next day, Bre-X applied for protection from creditors and an auditing firm was appointed to monitor the company's assets and records.[51]

With de Guzman's untimely death, we'll never know the full story. However, a report issued in October 1997 by Forensic Investigative Associates Inc. (FIA) concluded "evidence establishes reasonable and probable grounds to believe" that de Guzman was involved in the tampering.[52] De Guzman was thought to have salted the samples with gold dust. On November 5, Bre-X made an assignment into bankruptcy.[53]

Class action suits against Bre-X were filed in both Canada and the U.S. Then in June 1998, Walsh died, in the Bahamas, where he had lived since 1996. It was reported that, at the time of his death, his assets were valued at less than $40,000.[54] Previously, Walsh had sold more than $5 million worth of Bre-X shares, while Felderhof had sold about $24 million.[55] In May 1999, Felderhof was charged by the Ontario Securities Commission for allegedly breaching the Ontario Securities Act. However, the Royal Canadian Mounted Police indicated they would not be pursuing criminal charges.[56]

RED FLAGS

How could the Bre-X saga have happened, resulting in the loss of billions of dollars of shareholder money? The *Washington Post* implied that it was a classic case of overoptimism and confirmation bias. Paraphrasing Toronto Stock Exchange president Rowland Fleming, "In the end, each investment decision, each positive news story, each company statement gave Bre-X a tougher veneer of legitimacy and made it less likely for the next person in line to question the underlying facts."[57]

For example, in its 1995 annual report (released in February 1996), Bre-X included quotes from sensational news stories. A February 10, 1996, Reuters article reported 40 million ounces in gold deposits, and quoted Indonesia's director-general of mining (not Bre-X itself): "This is one of the largest gold deposits in the world."[58] Most investment professionals and analysts appeared to be willing to take at face value everything that management told them, or what others said about Bre-X. A mining executive commented, "It was a story a lot of people wanted to believe in."[59] Freeport agreed to come on board because the bigger the pronouncements of the size of the Busang find, the more Freeport believed it must be the real deal.[60] And even after the release of the damning Strathcona report, there were still some people who believed there was actually a significant amount of gold in Busang.[61]

According to the Strathcona investigation and the FIA report, there were a number of overlooked red flags.[62] The apparent gold deposit represented about 8 percent of all known gold resources in the world, and the largest single deposit. The gold in the Bre-X samples had qualities that resembled those in moving bodies of water, not what would be expected in the dense jungles of Busang. Bre-X didn't follow the standard practice of splitting the drill core samples and keeping half for subsequent testing. The Bre-X samples weren't taken directly from Busang to the lab at Balikpapan, nor were they stored in a secure facility while on the trip. Finally, there was a lack of visible gold in the samples. Often, we hear what we want to hear, and don't question anything other than rosy news that reconfirms our positive outlook.

After the blowup, one stock analyst cautioned, "The amateurs always buy at the wrong time and sell at the wrong time. You don't just buy a stock because you heard someone else say it's really good. Investing takes work, time, diligence."[63] Interesting advice, but it overlooks the losses by professional institutional investors, including C$45 million for the Ontario Municipal Employees Retirement Board, C$70 million for Caisse de dépôt et placement du Québec, and C$100 million for Ontario Teachers' Pension Plan Board.[64]

Consider the incentives that various parties had to overlook any of the red flags. Analysts who issued favorable research reports were given access to tour the Busang property, and then they often issued even rosier reports. Stockbrokers also had incentives to promote the stock. As one commentator observed, "Put yourself in [a broker's] shoes. Here is a stock that is going up like crazy. . . . All the officials are eager to have it traded. That is their business. When we fake a resume and get one person to accept it, they go easier the next time around, and pretty soon you're a neurosurgeon performing surgery with a degree from the Garage University."[65]

The Bre-X saga is one of the earliest cautionary tales for relying on investment information from online chat groups. As of the beginning of 1996, the internet was just starting to be a go-to place for information. There were still only an estimated 100,000 websites.[66] And yet there were sites specifically dealing with gold-mining stocks. One such site was quite transparent: "This thread is open to post RUMOURS!"[67] Mainstream media were encouraged to monitor the thread. It's been suggested that such rumors repeated in the mainstream media fueled Bre-X's rising and then falling stock price.[68]

We've seen this movie before. About a dozen years before Bre-X was starting to search for gold at Busang, eventually perpetrating massive fraud, an eerily similar scandal occurred. In 1980, a Canadian junior gold mining company, New Cinch Uranium Ltd., saw its stock price surge from C$2 per share to C$29 in only four months.[69] The company claimed to have found a rich gold deposit in New Mexico. Another company, Willroy Mines Ltd., paid $26 million for a 15 percent stake in New Cinch. But when Willroy conducted its own drilling, it couldn't find any gold. Sure enough, New Cinch's assays turned out to have been salted. The stock flamed out. And like with the Bre-X saga, this story also involved a death—the murder of an employee of El Paso Chem-Tech Laboratories, which had performed the assay work for New Cinch.[70]

More recently, traditional mining scams have been replaced by cryptocurrency scams. A common tactic was known as rug pulls.[71] A promoter touted high returns, but then vanished with investor funds. In 2021 alone, an estimated $2.8 billion in crypto funds were scammed. Some notable cryptocurrency scams between 2014 and 2023 were OneCoin, Thodex, Anubis Dao, Luna Yield, StableMagnet, and Swaprum. The common thread with Bre-X is that we often want to get rich quick, and don't want to believe that something shady is going on.

POSTSCRIPT

John Felderhof was the only Bre-X executive prosecuted for the gold fraud.[72] The Ontario Securities Commission accused him of insider trading. He was alleged to have sold $84 million of Bre-X stock while having material information that wasn't disclosed to the public. Felderhof was found not guilty in 2007. Two civil lawsuits wound their way through the courts and were dismissed in 2014. Most of Felderhof's savings were lost in a divorce settlement with his ex-wife. He eventually started a new life in the Philippines, got remarried and adopted a new family, and ran a small variety store and laundromat. He was reported to be very happy and enjoyed his new life. He died in 2019, at the age of 79. His lawyer, Joe Groia, was convinced that Felderhof had nothing to do with the fraud. "He was deceived like everyone else was deceived."[73]

FALSE HOPE

On March 28, 1997, just after Bre-X stock had its one-day drop in price of 83 percent, but before the mining consulting firms released their final report of what really happened, the *New York Times* interviewed investor Victor Mailoux.[74] He was 41 years old, from St. Paul, Alberta, and owned a hardware store. He had invested in Bre-X shares about a year earlier, on the advice of a local broker. He was hoping to strike it rich. "I'm not feeling very good about this now," Mailoux said. He was "waiting out the ride," just like many other investors, hoping the story would straighten itself out.[75] But not all investing stories straighten themselves out.

NOTES

1. Wells, Jennifer, "The Bre-X Bust," *MacLean's*, April 7, 1997.
2. Goold, Douglas, and Andrew Willis, *The Bre-X Fraud* (Toronto, ON: McClelland & Stewart, 1997), 9.
3. Ibid., 10–11.
4. Wells, Jennifer, *Fever: The Dark Mystery of the Bre-X Gold Rush* (Toronto, ON: Viking, 1998), 10, 19, 20.
5. Ibid., 350.

6. Irwin, Warren, 2022, "25 Years After Bre-X by the Man Who Made a Fortune Going Long & Short of the Biggest-Ever Mining Fraud," Uncommon Sense Investor, September 19. https://uncommonsenseinvestor.com/25-years-after-bre-x-by-the-man-who-made-a-fortune-going-long-short-of-the-biggest-ever-mining-fraud/.

7. Ibid.

8. Ibid.

9. Ibid.

10. Wilton, Suzanne, "The Mystery of Michael de Guzman," *Calgary Herald*, May 26, 2007.

11. The history of gold recounted here is primarily based on "Gold: The Most Precious of Metals," Focus Economics, May 29, 2023, https://www.focus-economics.com/blog/gold-the-most-precious-of-metals/#:~:text=Gold%20was%20generally%20used%20for,of%20exchange%20for%20international%20trade.

12. Burns, Peter, "Has Gold Been a Good Investment Over the Long Term?" *Money*, June 27, 2023, https://money.com/has-gold-been-a-good-investment-over-the-long-term/.

13. Ibid.

14. Unless otherwise noted, the Bre-X history is based on Nicholls, Christopher, "The Bre-X Hoax: A South East Asian Bubble," *Canadian Business Law Journal* 32 (1999): 2, 173–222.

15. Goold and Willis, *The Bre-X Fraud*, 17.

16. Ibid.

17. Francis, Diane, *Bre-X: The Inside Story* (Toronto, ON: Key Porter Books, 1997), 14–15.

18. Ibid., 14.

19. Goold and Willis, *The Bre-X Fraud*, 15.

20. Francis, *Bre-X: The Inside Story*, 36.

21. Wells, Jennifer, "Greed, Graft, Gold," *MacLean's*, March 3, 1997.

22. Wells, Jennifer, "King of Gold," *MacLean's*, December 9, 1996.

23. Ibid.

24. Wells, *Fever*, 266.

25. Wells, "King of Gold."

26. Ibid.

27. Robinson, Allan, "Placer Dome Enters the Bre-X Fray," *Globe and Mail*, December 3, 1996.

28. Ibid.

29. Ingram, Mathew, "Bre-X to Get Bigger Payoff: CEO," *Globe and Mail*, December 21, 1996.
30. Northfield, Stephen, "Bre-X: Buy, Sell or Hold," *Globe and Mail*, December 13, 1996.
31. Ibid.
32. Barnes, Angela, "TSE Adds Bre-X to TSE 300," *Globe and Mail*, December 13, 1996.
33. Ibid.
34. Robinson, Allan, "Bre-X and Barrick Submit Busang Proposal," *Globe and Mail*, December 17, 1996.
35. Nicholls, "The Bre-X Hoax."
36. Watkins, Michael, and Samuel Passow, "Bre-X: The Battle for Busang (B)," Kennedy School of Government Case Program, CRI-97-1388.0, 1997.
37. Nicholls, "The Bre-X Hoax."
38. Ibid.
39. Ibid.
40. Ibid.
41. Francis, *Bre-X: The Inside Story*, 13.
42. Ibid., 15.
43. Ibid.
44. Wells, *Fever*, 338.
45. Goold and Willis, *The Bre-X Fraud*, 10.
46. Nicholls, "The Bre-X Hoax."
47. Ibid.
48. Watkins and Passow, "Bre-X: The Battle for Busang (B)."
49. Ibid.
50. Nicholls, "The Bre-X Hoax."
51. Ibid.
52. Ibid.
53. Ibid.
54. Ibid.
55. Depalma, Anthony, "Canadian Gold Stock Investors Strike It Poor," *New York Times*, March 28, 1997.
56. Nicholls, "The Bre-X Hoax."
57. Schneider, Howard, "A Lode of Lies: How Bre-X Fooled Everyone," *Washington Post*, May 18, 1997.
58. Bre-X Minerals Limited, "Annual Report," 1995.

59. Israelson, David, "Blanket of Silence at Bre-X Office," *Toronto Star*, May 6, 1997.

60. Wells, *Fever*, 325.

61. Israelson, "Blanket of Silence at Bre-X Office."

62. Nicholls, "The Bre-X Hoax."

63. Israelson, "Blanket of Silence at Bre-X Office."

64. Wells, Jennifer, 1997, "The Blame Game," *MacLean's*, May 19.

65. Schneider, "A Lode of Lies."

66. "A Short History of the Internet," National Science and Media Museum, https://www.scienceandmediamuseum.org.uk/objects-and-stories/short-history-internet#:~:text=Consequently%2C%20the%20number%20of%20websites,around%2010%20million%20global%20users.

67. Nicholls, "The Bre-X Hoax."

68. Laver, Ross, "Web of Deception," *Maclean's*, June 16, 1997.

69. Wells, "The Bre-X Bust."

70. Ibid.

71. "Five worst cryptocurrency rug pull scams in history," CNBCTV, https://www.cnbctv18.com/cryptocurrency/five-worst-cryptocurrency-rug-pulls-scams-in-history-16807801.htm.

72. Healing, Dan, "Former Bre-X Chief Geologist John Felderhof Dies in the Philippines," *Canadian Press*, October 28, 2019.

73. Ibid.

74. Depalma, "Canadian Gold Stock Investors Strike It Poor."

75. Ibid.

CHAPTER TWELVE

AUTOPILOTS GONE WRONG

"Take Our Daughters to Work Day" (and later sons as well) was created in 1993 by American feminist Gloria Steinem.[1] Perhaps you've participated, as a child or as a parent. It's usually a fun bonding activity for parent and child. However, when your workplace is a commercial airline flying at 33,000 feet, a parent-child bonding exercise can be a different experience. And that's where this story begins, on March 22, 1994, aboard 14-hour Aeroflot flight 593 flying from Moscow to Hong Kong.

AEROFLOT FLIGHT 593

Aeroflot 593, an Airbus A310-308, had 75 people on board: three flight crew members, nine cabin crew members, and 63 passengers. The flight was under-booked and so about 30 airline employees and family members joined for a free trip.[2] Thirty-nine minutes after takeoff, the flight reached its cruising altitude at a speed of 329 mph. The plane was flying on autopilot, and everything was going according to its flight plan.

The pilot in command (PIC), Viktorovich Danilov, was in the passenger cabin, resting. Backup PIC, Yaroslav Vladimirovich Kudrinsky, was sitting in the left seat. Co-pilot Igor Vladimirovich Piskarev was in the right seat. All pilots were highly experienced.

TAKE YOUR KIDS TO WORK

Our story revolves around backup PIC Kudrinsky and his two children who were on the flight: 12-year-old daughter Yana and 16-year-old son Eldar. The story starts when another pilot, Vladimir Makarov, who was flying as a passenger, arrived in the cockpit along with Kudrinsky's children. It ends 18 minutes and 1 second later, with Kudrinsky saying, "Everything's fine." To give you a sense of where we are in time relative to "Everything's fine," we'll set a timer or countdown clock, starting at 18:01 and ending at 00:00.

At 18:01 (countdown clock time), Makarov entered the cockpit with Yana and Eldar. Then three and a half minutes later, at 14:31, Kudrinsky invited his daughter Yana to sit in the left seat where he had been sitting: "Come and sit here now, in my seat, would you like that?" He proceeded to stand up. Yana sat down in the seat and Kudrinsky raised it up for her. At 10:55 Kudrinsky invited his daughter to "fly the airplane a bit. . . . Hey, Yana, are you going to fly it? Go ahead, take the controls." Kudrinsky then set the autopilot so that the plane would make a slight turning maneuver.

Kudrinsky directed her about what to do with the control wheel. For the next 2 minutes and 40 seconds, until 08:15, the plane gently turned left, and then right, back to the original heading. This gave Yana the impression she was causing the plane to turn. All this time, father and daughter were chatting, which distracted the crew from monitoring the flight. At 06:49, after the plane was continuing on its original heading, Yana got out of the seat.

At 06:06, Eldar took the seat, with his father's permission. Kudrinsky wanted to show Eldar how to "fly" the plane as well, using the same autopilot maneuver he had just done for Yana. At 03:21, Kudrinsky again set the autopilot. Eldar asked his father if he could turn the control wheel, and Kudrinsky said yes. Kudrinsky then instructed his son, "Okay, watch the ground, where you're going to turn. Go to the left, turn to the left!"

After the left turn, the autopilot was then maneuvering the right. But what was different this time, compared with Yana, was that Eldar applied more force to the control wheel than his sister had done. Eldar was turning the control wheel so that the plane would turn at a 15-degree angle, while the autopilot was trying to hold the control wheel at 3 to 5 degrees, in order for the plane to come out on the assigned course.

AUTOPILOT OVERRIDE

Autopilot functions were invented in 1912, only nine years after Wilbur Wright's first flight. The inventor was American Lawrence Sperry, whose father was a prolific inventor.[3] Sperry's father had created a gyroscopic heading indicator that was used to operate a plane's elevators. Sperry attached it to a rudder, in order to balance the plane. After some testing in the U.S., on June 18, 1914, Sperry showcased his invention to the European public at the Airplane Safety Competition in Paris. Sperry's aircraft, a single-engine Curtiss C-2 biplane, was the last on the program of 57 entries.

While flying over the banks of the Seine lined with onlookers and past the judge's stand, Sperry engaged the stabilizer device. He then raised his arms over his head while letting the autopilot balance the plane. The crowd stood and cheered, *"Remarquable!"* *"Extraordinaire!"* *"Formidable!"* On the next lap, more dramatically, his passenger, French engineer Emil Cachin, climbed onto the wing of the plane to demonstrate the autopilot's balancing ability. The crowd again responded enthusiastically. And as a tribute, the band delivered a spirited rendition of "La Marseillaise." Then on the third and final lap, both Cachin and Sperry stood on the wings, waving to the crowd, while the plane flew itself. The judge cried out, *"Mais, c'est inouï!"* ("But that's unheard of!") Later, Sperry showed a French military commander a device he had installed on the plane to perform an unassisted takeoff and landing. Needless to say, Sperry was awarded first prize.

If you drive a fairly new vehicle with enhanced safety features, chances are it has lane assist technology. If the function is switched on, it will help to keep your car in its lane. If the system detects that you are veering to the left or right, it will actively and gently steer the car back into its lane. If, say, you are veering to the left, you will feel some slight resistance on the wheel, as the car nudges to the right, back into its lane. But if you want to switch lanes, say to pass a vehicle, then as you apply pressure as you turn the wheel, you will override the lane assist. In effect, the car has a type of autopilot, and you can easily override this function.

Now back to Aeroflot flight 593. Inadvertently, that's like what Eldar Kudrinsky did. He overrode the autopilot function that controlled the angling of the plane. By a quirk of the design, there was no indication from the instruments that the override had happened. If co-pilot Piskarev was the only person at the controls, he would have noticed the autopilot disconnect. But since both Eldar and Piskarev were handling control wheels, the autopilot disconnect wasn't noticeable to Piskarev. At 02:33, Eldar was still turning his control wheel to the right. But now with the autopilot disengaged, and unbeknownst to either Piskarev or Kudrinsky, the right bank began to gradually increase. By 02:12, it passed the operating limit of 45 degrees.

"WHY IS IT TURNING?"

Back at 02:25, Eldar had first noticed there was something he didn't understand and tried to bring it to the attention of his father, who was busy chatting with Yana.

Eldar:	"Why is it turning?"
Kudrinsky:	"It's turning by itself?"
Eldar:	"Yes."

The pilots in the cockpit tried to figure out what was going on. Makarov, who had come in to the cockpit with Kudrinsky's children, suggested the plane might have entered a holding pattern, like when a plane is circling an airport and waiting for landing instructions. Piskarev concurred.

By 02:09, the plane was now turning at a 50-degree angle. But still neither the co-pilot nor pilot reacted. The autopilot had had some functionality until the plane reached a 45-degree angle and had used auto-throttle to stabilize altitude and airspeed. But past that angle it was no longer engaged, and the plane began to descend. It also started to vibrate.

While this was happening, within two seconds, the plane's angle of attack increased from 4.5 degrees to 10 degrees. The vertical load factor or g-force was drastically increasing as well, making it difficult for Kudrinsky to get into the seat where his son was. Makarov reacted: "Hey guys!" and Kudrinsky exclaimed to both Eldar and Piskarev: "Hold on! Hold the [control wheel], hold it!" Eldar interpreted this command literally as he held the control wheel close to the neutral position, while co-pilot Piskarev correctly understood what Kudrinsky really meant: the need to counter the plane's roll.

"TURN LEFT!"

Piskarev began attempting to counter the roll six seconds after the plane had reached a 45-degree angle, but it was too late. To have succeeded, he would have needed to act when the angle was no greater than 40 degrees. At 02:07, the plane was angling to the right at 63 degrees. Seconds later, the angle exceeded 90 degrees.

During this time, the plane was losing altitude, and the aircraft began to stall. After Piskarev moved his control wheel to the left, for some reason there was a short, sharp deflection of the wheel to the right, which increased the bank further. During this time, Piskarev, Kudrinsky, and Makarov were all commanding Eldar: "The other way!" "Turn left!" "Left!" as Eldar was turning the left control wheel. That interfered with what Piskarev was trying to do with the right control wheel. Eldar replied, "I am turning it to the left!" Piskarev and Kudrinsky then told him to turn to the right. Piskarev asked, "Can't you see, or what?" To make matters even more challenging, Piskarev, who was only 5 feet 3 inches in height, was harnessed and had previously pushed his seat back almost as far as possible before Kudrinsky's children entered the cockpit. This limited his ability to fly the plane.

WARNINGS

Between 02:03 and 01:50, warnings were sounding: "altitude discrepancy," "stall warning," and "autopilot off." With the plane now in a dive at 460 miles per hour and at an angle of between 80 and 90 degrees, and with the increased g-force, the pilots were disoriented.

Then at 01:43, Piskarev was able to reestablish lateral orientation and shouted to Eldar, "To the left! There's the ground!" The g-force was now exceeding the structural limits of the plane. Kudrinsky was trying to get into the left seat, yelling repeatedly at Eldar, "Get out!"

Piskarev recognized the current primary danger of the high speed, and at 01:27 exclaimed, "Throttle to idle!" Piskarev was able to pull out of the dive, but he overcorrected as the plane climbed almost vertically and started to stall again. The airspeed had dropped dramatically to around 125 miles per hour. At 01:20, the plane started rolling uncontrollably, in a classic spin. The plane began angling to the left at 80 to 90 degrees, nose down. At 01:07, noticing the low speed, Piskarev yelled out in an emotional tone, "Full power! Full power! Full power!" A second later, Kudrinsky finally regained his seat.

"EVERYTHING'S FINE"

At this point, Kudrinsky and Piskarev were desperately trying to regain control of the plane.

Kudrinsky:	"Got full power, got it."
Piskarev:	"Full power!"
Kudrinsky:	"Got it . . ."
Piskarev:	"Full power!"
Kudrinsky:	"I gave it full power, I gave it!"
Piskarev:	"What's the speed?"
Makarov:	"Look on the left, it's [211 miles per hour]."
Kudrinsky:	". . . Okay . . . [sobbing] Full power!"

At 00:50, the plane's rotation had slowed. For the next 35 seconds, Kudrinsky was alternating the rudder pedals trying to stop the rotation completely and succeeded at 00:05, but the speed had again increased, to 230 miles per hour, and the altitude now was very low, only 1,000 feet.

Piskarev:	"We're coming out, we're coming out!"
Kudrinsky:	"Done."
Piskarev:	"Gently! . . . Shit, not again!"
Kudrinsky:	"Don't turn it right! The speed. . ."
Piskarev:	"There!"
Kudrinsky:	"We'll get out of this. Everything's fine . . . Gently, gently . . . Pull up gently!"

At 00:00, the plane crashed into the Kuznetsk Alatau mountain range, in southern Siberia. All 75 on board were killed.

AUTOPILOT FAILURES

The autopilot function has played a major role in other airline disasters as well. On May 31, 2009, Air France flight 447, an Airbus A330, took off from Rio de Janeiro on route to Paris.[4] About two hours into the flight, shortly after the pilot left the cockpit, the crew made a course change due to weather. Soon after, a pitot tube, which measured airspeed, became obstructed with ice crystals. This caused incorrect speed indications and disconnected the autopilot system. A gust of wind then caused the plane to depart from its path and roll to the right.

Once the autopilot disconnected, the crew wasn't aware of what the problem was, and the roll caught them by surprise. They didn't know that they had simply lost airspeed information. The crew became confused, and the situation quickly spiraled into what the crash report later called "the total loss of cognitive control." Unprepared by a lack of high-altitude training in manual airplane handling, and less than five minutes after the autopilot disconnected, the plane crashed into the sea. All 228 people on board were killed.

Automation was also at the heart of two devasting crashes of Boeing 737 Max-8 planes. Indonesian Lion Air flight 610, flying from Jakarta to

Pangkal Pinang in Indonesia crashed into the Java Sea shortly after takeoff on October 29, 2018. The crash killed all 189 people on board. Then less than six months later, on March 10, 2019, Ethiopian Airlines Flight 302, flying from Addis Ababa to Nairobi, Kenya, crashed into a field shortly after takeoff. All 157 people on board that plane were killed.

The Boeing 737 Max-8 had heavy engines that were placed farther forward on the wings than other similar-sized Boeing planes. Because of this, a computerized system, known as the Maneuvering Characteristics Augmented System (MCAS) was installed to compensate for the tendency of the plane to point its nose upward. When the MCAS repeatedly switched on during both tragic flights and pointed the nose toward the ground, the pilots struggled to keep the planes steady.[5] According to a veteran airline pilot, while automation helped make flying the safest means of travel, an overdependence on it had become an issue, and pilots needed "to be comfortable and capable of flying the plane manually."[6] A Transportation Department inspector noted that the 737 Max automation system raised "concerns about pilot's abilities to recognize and react to unexpected events."[7]

AUTOPILOTS FOR INVESTORS

We rely on automation and autopilots in investing as well. Just like pilots, most of the time we don't really think about it. Sometimes we don't really understand how investing automation works and what the limitations are of investing autopilots. In many ways, just like how automation has made aviation safer, automation has made investing more efficient. For example, index funds that invest in a basket of stocks, like the 500 largest in the U.S., the S&P 500 index, have drastically reduced the fees that investors pay compared with actively managed funds. And there's really nothing to manage. Index funds are the ultimate investing autopilot.

Although we don't give them much thought, not all index funds are created equal. Suppose you wanted to diversify geographically. You decided you wanted exposure to Canadian stocks and so you invested in a Canadian index fund that invested in the largest 250 Canadian stocks. What you may not be aware of is that the three largest sectors in Canada are financials, energy, and materials. In contrast, the three largest sectors of the S&P 500 index are information technology, healthcare, and a relatively much smaller stake in financials. You may think you're getting geographic exposure, which you are. But you're also getting major sector concentration.

Concentration in index funds can be even more pronounced, down to the individual stock level. For example, around the peak of the so-called dot-com bubble in early 2000, one stock, Nortel Networks Corporation, represented over a third of the Canadian stock index of the largest 300 firms. It was even more severe in Finland, where Nokia Corporation made up about 70 percent of the Finnish index. If you were invested in funds that replicated these indexes, you probably weren't getting the diversification you were expecting, and you actually had huge individual stock risk exposure.

There are lots of other investing autopilots, such as target date or life-cycle funds, which invest in a mix of stocks and bonds that reallocate through time. These funds are designed so that as an investor ages, their exposure to riskier equities decreases and the exposure to less risky bonds increases. These types of funds are becoming increasingly popular among defined contribution pension plans, often as the default option. Nobel laureate Robert (Bob) Merton has criticized[8] target date funds because the investment strategy never uses any new information about investor risk preferences or tolerance to update asset allocation. Instead, these funds assume that the only factor that impacts an investor's risk is their age. So, while these types of funds sound like terrific investing autopilots, they may not be appropriate for every investor at the same age. That's why it's important to understand how each of your investing autopilots actually work.

Here's another autopilot example. A major investing trend is known as ESG investing, which stands for environmental, social, and governance. Originally known as "socially responsible investing" or "ethical investing," the idea is to avoid or exclude stocks whose company's practices and values are inconsistent with those of the investor.[9] For example, such a fund might exclude tobacco companies.

The focus then shifted to choosing stocks to be included in an ESG portfolio based on positive ESG attributes. For example, under the E category are considerations like how a firm deals with natural resources such as energy, emissions, and water. The S category includes what rights employees have and how diverse, equitable, and inclusive the workforce is. And under the G category is how independent and diverse the board is. Estimates varied widely, but there may have been over $4 trillion in ESG assets under management as of 2022.

So investors now have a plethora of autopilot ESG funds that track a growing number of ESG indexes.[10] But unlike broad-based traditional index funds like those that mimicked the S&P 500 index, ESG index funds vary widely in terms of their approach and thus which stocks are included or excluded. ESG index funds often rely on scoring mechanisms that aggregate very difficult to measure components. For example, Tesla once got a high "AA" rating from one rater, a low rating from another, and a rating in the middle by yet another. In the case of Meta (owner of Facebook), one rater had its E score in the top 1 percent, while another had it in the bottom 4 percent. It's not surprising, then, that correlations of rankings across these ratings firms are quite low, and so funds replicating ESG indexes might contain very different stocks and perform very differently.

Another type of autopilot is a stop-loss order, that, as the name suggests, is designed to limit losses. Let's suppose you bought a stock at $20 and wanted to protect yourself on the downside. You could place a stop-loss order at, say, $15, to protect yourself on the downside. That means you are automatically requesting that the stock be sold when it hits the $15 price. The problem with this autopilot is that, particularly in a volatile market when prices are quickly declining, there is no guarantee you can sell the stock at the stop-loss price. You might think that the worst you could do was lose 25 percent, but that isn't the case.

While it's easy to criticize autopilots, we override them at our peril. There's an important footnote to the story of Aeroflot flight 593. Despite all the attempts by Kudrinsky and Piskarev to save the plane, it was later determined that had they just let go of the control wheel, the autopilot would have prevented the stalling, and the plane wouldn't have crashed. The beauty of buying and holding a well-diversified index fund is that it takes our emotions out of play and helps us to avoid mistakes we might otherwise have made. Studies have shown that individual investors—particularly men—tend to be overconfident in their trading abilities and trade excessively. But this excessive trading hurts their performance, and they would have been better off simply buying and holding an index fund.[11]

There's a final lesson that investors can take from the world of aviation. When disaster strikes—and it will for almost every investor—we need to recover the black box, understand what went wrong, and learn from our mistakes. Every investor makes mistakes, even Warren Buffett. Sticking with our theme, he actually lost a lot of money by investing in airline stocks. He once quipped, "If a far-sighted capitalist had been present at Kitty Hawk, he would have done his successors a huge favor by shooting Orville down."[12] But at least Buffett admits to his mistakes and learns from them.

LAWRENCE SPERRY CROSSES THE CHANNEL

Finally, back to the inventor of the first autopilot, Lawrence Sperry, who thrilled onlookers at the 1914 Airplane Safety Competition in Paris. Between 1915 and 1923, Sperry acquired 23 patents, and racked up 4,000 hours of flight time.[13] On December 13, 1923, a day after his 31st birthday, Sperry took off from Britain for a short flight across the Channel to France. He was flying in his personal aircraft that was fully equipped with the instruments he had designed. Sperry was undeterred by the fog—he confidently relied on the automations he invented. Whether or not due to mechanical failure related to the autopilot, tragically, Sperry's plane went down. His body was recovered several weeks later.

NOTES

1. Smith, Stacey Vanek, "A History of Take Our Daughters to Work—and Why It Now Includes Sons," Marketplace, April 15, 2013, https://www.marketplace .org/2013/04/25/history-take-our-daughters-work-and-why-it-now-includes-sons/.
2. Goldberg, Carey, "Pilot's Son May Have Caused Air Crash in Russia," *Los Angeles Times*, April 3, 1994, https://www.latimes.com/archives/la-xpm-1994-04-03-mn-41784-story.html. All flight facts below are from Aviation Safety Network, "Report on the Investigation into the Crash of A310-308, Registration F-OGQS, on 22 March 1994 Near the City of Mezhdurechensk," https://reports .aviation-safety.net/1994/19940323-0_A310_F-OGQS.pdf; and Lanfermeijer, Stephan, "23 March 1994—Aeroflot 593," Tailstrike.com, https://tailstrike. com/database/23-march-1994-aeroflot-593/.
3. See Scandinavian Traveler, "The Story of the World's First Autopilot," https://scandinaviantraveler.com/en/aviation/the-story-of-the-worlds-first-autopilot; and Scheck, William, "Lawrence Sperry: Genius on Autopilot," Historynet.com, November 15, 2017, https://www.historynet.com/lawrence-sperry-autopilot-inventor-and-aviation-innovator/.

4. BEA Bureau of Enquiry and Analysis for Civil Aviation Safety, "Final report on the accident on 1st June 2009 to the Airbus A330-203 registered F-GZCP operated by Air France flight AF 447 Rio de Janeiro–Paris," July 2012, https://bea.aero/docspa/2009/f-cp090601.en/pdf/f-cp090601.en.pdf.

5. Woodyard, Chris, "On autopilot: 'Pilots are losing some of their basic flying skills,' some fear after Boeing 737 Max crashes," *USA Today*, May 25, 2019, https://www.usatoday.com/story/news/2019/05/25/boeing-737-max-8-autopilot-automation-pilots-skills-flying-hours-safety/1219147001/.

6. Ibid.

7. Ibid.

8. Baskin, Kara, "Wall Street Gurus: How to Invest in a Volatile Market," MIT Management Sloan School, June 6, 2022, https://mitsloan.mit.edu/ideas-made-to-matter/wall-street-gurus-how-to-invest-a-volatile-market.

9. This discussion relies heavily on Sundaram, Anant, "ESG Investing," 2022, *Handbook of Business and Climate Change*, ed. A. K. Sundaram & R. G. Hansen (Edward Elgar Publishing, 2023), https://papers.ssrn.com/sol3/papers.cfm?abstract_id=4158029.

10. For an example of such funds, see Brock, Catherine, "ESG Funds for Responsible Investors," Fool.com, June 30, 2022, https://www.fool.com/investing/stock-market/types-of-stocks/esg-investing/esg-funds/.

11. Barber, Brad, and Terrance Odean, "Boys Will Be Boys: Gender, Overconfidence, and Common Stock Investment," *Quarterly Journal of Economics* 116 (February 2001): 261–292, https://faculty.haas.berkeley.edu/odean/papers/gender/boyswillbeboys.pdf.

12. Barro, Josh, "Warren Buffett Should Have Listened to Warren Buffett About Airlines," *New York Magazine,* May 4, 2020, https://nymag.com/intelligencer/2020/05/warren-buffett-should-have-listened-to-himself-on-airlines.html.

13. Facts in this paragraph are from Scheck, "Lawrence Sperry: Genius on Autopilot."

CHAPTER THIRTEEN

A HOSTAGE CRISIS AND THE BIRTH OF GOVERNMENT BONDS

Bonds—along with stocks—are known as traditional investments because they've been around for many centuries. Most investors own bonds either directly, or indirectly such as through pension plans. A bond is simply an IOU. While we think of buying a bond as investing, it's actually a form of lending, either to governments or corporations. Governments borrow when current spending needs exceed current revenue. Borrowers promise to compensate lenders through regular interest payments, say 5 percent of the money borrowed, paid each year. Bonds are considered to be a relatively safe investment compared with stocks, particularly when the issuer is a government. Government bonds are also liquid. After a government bond is issued, there's an active secondary market for buying or selling.

Who invented government bonds, when, and why? To answer those questions, our story takes us back to 12th century Venice. That's where the precursor to government bonds, as we know them today, were issued in 1172. Government bonds have been an incredible success story for both governments and investors for over 850 years. Governments get money to spend. Investors typically get steady returns. These bonds were accidentally born out of necessity and failure, during a time of political strife. Our story involves trumped-up charges, conflict, deceit, a plague, and an angry mob. The birth of bonds is a happy story for today's investors. Unfortunately, it wasn't a happy ending for our protagonist, Doge Vitale Michiel.

DOGES OF VENICE

Venice was established in the fifth century, around the fall of the Roman Empire. Nearby refugees flocked to its marshy islands to get away from Germanic and Hun invasions. The eastern half of the Roman Empire survived as the Byzantine Empire. In 565, Byzantine Emperor Flavius Justinianus (Justinian I) conquered Venice and made it the westernmost post of the Byzantine Empire. By this time, the city of Byzantium had become Constantinople, now known as Istanbul.

In the late seventh century, Venice was facing an internal crisis. Venice originated from 12 early settlements. Each had their own elected official or tribune. Various family feuds and ambitious tribunes had led to bloody clashes and the plundering of churches. Venice was threatened with anarchy. A church official from one of the settlement areas, the Patriarch of Grado, called a general meeting to try to preserve the churches and maintain public order. It was proposed that all of the tribunes be relegated to purely local offices, and a capo or chief, known as the doge, be elected for life. The policy was approved and in 697, the first doge, Paoluccio Ana-festo, was chosen. Except for a short six-year interruption, the Dogeship of Venice endured for 11 centuries.[1]

The doges had immense powers. They could nominate, degrade, or dismiss all public officials. They could convoke or dissolve general meetings. They could veto the appointment of bishops and patriarchs. The military authority reported to the doge. They handled foreign affairs, although approval was required from the people to declare war or conclude peace. They could impose taxes or exact forced labor in lieu of taxes. The doge often sat on his ivory throne, holding a scepter, dressed in a silk outfit with gold clasps, and wearing a horned cap. When they went abroad, they were surrounded by guards and a state umbrella was held over the doge, with nearby trumpets blaring and banners waving. Doges were generally democratically elected over the next seven centuries. As for their typical day, they "rose before dawn, heard mass, went forth to judge the people and transact the business of the day."[2]

It wasn't always easy being a doge.[3] The first doge, Anafesto, died in 717 during a revolt and conflict between two powerful Venetian families. The third doge, Orso Heraclea, was murdered during a two-year civil war and his son was banished. The dogeship was then abolished during a disastrous experiment with the appointment of the Master of Soldiers as the head of state. Eventually, Deodato Heraclea, the son of the previous doge, became the new doge. In 1117, Doge Ordelafo Faliero, was leading Venetians in battle against Hungarians near Zara on the Adriatic coast. Unfortunately his horse stumbled on a dead body and while he lay defenseless, he was slain by the enemy.

THE RISE OF VENICE

As we've seen, the history of Venice was associated with conflicts. The first major battle between the Western and Eastern Empires took place in Venice, along the beaches of the Lido. That's where Venetian-Byzantine forces turned back Charlemagne (Charles the Great), which eventually resulted in a peace treaty in 814. Charlemagne renounced all claim to Venice. Over the next two centuries, Venice continually assisted the Byzantine Empire in battles and was rewarded with its official independence in 992.[4]

Shortly after Venice's independence, the Commercial Revolution commenced in Europe. It included long-distance trade between Western Europe and Levant, the region along the eastern shores of the Mediterranean, which included Constantinople. Venice was fortunate to be strategically positioned midway on a major route between Western Europe and Constantinople. That made Venice a natural trading partner with Constantinople. Much of the trade included wheat, timber, and salt.[5]

In 1071, a pivotal year for the Byzantine Empire and consequently for Venice, the Byzantine Empire lost decisively to the Seljuk Empire in the Battle of Manzikert. Seljuk Turks were now at the doorstep of Constantinople. In that same year in the West, Normans banished the Byzantine army from southern Italy. A new Byzantine emperor recruited Venice to disrupt their mutual enemy, the Normans, from crossing the Adriatic. A subsequent pact, the Golden Bull of 1082, was a major boost for Venetian trade. It granted Venice duty-free access to 23 of the most significant Byzantine ports. Venetian merchants were given property-rights protection from corrupt Byzantine administrators. Venetian traders became the first foreigners to have their own Quarter in Constantinople, home to 20,000 Venetian merchants over the next century. The Golden Bull precipitated a long expansionary period for Venice into the eastern Mediterranean.[6]

In the summer of 1147, Venice again came to the aid of the Byzantine Empire.[7] A Norman fleet sailed across the Adriatic to capture the island of Corfu, part of the Byzantine Empire. Unimpeded, it then plundered the Greek coast. The Byzantine emperor, Manuel I, turned to Venice for assistance. There was no question that Venice would agree to help. It was in Venice's interest to have a stable and peaceful Byzantine Empire from both a strategic and economic perspective.

In October, Emperor Manuel quickly dispatched another Golden Bull that confirmed all of the commercial interests that Venice had. The Doge of Venice, Pietro Polani, the son-in-law of the previous doge, took command of the Venetian fleet to confront the Normans on Corfu. The Venetians successfully defeated the Normans, but Polani died on the voyage. In an act of gratitude toward Venice, Emperor Manuel considerably expanded the Venetian Quarter in Constantinople. This was the highwater mark in the relationship between Venice and Constantinople. The association would soon deteriorate, and tensions would reach a boiling point in 1171.

HOSTAGE CRISIS

In the years following Venice's defeat of the Normans on Corfu, relations between Venice and Emperor Manuel worsened.[8] Manuel had again reached out to Venice for help, this time for his planned invasion of southern Italy. But on this occasion, Venice refused. In retaliation for the snub, Manuel reached out to Venice's commercial adversaries, Genoa and Pisa, nurturing these new relationships. He even granted both of them their own quarters in Constantinople, right near the Venetian Quarter. Manuel must have known that this would create a stir, and it did.

Venetians living abroad, and in Constantinople in particular, had quite a reputation—not in a good way. Many of the merchants had become quite wealthy. According to one observer, they had become "so arrogant and impudent that not only did they behave belligerently . . . but they also ignored imperial threats and commands."[9]

One day in 1171 in Constantinople, in a purported incident, a group of Venetians were said to have raided the Genoese Quarter. According to reports, Genoese were killed before the imperial guard eventually subdued the violence. However, the charges against the Venetians appear to have been fabricated.[10] Nonetheless, Venice's Doge Vitale Michiel tried to defuse the situation by sending high-level ambassadors to meet with the emperor. Manuel assured the ambassadors that everything was fine between them. Relieved, the ambassadors returned to Venice with the good news.

Or so they thought it was good news. This supposed incident occurred when Manuel was convinced that he no longer needed to rely on Venice as an ally. Genoese warships were as numerous in the Aegean as Venetian warships. Manuel felt he could have Byzantine defenders without the arrogance of the Venetians. So in early 1171, he sent out secret messages to officials across the Byzantine Empire. They were asked to prepare to arrest and imprison every Venetian they could round up, and confiscate their property. Incredibly, the upcoming plan remained secret. Manuel's decree was triggered on the morning of March 12.

All across the Byzantine Empire, every Venetian man, woman, and child was rounded up and tossed into prisons as hostages. Once prisons were full, they were thrown into monasteries. All of their possessions were confiscated, including shops, vessels, and houses. Over ten thousand Venetians were arrested in Constantinople alone, and another ten thousand across the rest of the Byzantine Empire.

One of the few Venetians to escape from Constantinople was a rich merchant and shipowner, Romano Mairano. His wealth came primarily from two sources: his wife's estate that he inherited after she died, and from a substantial dowry from his second wife. Like other Venetians, Mairano had been arrested and tossed into an overcrowded prison. However, along with a few other wealthy Venetians, officials agreed to release him after he posted a huge bail. But he didn't plan to stick around. In the dead of night, he made it to the wharves, where his ship, the *Kosmos,* was anchored. It was the largest merchant ship in Venice. It was also well protected from flaming arrows and catapult stones by a covering made from animal hides soaked in vinegar.

The Venetian escapees slowly sailed out of the Golden Horn, Constantinople's secure harbor. By dawn, the fugitives realized that the seas were filled with ships carrying Byzantine officials looking to arrest Venetians. One such vessel approached the *Kosmos* and ordered it to stop for an inspection. In response, the Venetians put up all of their sails to get away as fast as they could. The Byzantines then tried to destroy the ship with fire projectiles, but the *Kosmos* was too well protected. Mairano and the other Venetians on board were able to make it to the safe harbor of Acre, along the eastern Mediterranean coast, where they told their harrowing tale to countrymen.

OUTRAGE

The news of the Venetian arrests and property confiscation soon reached Venice[11] and was met with shock and outrage. The ambassadors who had met with Manuel were embarrassed by how they had been tricked. Doge Michiel convened a meeting with his high councilors or wise men, the *sapienti*. This council had been set up by the previous doge, Polani, to comprise important members of the community. It included Venice's richest man and the brother of the patriarch.[12] Given the unbelievable-sounding reports of the mass arrests, the sapienti advised a cautious tactic. They suggested a three-pronged approach: first, sending an envoy to Constantinople on a fact-finding mission; second, if the reports were true, ascertaining Manuel's reasoning behind the arrests; third, then demanding that all the hostages be released, and property returned. The doge agreed. But events soon spun out of control.

Soon after the sapienti had convened, a large convoy of 20 Venetian ships with escapees arrived noisily at Venice's harbor. The passengers disembarked and passionately told their distressing tales to anyone who would listen. Residents poured out of their houses and were enraged—they wanted revenge! The residents gathered together to exert their rarely used power to form the *arengo,* a special assembly. The ad hoc assembly of the people usually only met when the doge sought approval on important matters. But when they met and decided on something, the doge and government had to obey.[13]

The arengo demanded a retaliatory strike against the Byzantine Empire. They ordered Doge Michiel to personally lead a war fleet. The fleet was to consist of 100 galleys and 20 transport vessels. The objective was to win the release of all of the hostages, as quickly as possible. Michiel had no choice but to agree.

BIRTH OF A GOVERNMENT BOND

Imagine the corner into which Doge Michiel was painted. He needed to quickly make a huge, unplanned infrastructure investment, in a time of crisis. And not only in building the fleet, but also financing the upcoming conflict itself. Where could he get the money? The traditional method of taxation? Direct taxation was detested by citizens and so rulers usually took a softer approach to meet regular expenditures through indirect taxes on goods rather than people, such as on salt, wine, or customs duties.[14] But that wouldn't meet the immediate needs.

The main aim of the Venetian state from a commercial perspective was to protect and develop trade.[15] In the case of an extraordinary event like a war, the level of anticipated expenses determined the revenue required.

Nonetheless, new or increased "exceptional" taxation soon became regular and often permanent. Costs related to war were both immediate and ongoing. Building and equipping galleys for warfare required materials including wood, hemp, linen, metal, gunpowder, and arms. It also included the wages for the tradespeople: carpenters, caulkers, sailmakers, oar makers, rope makers, cannon makers, and cross-bow makers. Not only did Doge Michiel need to finance the building of a large fleet, but also the wages of the sailors, who insisted on being paid immediately in gold rather than promises of future payment.

What would a modern government do facing increased expenditures related to a war? It would issue a bond, with a set interest payment. But in 12th-century Venice, it wasn't that simple. One of the biggest obstacles: the Catholic Church's ban on usury—the lending of money while collecting interest. The notion was that a usurer was taking advantage of someone in need of money, and thus usury was considered a sin. Usury was thought to be on the same level as committing a violent robbery.[16] In the 12th century, usurers were excommunicated by the Catholic Church and couldn't be buried on consecrated grounds.[17] Given the close link between the Church and state, rulers were often persuaded to enforce the ban on usury. There were some illicit work-arounds, such as disguising a loan as a sales contract with a specified future payment. However, if the future price was deemed to be fair, and if a lower cash price was deemed to be a generous discount, then the contract might be deemed to be legitimate.[18]

Despite the usury ban, medieval governments needed to rely on some form of borrowing since powers to tax were often limited and they were often engaged in expensive wars. In 1149, Genoa created a unique way to fund debts. It agreed to give a consortium of lenders control over a *compera,* which was a consolidated fund of tax revenues.[19] Then in 1164, Venice used a similar mechanism for a loan of 1,150 marks. The state of Venice provided a group of 12 prominent Venetian lenders with tax revenues from rents from the Rialto market, the financial and commercial center of Venice, for 11 years.[20]

Necessity, as they say, is the mother of invention. During the current crisis, Doge Michiel devised a clever borrowing scheme that was implemented the following year, in 1172. It didn't involve direct taxation. It didn't involve a small number of lenders. Rather, his innovation was to create a forced loan from all Venetians who could afford it.[21] He divided Venice into six districts: Castello, Cannaregio, Dorsoduro, Santa Croce, San Polo, and San Marco. The wealth of the citizens in each district was estimated, and based on that amount, a portion was collected and forwarded to the Grand Council, or sapienti.

To make it palatable, a unique feature was that each of those who provided the forced loan were promised 5 percent interest until the forced loan was paid back. This forced loan was known as a *prestiti*. What was fascinating about this new arrangement was that there was now a borrower-lender relationship between the city-state and its citizens. Thus the precursor to today's government bond was born. In many ways, it was a win-win. The state got immediate access to funds it desperately needed, and the lenders got the promise of a steady stream of reliable future income.

OUTFOXED

In July 1171, four months after the decision to retaliate against Manuel, the Venetian fleet was ready to sail.[22] Doge Michiel led the armada along the coast of Dalmatia. They landed on the Greek island of Negroponte and laid a siege to the capital, Chalkis. Realizing the gravity of the situation, the local Byzantine governor requested to meet with Michiel and his councilors. The doge tipped his hand. He made it clear that the Venetians preferred a diplomatic rather than a military solution. The governor took this information and ran with it. He proposed sending an envoy to

Constantinople to urge Manuel to release the Venetian hostages in return for the withdrawal of the Venetian forces at Chalkis. Michiel agreed.

The Venetian fleet retreated to the island of Chios, where they spent the winter waiting for Manuel's reply. Meanwhile, Manuel refused to receive the envoy from Chalkis. Instead, Manuel sent his own envoy to Chios, urging *the Venetians* to send an envoy to Constantinople. While not clear to Michiel, Manuel was displaying a classic case of masterly inactivity that we saw in a previous story (Chapter 2): biding his time while preparing his own troops. His stalling tactic worked brilliantly. Not realizing what Manuel was up to, Michiel dispatched an envoy.

Shortly after Manuel's envoy departed, and perhaps not coincidentally, the Venetians were overcome with a deadly plague. More than a thousand Venetians perished in the first few days. It was suspected that Byzantine agents had poisoned the wells. Michiel's leadership was being questioned. In March 1172, the Venetian fleet moved to the island of Panagia, hoping to leave the plague behind. But it followed them. Later that month, Michiel's envoy finally returned. The envoy had been denied an audience. However, Manuel sent yet another Byzantine envoy to Michiel, with a promise that if a third envoy was sent, Manuel would receive it.

Evidently Michiel didn't know the old proverb "Fool me once, shame on you. Fool me twice, shame on me." He sent two trusted men, including the nephew of the patriarch, to meet with Manuel. In a desperate attempt to outrun the continuing plague, he moved his fleet first to the island of Lesbos and then to Skyros, but no luck; the death toll continued to grow. It finally dawned on Michiel that his depleted fleet was no longer a threat to Manuel. Meanwhile, the discouraged survivors ordered the doge to take them back to Venice. He capitulated. Manuel was victorious in a battle he didn't even fight. And to shove salt into his wounds, Manuel sent a nasty letter to Michiel, calling his behavior and tactics stupid, and saying that he had made himself a laughingstock. After this humiliation, matters were to get even worse for Michiel. We'll get to that in a bit.

EVOLUTION OF THE PRESTITI

With a weakened Venice, the prestiti issued in 1172 were never fully repaid. Steady interest payments were made but the debt became permanent. However, there was a silver lining. Because of the failed expedition to rescue the hostages, the debt had a long life. In 1262, all previous Venetian debt was consolidated into one fund upon which 5 percent interest of the face value was paid semi-annually. Semi-annual interest payments are a standard feature on almost all bonds today. The repayment obligations were transferable, and eventually an active secondary market developed in the Rialto market, where they were bought and sold. Another feature was that the government couldn't retire the loans by repaying the principal, although the government could repurchase them in the secondary market. These types of prestiti helped to fund Venetian wars and more over the next few centuries as well.[23]

MODERN-DAY BONDS

Diversification is the cornerstone of investing principles. That means not only within asset classes like stocks and bonds, but across them as well. Stocks and bonds go together like Oreo cookies and milk. For at least four decades and probably since the 1960s, an asset mix "rule" to achieve an optimal risk/return tradeoff was to invest 60 percent of your wealth in stocks and 40 percent in bonds.[24] Within bonds, those issued by governments— particularly the U.S., but most major developed countries as well—typically dominated because they were generally viewed as riskless, with no chance of default. The premise is that if stock and bond prices aren't perfectly correlated, then losses in one of the asset classes should be at least partially offset by gains in the other. Think of bonds as acting like a shock absorber for stock losses. Of course, there have been exceptions, such in 2022, when both stocks and bonds did poorly. But in general, we have Doge Michiel to thank for creating the precursor to today's government bonds, now a major component of most portfolios.

FINAL ASSEMBLY

Back to the chastened Doge Michiel. The remainder of the Venetian armada finally hobbled into Venice in May 1172. The fleet had set out looking for revenge. It returned in defeat, humiliated, and with the plague. As before, Venetians took matters in their own hands and demanded a general meeting with the doge and his councilors to discuss what had gone wrong. On May 27, the assembly took place at the Ducal Palace.

The meeting went badly right from the beginning. Widows and friends were crying for their lost beloveds. Anger engulfed the throngs. How could the doge have messed up so royally? He had been given a clear mandate to retaliate and bring home the hostages. He had been provided with the means to do so, with a powerful fleet, financed through the forced loans from Venetians. What did he use it for? Diplomacy! Many of the survivors condemned the doge, claiming they were poorly led and betrayed. It was his fault. Within the assembly, stones and knives began to appear. While Michiel was trying to reason with the angry congregation, the councilors took the cue and quietly slipped out one by one.

Michiel soon realized he was alone on stage. As the crowd grew angrier, he made a break for the nearby Church of San Zaccaria, hoping it might be a sanctuary. He never made it. An angry mob overtook him and stabbed him to death. He joined the list of doges of Venice who met an untimely death.

We often act impulsively, both in our investments and in other decisions as well, and this often leads to regret. The same was true for the

Venetians who were part of the angry assembly. As the doge was being prepared for burial, they realized how wrongly they had acted. They were the ones who had put Michiel in an intolerable predicament. So they then made a scapegoat of his assassin, Marco Casolo, who was executed. It would take more than a decade for the hostages to be released.

NOTES

1. Okey, Thomas, *Venice and Its Story* (London: J. M. Dent & Sons, Ltd., 1903).
2. Ibid.
3. Ibid.
4. Puga, Diego, and Daniel Trefler, "International Trade and Institutional Change: Medieval Venice's Response to Globalization," National Bureau of Economic Research, 2012, Working Paper 18288.
5. Ibid.
6. Ibid.
7. Madden, Thomas, *Venice: A New History* (New York: Penguin Group, 2012), 82–84.
8. Accounts of the hostage crisis and aftermath are primarily from: Madden, *Venice*, 85–91; and Abulafia, David, *The Great Sea: A Human History of the Mediterranean* (London: Penguin, 2014).
9. Magoulias, Harry (translator), 1984, *O City of Byzantium, Annal of Niketas Choniates*. (Detroit: Wayne State University Press).
10. Goetzmann, William, 2016, *Money Changes Everything*; (Princeton, NJ: Princeton University Press).
11. Events described in this section are primarily from Madden, *Venice*, 82–84.
12. Madden, Thomas, 2010, "A History of Venice: Queen of the Seas," audiobook.
13. Ibid.
14. Mueller, Reinhold, *The Venetian Money Market: Banks, Panics, and the Public Debt, 1200–1500* (Baltimore: Johns Hopkins University Press, 2019).
15. See Hocquet, Jean-Claude, "Venice," in Bonney, Richard, ed., *The Rise of the Fiscal State in Europe c. 1200–1815* (Oxford, 1999).
16. Munro, John, "The Medieval Origins of the Financial Revolution: Usury, Rentes, and Negotiability," *International History Review* 25, no. 3 (2003): 505–562.
17. Ibid.
18. Ibid.

19. Ibid.

20. See Munro, "The Medieval Origins of the Financial Revolution," and Goetzmann, *Money Changes Everything*.

21. Goetzmann, *Money Changes Everything*.

22. This account is based on Madden, *Venice*.

23. Goetzmann, *Money Changes Everything*.

24. For example, see the reference to the "old" 60/40 rule in Ambachtsheer, Keith, "In Defense of the 60/40 Equity/Debt Asset Mix," *Financial Analysts Journal* 43, no. 5 (1987): 14–24.

CHAPTER FOURTEEN

A REVOLUTIONARY INNOVATION TO FIGHT INFLATION

In the late 1770s, the Revolutionary War wasn't going well for the American colonies. The British army was making gains in America's south, and the British navy was blockading the eastern coast. American army morale was low—the troops were poorly clothed, poorly fed, and often in need of medical attention. Mutinies were a real threat. Also sapping morale was another enemy: soldiers were facing a loss of the value of their pay due to inflation, jeopardizing their ability to support their families.

What happens when inflation runs rampant? To this day, central banks and governments continue to grapple with this issue. In 1780, the Commonwealth of Massachusetts rode to the rescue, with a financial innovation that was truly revolutionary. The invention played an important role in the eventual turnaround in army morale, and consequently America's fortunes. That famous midnight horseback rider, Paul Revere, even contributed, but not at all in a way you might have expected from what we know of Revere from history books. Largely forgotten for centuries, the financial innovation was reinvented in the 20th century. That was in time to fight that same enemy—inflation—that returned worldwide with a vengeance in 2021.

Inflation is the change in price of a basket of goods and services. Hitching financial returns, such as a bond's coupons and principal, to inflation was the revolutionary idea. We now refer to this as inflation indexing. W. Stanley Jevons[1] credited work by Joseph Lowe published in 1822[2] for first proposing an inflation indexing scheme that was "probably invented by him."[3] But both Jevons and Lowe overlooked the reality that inflation indexing *in practice* essentially predated the purported invention. Inflation indexing was actually enacted in legislation in Massachusetts both in 1777 and in 1780, and that's when our story takes place.

THE REVOLUTIONARY WAR AND PAUL REVERE'S MIDNIGHT RIDE

Here's some context and key events related to the Revolutionary War, also known as the American Revolution. Occurring between 1775 and 1783, it involved an insurrection by the 13 American colonies against British rule, leading to America's independence.[4] In the decade prior to the initial armed conflict, tension between the British authorities and the colonists had been growing. In 1773, the British government attempted to raise revenue through colonial taxation with the Tea Act.

To show their displeasure, a faction of Bostonians dumped 342 chests of tea into the Boston Harbor, an act famously known as the Boston Tea Party. The outraged Brits enacted a number of measures, known as the Coercive

Acts, to reassert control in Massachusetts. A group of colonists, including George Washington and Samuel Adams, convened in Philadelphia in September 1774 to voice their grievances in the First Continental Congress. But merely raising complaints didn't prevent the pending military conflict.

On the night of April 18, 1775, British troops marched from Boston to Concord, Massachusetts, to seize a cache of colonial arms. That's when Paul Revere (and others, less celebrated) made a famous ride to warn the colonial militiamen of the pending British action. Among various jobs, one of which we'll describe later, Revere was employed as an express rider by the Boston Committee of Correspondence and the Massachusetts Committee of Safety.[5]

On that fateful night, Revere was called upon to ride to Lexington with the news of the British movement, and also the apparent plans by the Brits to arrest Samuel Adams and John Hancock. In fact, as it turned out, the British had no such plans for arrests. Revere instructed a friend to hold two lit lanterns in the Tower of Christ Church as a signal that the British troops were planning to row by sea to Cambridge across the Charles River.

After rowing across the river, himself, Revere borrowed a horse and at around 11 o'clock set off, narrowly avoiding capture. He eventually made it to Lexington to warn Adams and Hancock. He then continued on to Concord to make sure military supplies were hidden. Just outside of Lexington, Revere was stopped by a British patrol, questioned, had his horse confiscated, and was then let go.

On April 19, 1775, British troops and colonists clashed in the Battles of Lexington and Concord. The initial gunfire was immortalized as the "shot heard round the world." The Revolutionary War had begun. In June 1775, at the first major confrontation in Boston, the Battle of Bunker Hill, the British were victorious. However, the Americans inflicted heavy casualties and the revolutionary forces were encouraged. On July 4, 1776, the Colonial Congress voted to adopt the Declaration of Independence.

After suffering a number of losses, the tide turned for the Americans with a victory in the Battle of Saratoga on September 19, 1777. This prompted

France to enter the war in support of the colonists. Many battles in the north in 1778 ended in stalemates. Between 1779 and 1781, the Americans suffered a number of setbacks, including the defection of General Benedict Arnold and defeats in Georgia and South Carolina. But in the fall of 1781, the Americans triumphed in the conclusive Battle of Yorktown. In 1782, Britain began removing troops from Charleston and Savannah as the war started to wind down. By late November 1782, preliminary peace plans were negotiated. On September 3, 1783, Britain formally recognized America's independence through the signing of the Treaty of Paris.

MASSACHUSETTS'S ACTS

Let's return to what was happening in Massachusetts, particularly between 1777 and 1780. That's when eventual colonial victory was far from certain. After a decade with virtually no inflation between 1765 and 1775, with the onset of the Revolutionary War, prices throughout the colonies started rising at a brisk rate. More recently, scholars have estimated inflation across the colonies was 14 percent in 1776, 22 percent in 1777, and 30 percent in 1778.[6]

Between 1776 and 1780, eight conferences were held among the colonies in an endeavor to harmonize price controls, with Massachusetts making the first attempt.[7] On January 25, 1777, Massachusetts enacted a new law to control prices, the "Act to Prevent Monopoly and Oppression." The Act covered the prices of more than 50 staples, including food and clothing. But the Act didn't last long. The pricing scale was below the costs of procuring goods, and there were other complaints. So the Act was repealed on October 13 of the same year. However, the silver lining was to bring attention to the harshness that many were facing because of rapid price increases, particularly for those serving in the army.

Early in 1777, Rhode Island passed a law providing soldiers from that state with certain supplies at earlier lower prices rather than currently higher prices. Massachusetts passed a similar law on October 10, 1777, just before a repeal of the earlier act. But the resolution fell into disuse. In January 1779, four Massachusetts battalions officially complained that because of the depreciation of the money that they received for their pay, they were effectively losing seven-eighths of it due to inflation. They asked for new legislation so their wages would reflect their original purchasing power. Despite new legislation that was extended to all of Massachusetts's battalions, the soldiers and their families continued to suffer from inflation.

According to economics professor Willard Fisher's 1913 account, the situation had grown dire enough in 1779:

> ... to induce the State to give most serious attention to the condition of the troops and their demands. The general military situation was by no means favorable. The French alliance had not yet yielded important results. The South and many parts of the North were overrun by the British. The financial and monetary systems of the states, as of Congress, were at a point of collapse. The American troops were in dire want, unpaid and scantly supplied, suffering themselves and anxious for their families; they were all but discouraged. Their patriotism and their human endurance had been drawn almost to the limit.[8]

Congress and Massachusetts were becoming anxious about the maintenance of the army. Massachusetts passed new resolutions complimenting the patriotism of their soldiers and offering bonuses to those who agreed to reenlist. A committee was arranged to hear each soldier's account by the end of the year. In October, the committee met with Washington in West Point, where his main army was, to preview what they planned to offer the soldiers. Washington readily approved. By this point, the committee reported that the army was impoverished, "as near half are now barefooted—and a great proportion entirely destitute of Hatts, Stockings, or Blankets so indispensably necessary especially at this season and in that rugged country." Desertions were rampant, with former soldiers willing to work for farmers at low wages.

A committee of officers was assigned for closer discussions of the issues and eventually met with the state committee. In November 1779, a resolution was approved to accept the claims of the soldiers and to act in haste. On January 13, 1780, an act was passed to fix a settlement related to the lost purchasing power of soldiers' wages. At this time there were still major differences between the army and state committees as to terms. The main difficulty was to precisely determine the nature of compensation, which essentially involved determining an appropriate rate of inflation between January 1, 1777, and January 1, 1780.

Keeping with the verboseness of the times, the 1780 act was called "An Act to provide for the Security and Payment of the Balances that may appear to be due by Virtue of a Resolution of the General Assembly of the sixth of February, One Thousand Seven Hundred and Seventy-nine, to this States Quota of the Continental Army, agreeable to the Recommendation of Congress, and for Supplying the Treasury with a Sum of Money for that Purpose." To make matters more manageable, rather than considering the 50-plus prices that were listed in the 1777 act, only four were reflected in order to estimate the "rate of depreciation" of money previously paid (the inflation rate): prices of beef, corn, wool, and leather.

THE EARLIEST KNOWN INFLATION-INDEXED BONDS

The Committee of the Army set out to gather monthly prices for the three-year period. The final calculation was a simple average of the four rates of price increases. The committee concluded that the January 1, 1780, price of goods was 32 and a half times the amount on January 1, 1777. Officers and soldiers who agreed to enlist for the duration of the war were to be paid in four equal interest-bearing notes that were due on March 1 of 1781, 1782, 1783, and 1784 to make up for their losses due to the rate of depreciation of money, or what we now call inflation. Those who refused to serve through the war would still be compensated, but their payments would be deferred by an additional four years. To fund the payments, new taxes were arranged, which amounted to £1,000,000 per year for eight years. But uniquely, the future amounts to be paid would reflect the prevailing cost of the four goods as of 1781 through 1784. In other words, the future payments were indexed to inflation.

Known at the time as "depreciating notes," the face of each note indicated: "Both Principal and Interest to be paid in the current Money of said State, in a greater or less Sum, according as Five Bushels of Corn, Sixty-eight Pounds and four-seventh Parts of a Pound of Beef, Ten Pounds of Sheeps Wool, and Sixteen Pounds of Sole Leather shall then cost, more or less than One Hundred and Thirty Pounds current Money, at the then current prices of the said Articles."

All well and good, but implementation was another matter—how would the future amounts be estimated? The answer, as is often the solution of governments, was to strike another committee. This one was a group of a dozen prominent citizens (all male), whose task each month was to collect and keep account of prices "according to the best of their judgments." Furthermore, justices of the superior court were available to assist the committee in their calculations. As Fisher later commented, more than a century ago, "Nowadays it would be quite intolerable to entrust valuations to any body of men on the basis of 'whatever certain information they may be able to obtain,' much less upon 'their own judgment in the premise.'"[9]

Massachusetts's General Assembly then reached out to Congress, explaining their actions, and sought funding from Congress for the Act.

They claimed that without the Act, there wouldn't be any prospects of men reenlisting in the army. Recognizing the urgency, the day after the new law was enacted, the Assembly quickly authorized payments of half the balances, in order to settle as soon as possible. Later in the Revolutionary War, this custom was widely adopted across other states.

What happened next was somewhat anticlimactic. There was evidence that the notes weren't regularly paid at maturity.[10] Many individuals petitioned Massachusetts's General Assembly for payment of overdue notes. There was even the passage of an act on February 14, 1782, specifically directing the payment of notes that were due on March 1, 1781. The depreciating notes weren't used like currency. Transfers of the notes weren't always allowed. In some cases, officers drew upon the notes of their soldiers through forged orders.

The prominent citizens tasked with collecting and accounting for price increases faced challenges because many towns and counties failed to send price reports, despite legislative orders. While the notes continued to have value for a number of years, they were eliminated prior to the full eight-year period. As the war appeared to be approaching a successful ending for the colonies, the Massachusetts legislature was already pushing for readjustments of the terms.

There is at least one indication that inflation-indexing was used in a manner beyond the law meant to compensate soldiers for price increases.[11] Reverend Doctor Samuel Langdon was a graduate of the Harvard class of 1740 and the 12th president of Harvard College (1774–1780), the first president selected from outside Massachusetts.[12] Langdon was chaplain of a regiment and took part in the capture of Louisburg. In 1788, he was a delegate to the New Hampshire convention that adopted the Constitution.

Around the time of Langdon's resignation as president of Harvard, on October 3, 1780, the House of Representatives agreed to pay Langdon

£497 10s "in the new money & in consideration of his faithful Discharge of the office of President of Harvard College & to enable him to remove his Family & Effects."[13] The agreed-upon payment was a nontrivial amount, equivalent to perhaps $120,000 today.[14] Accompanying documents indicated that the amount determined was based on applying the depreciation scale applied to soldiers. Beyond such an isolated occurrence, there didn't appear to be an attempt to establish any inflation-adjustment standard.

HOW INFLATION IS MEASURED TODAY

What do we have today in place of that 1780 group of a dozen prominent citizens charged with measuring the price of beef, corn, wool, and leather? Inflation is measured by monthly price changes in the typical basket of goods and services that the average household consumes, resulting in a consumer price index (CPI) as compiled by the Bureau of Labor Statistics (BLS).[15] It's constructed each month based on the prices of 80,000 goods and services paid by urban consumers. BLS representatives visit or contact stores across the U.S., collecting data on the prices of the same goods and services as the previous month. A separate housing survey is based on visits or calls to 50,000 residents.

The major categories of consumer spending are housing, transportation, food, recreation, medical care, apparel, education (which includes communication), and other goods and services.[16] Of course, each household's basket looks different, but we now have a standard method of measuring inflation, which is the first important step in creating an inflation-indexed bond.

THREE CENTURIES OF INFLATION

Now that we understand how inflation is measured, let's look at its record. Historians have meticulously created price indexes in America going back to 1700. While certainly not as broad as today's inflation measures, researchers have been surprised that a price series tracking only a few goods highly correlates with price series based on a much larger number of goods.[17]

The overall average annual change in consumer prices was 1.3 percent. Inflation was well below average in the 1700s (0.6 percent), slightly negative in the 1800s (−0.2 percent), much higher in the 1900s (3.2 percent), and then a bit more muted but still above the long-term average in the 2000s (2.5 percent). The volatility of price changes has declined steadily. Lower volatility of inflation in the 20th and 21st centuries makes sense, coinciding with the creation of the Federal Reserve in 1913, in part to control inflation.

In the past century alone, we have seen a number of different inflationary regimes. Since 1914, inflation averaged 3.3 percent. During and just after both World Wars (1914–18, 1939–45), prices increased at rates approaching 15 percent or higher, but not as dramatically around the start of the Korean War (1950–53), and in the 1960s around America's involvement in the Vietnam War. Energy price increases also played a big part in inflation rises in the 1970s. The highest inflation since the Second World War occurred in 1980, when the rate was just below 15 percent. It took major action by Federal Reserve chair Paul Volcker, who substantially increased interest rates, to wrestle inflation at the cost of a major recession. The Covid-19 pandemic disruption contributed to the 2021 inflation spike.

We've also seen some periods of *deflation*, when prices actually dropped (not to be confused with *disinflation*, which refers to rising prices, but at a lower rate of increase than previously experienced). The most severe cases of deflation occurred around 1921, then again during the Great Depression, particularly between 1930 and 1933. In both of those instances, prices dropped at an annual rate of 10 percent. Sustained periods of deflation were common in the 1700s and 1800s. Deflation has been virtually nonexistent in America since the 1930s (although during the Global Financial Crisis, prices dropped marginally between March and October of 2009). Sustained deflation is bad because if it becomes ingrained and prices are expected to drop, consumers will postpone purchases, and reduced demand can cause economic activity to stagnate. Japan has experienced this since the early 1990s after bursting asset bubbles in stocks and real estate. In such a liquidity trap, there is little room for central banks to stimulate through reducing interest rates.

The Federal Reserve's mandate is to foster economic conditions that achieve stable prices, or inflation of around 2 percent annually (along with moderate long-term interest rates and maximum employment). In the three decades prior to the spike in inflation in 2021, we witnessed ideal price stability. Between 1992 and 2020, inflation averaged 2.2 percent annually. That's why 2021 price increases sounded alarm bells.

Why is price stability so important? Imagine you own a business manufacturing and selling widgets. You employ a vast labor force. Business is good and you're looking to expand your facilities. You need millions of dollars in capital—equity and loans—in order to invest in the expansion. If you do invest, you will be satisfying growing demand and also providing more jobs. It's easy to make that decision with low and steady inflation. You aren't expecting much of an increase in per-employee labor costs.

Contrast that with a high inflation environment—there is much more uncertainty. Facing increasing inflation, will your employees demand higher wages? What will be the impact on increasing costs associated with the investment? Will your customers tolerate higher widget prices? Thus low and steady inflation is beneficial because it removes uncertainty.

MODERN INFLATION-INDEXED BONDS

After being largely forgotten for over 160 years, the inflation-indexed bond concept was resurrected in the 20th century. In 1945, Finland became the first country in modern times to introduce inflation-indexed bonds. The list of countries issuing these bonds grew, notably the U.K. in 1975, Canada in 1991 (which subsequently stopped issuing inflation-indexed bonds in 2022), and the U.S. in 1998.

The U.S. bonds are known as Treasury Inflation-Protected Securities, or TIPS. Both the interest (semi-annual coupons) and principal (amount owing at maturity) are adjusted as the CPI changes. The government has issued a variety of TIPS with different maturities. When 30-year TIPS were initially issued in 1998, they offered a guaranteed real return (in excess of inflation) of around 3.63 percent when held to maturity. To put this real return in perspective, since 1926, stocks had average real annual returns of around 9 percent, albeit with much more risk than government bonds. The beauty of TIPS is that you lock into a return without worrying about inflation—so long as you hold the bond to its maturity.

When TIPS were first issued, it wasn't clear how much demand there would be. As recounted by Nobel laureate in economics Robert (Bob) Shiller, a couple of years prior to the issuance of TIPS he was told about a joke circulating in the U.S. Treasury Department. If and when inflation-indexed bonds were issued, the Treasury Department should send the prospectus to all the members of the American Economic Association, since they were likely the only people who would be interested in the bonds.[18] Joking aside, many proponents of TIPS include investment luminaries such as Bill Sharpe, Bob Shiller, Bob Merton, and Jeremy Siegel.[19] Demand has been strong: a recent estimate indicates that investment funds have over $250 billion in assets under management in TIPS.[20]

WHY INFLATION MATTERS

We've already seen that inflation matters because it creates uncertainty, particularly for businesses looking to invest, and employees considering wage demands. We should pay attention to inflation because, like a tax, it impacts on our standard of living. While over long horizons stock returns tend to provide real returns well in excess of inflation, in the short-term stock prices tend to react negatively to increased inflation. The intuition is that stock prices reflect the discounted value of expected cash flows, and so when the discount rate increases because investors require higher nominal returns with higher inflation, then stock prices decline.

Inflation also hurts bond prices, in a more direct manner. Bond prices are inversely related to yields or interest rates. Higher inflation goes hand in hand with higher yields, bringing bond prices lower. If higher expected inflation becomes ingrained, there is a danger of inflation spiraling out of control, which is known as hyperinflation. With inflation of around 3 percent over the past century, prices doubled in about 24 years. The worst case of hyperinflation occurred in Hungary in 1946, when prices were doubling, on average, every 15.6 hours.[21]

PAUL REVERE'S OTHER REVOLUTIONARY CONTRIBUTION

Oh, and what was Paul Revere's small contribution to the innovative 1780 inflation-indexed bonds? When he wasn't out on a midnight ride to warn the colonial militia of a pending British attack, he had a day job—as a silversmith and engraver. As the official engraver for Massachusetts, he apparently engraved the border on the 1780 inflation-indexed bonds![22]

NOTES

1. Jevons, W. Stanley, *Money and the Mechanism of Exchange* (New York: D. Appleton and Company, 1877).
2. Lowe, Joseph, *The Present State of England in Regard to Agriculture, Trade, and Finance: With a Comparison of the Prospects of England and France* (London: Longman, Hurst, Rees, Orme, and Brown, 1822), https://play.google.com/store/books/details?id=esk_AAAAcAAJ&rdid=book-esk_AAAAcAAJ&rdot=1.
3. Jevons, *Money and the Mechanism of Exchange*, 329.
4. Unless otherwise noted, descriptions of the war are from "Revolutionary War," History.com, September 20, 2020, https://www.history.com/topics/american-revolution/american-revolution-history.
5. This account is from "The Real Story of Paul Revere's Ride," Paul Revere House, https://www.paulreverehouse.org/the-real-story/.
6. Source data are from McCusker, John J., "How Much Is That in Real Money? A Historical Price Index for Use as a Deflator of Money Values in the Economy of the United States," *Proceedings of the American Antiquarian Society* 101, no. 2 (October 1991): 297–373, https://www.americanantiquarian.org/proceedings/44517778.pdf.
7. Accounts are from Fisher, Willard, "The Tabular Standard in Massachusetts History," *Quarterly Journal of Economics* 27, no. 3 (1913): 417–454.
8. Ibid., 432–433.
9. Ibid., 450.
10. Ibid., 442–446.
11. Ibid., 448–449.
12. Biographical information is from *The National Cyclopaedia of American Biography*, vol. 6 (James T. White & Company, 1896), 416, https://books.google.ca/books?id=z9kbAAAAIAAJ&pg=PA416&redir_esc=y#v=onepage&q&f=false.
13. Fisher, "The Tabular Standard," 448.
14. Based on converting £1 from 1780 to 2022, via the website https://www.in2013dollars.com/uk/inflation/1780 and then converting to U.S. dollars at the prevailing exchange rate as of November 8, 2022, of 1.16.
15. This description is based on Salwati, Nasiha, and Davis Wessel, "How Does the Government Measure Inflation?" *Brookings*, June 28, 2021, https://www.brookings.edu/blog/up-front/2021/06/28/how-does-the-government-measure-inflation/.

16. U.S. Bureau of Labor Statistics, "Consumer Expenditures—2021," 2022, https://www.bls.gov/news.release/cesan.nr0.htm.

17. McCusker, "How Much Is That in Real Money?" 305.

18. Shiller, Robert, "The invention of inflation-indexed bonds in early America," NBER, Working Paper Series 10183, 2003, https://www.nber.org/papers/w10183.

19. Lo, Andrew, and Stephen Foerster, *In Pursuit of the Perfect Portfolio: The Stories, Voices, and Key Insights of the Pioneers Who Shaped the Way We Invest* (Princeton, NJ: Princeton University Press, 2021).

20. U.S. Treasury, "TIPS Supply," November 2021, https://home.treasury.gov/system/files/221/TBACCharge1Q42021.pdf.

21. Toscano, Paul, "The Worst Hyperinflation Situations of All Time," CNBC, February 14, 2011, https://www.cnbc.com/2011/02/14/The-Worst-Hyperinflation-Situations-of-All-Time.html.

22. Shiller, "The invention of inflation-indexed bonds in early America."

CHAPTER FIFTEEN

A MARKET CRASH, RECOVERY, AND CONSPIRACY THEORIES

This story takes place over two successive days: Monday, October 19, and Tuesday, October 20, 1987. The former and more famous date was known as Black Monday, while the latter and largely forgotten date was known as Terrible Tuesday. The first part of the story, on the Monday, involved a domestic commercial flight taken by former Federal Reserve chair Alan Greenspan. The second part of the story, on the Tuesday, was described by a general partner at a major asset management firm as "the most dangerous day we had in 50 years. I think we came within an hour" of a meltdown of the stock market.[1] What saved the world from financial Armageddon were some mysterious trades—possibly market manipulation—of a thinly traded stock index futures contract. If you're intrigued by conspiracy theories, this is a rare feel-good one.

BACK TO 1986–1987

Let's travel back in time to the last day of 1986 to see what was happening in the stock market. The Dow Jones Industrial Average (the Dow) closed that year at a level of 1896. (Coincidentally, 1896 was the year the Dow index originated.) That level was up from the previous year's close of 1547. During the year, the average daily point gain was 1.38. Typical for the time, the Dow's daily point changes were reported to two decimal places. This is a relevant tidbit for our story, as you'll see later.

On August 11, 1987, Ronald Reagan's vice president, George H. W. Bush (who appeared in our Bre-X story in Chapter 11), swore in Greenspan as the new chair of the Federal Reserve. Greenspan took over from Paul Volcker, who was known for his tough stance fighting inflation. Volcker was 6 feet, 7 inches tall. Greenspan's height was 5 feet, 4 inches. Greenspan had big shoes to fill, both figuratively and literally. The Dow closed at over 2680 that day, a new record. Further record highs would follow over the next two weeks. But, unbeknownst to market participants, the August 25, 1987, record of 2722 wouldn't be surpassed for another two years.

SETTING THE STAGE FOR A STOCK MARKET COLLAPSE

In early September 1987, Greenspan raised the Federal Reserve's discount rate for the first time in three years. He meant to send a message to the markets about his concern with a potential increase in inflation. Then in October, a number of events combined to contribute to market jitters. Higher-than-expected trade-deficit figures fueled fears of further declines in the dollar relative to major trading partners' currencies. Furthermore, the U.S. had entered into a currency-stabilization pact among G-7 nations. But the dollar was sent into a further decline when Treasury Secretary James Baker commented that the U.S. might let the dollar drop unless West Germany (this was before West and East Germany reunified in 1990) eased credit. The inflationary concern was particularly tied to oil prices with the continuing war between Iran and Iraq, two oil-rich countries.

There were psychological factors at play as well. Think of how we react to round number markers, and why an item selling for $10.00 seems a lot more expensive than one selling for $9.99. On October 14, 1987, long-term U.S. bond yield rose above 10 percent, catching investor attention, and making bonds look much more attractive relative to stocks. Then on Friday, October 16, the Dow dropped by more than 100 points for the first time ever, to a level of 2246.7—not the greatest percentage drop, although at 4.6 percent, quite large, and certainly a headline-grabber. Investors stewed nervously over the weekend, wondering what would happen when markets opened on Monday.

GREENSPAN'S FLIGHT

On Monday, October 19, 1987, a day now known as Black Monday, Greenspan was flying from Washington, D.C., to Dallas, Texas, to attend an American Bankers Association meeting. Despite the recent market turmoil, he decided to go because he was scheduled to give the keynote address the next day. These were in the days when commercial airline passengers had no communication with the outside world when flying. It was also the days before the World Wide Web and mobile phones. Once you entered an airplane, you became unaware of what was happening in the outside world, not only for the duration of the flight but until you could access a pay phone at the airport. Before Greenspan boarded his four-hour flight, the Dow was already down a stunning 200 points, or over 8 percent.

When Greenspan arrived in Dallas, the stock exchanges were closed for trading for the day. The first question he asked the official greeting him was "How did the market close?" The reply was "Down five-oh-eight."[2] Thinking the market had recovered and ended the day virtually flat, down just 5.08 points, Greenspan was fleetingly relieved. As he recounted, "'Great,' I said, 'what a terrific rally.' But as I said it, I saw the expression on his face was not one of shared relief."[3] Greenspan had the decimal points misplaced. The Dow had dropped a staggering 508 points, or 22.6 percent, from 2246.7 to 1738.7. This was the worst one-day loss in history. The entire year's gains were wiped out. No subsequent daily drop in the Dow, percentagewise, has come close. (On March 16, 2020, near the beginning of the Covid-19 pandemic, the Dow dropped almost 13 percent, the second-worst day on record.)

LOSING A QUARTER OF YOUR WEALTH IN A FEW HOURS

Imagine what Greenspan, who was arguably the person most able to impact the U.S. economy as well as the stock market, was feeling in that particular moment. Imagine going from relief to shock, when he suddenly realized the astonishing one-day wealth loss he and all stock market investors had suffered. And that loss of about a quarter of stock market wealth is based on investors who were well-diversified. Some of those who weren't faced even greater one-day losses.

We don't think about investment risk very often, perhaps only when we're forced to, such as when we open a new investment account. It's one thing to answer risk-related questions such as "How you would feel if you lost 10 percent of your portfolio?" while you're sitting on your comfy sofa sipping your morning latte on a warm, sunny weekend. But what's more difficult is trying to *really* reflect on how you would feel if something similar to October 19, 1987, happened today. And if you had tens of thousands or hundreds of thousands of dollars of your hard-earned money invested, would you feel disbelief? Fear? Anger? Sadness? Despondency? Would you panic, and liquidate your entire portfolio, as many investors did? The same goes for more recent although less severe one-day drops during the start of the Financial Crisis in 2007, and the start of the 2020 pandemic.

In hindsight, panic selling would not have served investors well. Despite the fall to a level below 1739, by June 1989 the Dow was again above 2500. Large drops in the stock market are often followed by large gains. One of the biggest one-day gains ever occurred two days after Black

Monday, when the Dow gained more than 10 percent. And that was after a gain of 6 percent on October 20, as we'll see shortly.

Of course, the Greenspan story could never be repeated today. If the Washington–Dallas flight had occurred nowadays, during the flight Greenspan would have internet access and would know what was happening in the market every second. Perhaps he could even have taken some immediate action or tried to calm the markets. On the other hand, there is nothing to stop such a one-day drop or even greater in the market today. Prior to 1987, the worst-case scenario we had as a reference point was a one-day drop of 12.8 percent on October 28, 1929. (That drop was followed the next day by an 11.7 percent drop, then the following day a gain of 12.3 percent.) Each major one-day drop has been unique. It's hard to anticipate all of the economic, geopolitical, psychological, and technical factors that went into the mix on October 19, 1987. A perfect storm perhaps. What might today's perfect storm look like?

A one-day drop exceeding Black Monday is extremely unlikely, and there is no indication of such a pending drop. But for *any* investment, it's important to understand what *could* happen, rather than what we expect or would like to happen. The best course of action? Having a plan, figuring out what you would do before such events occur, and then hopefully remaining calm if and when they occur. It's exciting to watch stock prices and other asset prices hit new highs. But stock prices—as well as cryptocurrencies, real estate, and any other assets—don't just move in one direction.

BLACK MONDAY CAUSES

On Black Monday, trading on the New York Stock Exchange (NYSE) reached a record of over 600 million shares, double the previous record, set on the prior Friday. The ratio of declining to rising stocks was 40 to 1.

(A ratio of more than 3 to 1 was generally considered to be a rout.) John J. Phelan, the NYSE's chairman, blamed the drop on at least five factors. Markets had increased steadily over the past five years without any substantial correction. There were inflation concerns. Interest rates were increasing. The military conflict between Iran and Iraq was causing geopolitical risk. And there was volatility in the derivatives markets.[4]

Let's drill down into the last factor. Derivatives are securities with prices that depend on the price of some other assets. Options contracts are agreements between two parties giving one the option to buy, or sell, shares in an asset at an agreed-upon price by a certain date. Another type of derivative security, futures contracts, is an agreement between two parties to exchange shares in an asset at a fixed price sometime in the future.

Stock index futures are traded on organized exchanges. They are based on standardized contracts and derive their prices from an underlying index like the S&P 500 index. This allows one party to buy the index in the future at a predetermined price. It stands to reason that when the market itself declines, we would expect the corresponding futures price to decline as well.

In 1987, trading in stock index futures was an important part of a strategy called portfolio insurance. Also known as program trading, portfolio insurance was implemented through the emerging technology of automated trading (like through Bernie Madoff's legitimate business, discussed in Chapter 4). In order to cushion their portfolios against drops in the market, sophisticated investors who owned stocks would buy portfolio insurance by selling stock index futures.

That meant that when the value of their portfolio of stocks went down, they were able to offset at least some of the losses. If there was extensive selling of the stock index futures, pushing down the price of the stock index futures, then traders known as arbitrageurs would step in. In order to capitalize on price discrepancies, the arbitrageurs would do the opposite of what other traders were doing: by *buying* stock index futures and *selling* the underlying stocks in the index. On October 19, the result of this process was a hastening of the decline of stock prices.

SPECIALISTS' DESPAIR

Back in 1987, as today, the NYSE's trading model involved humans trading on the floor of the exchange. They were known as designated market makers or specialists.[5] Operating both manually and electronically, their role was to "maintain fair and orderly markets for their assigned securities." If there was a preponderance of sell orders, then the specialists would step in to buy stocks in order to provide liquidity, adding to their inventory. The specialist firms had a lot of power and were usually very profitable. In 1987, there were 50 specialist firms handling all of the NYSE market making.

In the afternoon on Black Monday, according to James Maguire, chairman of one specialist firm, Henderson Brothers Inc., whose firm made markets in 70 stocks, "From 2 p.m. on, there was total despair. The entire investment community fled the market. We were left alone on the field." As buyers when everyone else was selling, Henderson Brothers ended the day with $60 million in stocks, three times the normal volume. At the time, investors had five days to settle stock transactions. So Maguire's firm had until the following Monday to pay for the stocks. That would require a lot of borrowing.

That evening, Maguire phoned his bank, one of the largest Wall Street lenders, asking for a $30 million loan. He was stunned by the reply: the bank wasn't in a position to commit to a loan. After five more calls until after midnight, the bank wouldn't budge. Other specialists faced similar predicaments and one was forced into a merger with a well-capitalized firm.

If the market continued to drop, specialist firms faced having to renege on their earlier buying commitments. The result of such an action would possibly be bankruptcy for the specialist firms, and most certainly market turmoil.

TERRIBLE TUESDAY: MORNING

By Tuesday morning, October 20, there were rumors that the NYSE might have to close, an extremely rare occurrence—like when the markets closed early when President Kennedy was shot. Credit markets are the oil that greases market transactions. By 8 a.m., credit markets were tightening. Not only were specialist firms rushing to borrow, but larger securities firms were as well, because they had grown their stock inventories by accommodating selling by major clients. Trading and borrowing in government securities swelled. Arbitrageurs who were trying to take advantage of pending takeovers were forced to put up more capital on their borrowings. Banks were reluctant to settle trades, fearing they might not get paid.

Sensing potential disaster, Federal Reserve chair Alan Greenspan, along with the Fed's New York president, E. Gerald Corrigan, jointly made a public statement. It indicated that the Fed was (at least temporarily) reversing its tightening stance. The Fed would be a "source of liquidity to support the economic and financial system" by flooding the market through buying government securities and driving down interest rates.

At 9:30 a.m. on October 20, the opening of trading on the NYSE, the Dow jumped about 12 percent, over 200 points, to 1949.77. However, some specialists resolved to wait until they received enough buy orders at higher prices before opening trading in their stocks. As specialists and large firms sold some of their huge inventories of stocks with the initial jump in some stock prices, buying dissipated. Stock index futures began to plummet. There were very few program traders stepping into the market even though the stock index futures were trading below the cash value of the underlying stocks. By late morning, both stocks and futures were being sold. This was the worst-case scenario for specialists with huge pending losses from Black Monday that they needed to cover.

Before noon, many of the 30 blue-chip stocks that were part of the Dow still hadn't opened or had started trading and then stopped because of sell orders overwhelming buy orders. These included DuPont, Merck, Eastman Kodak, and Philip Morris. USX also stopped trading at 12:51 p.m. Other large firms, including Sears, 3M, and Dow Chemical, stopped trading.

THE MAJOR MARKET INDEX

The Dow and the S&P 500 are the best-known U.S. stock indexes. Much less well known is the Major Market Index (MMI), which was established in 1983. Like the Dow, the MMI is a price-weighted index. As such, stocks that trade at higher prices have higher weights. (The S&P 500 index is weighted based on market capitalization.) The MMI contains 20 stocks, and 17 of them were also part of the Dow. That wasn't a coincidence as the MMI was created to mirror the Dow. At the time, options on the MMI index were traded on the American Stock Exchange, while futures were traded on the Chicago Board of Trade (CBOT). By early afternoon, this little-known index was about to save the world from financial Armageddon.

Ronald Shear, the senior specialist for the MMI on the American Stock Exchange, was dismayed by the lack of trading of many of the stocks that were part of the MMI. He was concerned about order imbalances in MMI options, just like the order imbalances in the underlying stocks that made up the MMI. He checked with a floor supervisor about the rules for index-options trading. The floor supervisor confirmed that if more than 20 percent of stocks that made up the underlying index capitalization weren't trading, then options trading should cease. By late morning, over half of the stocks in the MMI weren't trading. So, over a loudspeaker, Shear announced the halting of trading of MMI options.

TERRIBLE TUESDAY: AFTERNOON

Index derivative trading liquidity issues were occurring at other exchanges as well. By 12:15 p.m., the Chicago Board Options Exchange (CBOE) that traded options on the S&P 500 index had closed trading. Shortly afterwards, the Chicago Mercantile Exchange (CME) that traded S&P 500 futures also closed trading. Only the CBOT was still trading futures on one of the prominent indexes, the MMI, but not without concerns.

In theory, futures on a stock index should trade close to the value of the underlying index itself. On the morning of Black Monday, MMI futures were trading at a 30-point discount to their cash value. That meant it was potentially profitable for arbitrageurs to buy MMI futures and sell the underlying stocks at a profit. Except during a few periods in the afternoon, for much of the remainder of October 19 the MMI futures were trading near par. However, on October 20, Terrible Tuesday, it was a different story. At 12:15 p.m., the futures were trading at an incredible 50-point discount, the largest ever. This gave arbitrageurs an incentive to sell underlying stocks. But that could create an even greater trade imbalance, causing remaining stock trading to freeze up.

Around 12:15 p.m., the chairman of the CBOT, Karsten (Cash) Mahlmann, was on the phone with the NYSE, an intense rival of the CBOT.

Mahlmann was the son of a German grain importer.[6] At age 20, he began working for brokerage firm Daniel Rice & Company as a runner, delivering trade orders to the floor for trade execution. While working in the back office of securities firm Shearson Hayden, he had a job in the cash grain department, which is where he got his nickname. He joined the CBOT in 1963, and in 1983 became a member of the board of directors. While he often complained to reporters for overusing his nickname, even his wife called him Cash.[7]

Mahlmann was told the NYSE was considering shutting down trading. Mahlmann estimated that 17 of the 20 MMI stocks were still trading, albeit intermittently. Mahlmann had also received a call from the President's Council of Economic Advisers imploring him to keep the CBOT open for trading. Mahlmann recalled, "We felt we had to stay open to do our job, to provide liquidity." That fateful decision saved the day.

Pressure was mounting on the NYSE to shut down trading. Large investment firms with huge stock inventories were seeing the stock values drop. By noon, the Dow had dropped below Black Monday's horrific closing level. However, earlier in the day, NYSE chairman Phelan had talked to President Reagan's Chief of Staff Howard Baker, who urged the NYSE to stay open. According to Phelan, closing and then later reopening hundreds of stocks simultaneously could be a huge problem. "The strain on the country ... would be taken as an extremely bad sign. If we close it, we would never reopen it."

A MIRACLE

What happened next with MMI futures contracts was later described as a miracle. Around 12:38 p.m., in the space of about five minutes, the MMI cash-to-futures spread swung from a discount of almost 60 points to a premium of around 12 points. The rally in the MMI was equivalent to a

360-point rise in the Dow, or about a 20 percent increase compared with the Dow's noon level. Knowledgeable traders thought that in an attempt to prop up the Dow, a few major firms used MMI futures contracts to intentionally manipulate the markets.

The rally may also have started with a trade by Blair Hull, a well-known trader on the CBOE, whose trading firm also had a seat on the CBOT.[8] Hull needed to meet a margin call and since the CBOE was closed, he entered the MMI trading pit and started buying futures contracts to cover a short position that was costing him money. He was quickly swarmed by traders who were selling and he bought what he needed.

Given the low level of trading at the time, intense trading had a disproportionate effect. The swing in the MMI futures to a premium spurred arbitrageurs to rush in to buy the underlying stocks, as computer monitors on trading desks unexpectedly flashed green among a sea of red. This in turn enabled the NYSE specialists to resume trading in the previously dormant stocks. Consequently, the NYSE dodged the bullet of shutting down. A subsequent analysis by *Wall Street Journal* reporters suggested the buying of the futures contracts at that time was predominantly by major firms on Wall Street, and the contracts could have been purchased with as little as a few million dollars.

As news of the MMI rally spread, markets got more good news. Major firms including Shearson Lehman Brothers Holdings Inc., Merrill Lynch, Citicorp, Honeywell, ITT, Allegis, and USX announced stock buybacks. This sent a message that these CEOs felt their stocks were undervalued. Between noon and 1:00 p.m., the Dow increased almost 100 points, or almost 6 percent. By the end of the trading day, the Dow was at 1841.01, an increase of just under 6 percent from Black Monday's close. And after the Fed's earlier pledge to provide liquidity, banks agreed to continue lending, including to specialists. The immediate crisis had passed, albeit not before exposing market weaknesses.

COUNTERFACTUAL SCENARIO

Imagine this counterfactual: What might have unfolded if those mysterious MMI futures trades hadn't occurred around 12:38 p.m. on Tuesday, October 20, 1987? Trading on all U.S. stock and derivative exchanges would have ceased. Financial firms such as the specialist firms would have gone bankrupt. Bank lending would have dried up, creating a contagion effect beyond Wall Street into Main Street. A deep recession would have followed. Fortunately, none of this happened.

Liquidity—the ability to freely trade securities—matters. Liquidity matters most when investors are nervous. The financial ecosystem—including retail investors, institutional investors, market-making specialists, investment firms, the Fed, both stock and derivative-based exchanges, and regulators—is often delicately balanced. We shouldn't take it for granted.

Miracles can and do happen. But sometimes miracles need a nudge. A conspiracy among some of the large Wall Street firms? Perhaps, but at least this was a feel-good one. And if you need liquidity, who better to rely on than someone nicknamed Cash?

NOTES

1. The accounts and quotations regarding the events on October 20, 1987, are based on the Pulitzer Prize–winning article by Stewart, James B., and Daniel Hertzberg, "Terrible Tuesday: How the Stock Market Almost Disintegrated a Day After the Crash," *Wall Street Journal*, November 20, 1987, 1, 23, https://www.wsj.com/articles/BL-267B-259.
2. Murray, Alan, "Fed's New Chairman Wins a Lot of Praise on Handling the Crash," *Wall Street Journal*, November 25, 1987, https://www.wsj.com/articles/SB112404015636012610.

3. Greenspan, Alan, *The Age of Turbulence: Adventures in a New World* (New York: Penguin Press, 2007), 105.
4. Matz, Tim, Alan Murray, Thomas E. Ricks, and Beatrice E. Garcia, "Stocks Plunge 508 Amid Panicky Selling," *Wall Street Journal*, October 20, 1987, 1, 22.
5. "Trading Information," New York Stock Exchange, https://www.nyse.com/markets/nyse/trading-info.
6. Froehilch, Lee, "Fall from Grace at Board of Trade," *Washington Post*, September 4, 1990, https://www.washingtonpost.com/archive/business/1990/09/04/fall-from-grace-at-board-of-trade/a34487f5-6012-47d7-a9a7-887b7f0421c5/.
7. Greising, David, and Laurie Morse, *Brokers, Bagmen, and Moles: Fraud and Corruption in the Chicago Futures Markets* (Hoboken, NJ: Wiley, 1991), 134.
8. Henriques, Diana, *A First-Class Catastrophe: The Road to Black Monday, the Worst Day in Wall Street History* (New York: Henry Holt, 2017), 244.

ACKNOWLEDGMENTS

This book grew in part out of research for my most recent book, *In Pursuit of the Perfect Portfolio: The Stories, Voices, and Key Insights of the Pioneers Who Shaped the Way We Invest* (Princeton University Press, 2021). My co-author was MIT Sloan School finance professor Andrew Lo, to whom I owe a huge debt of gratitude. I first met Andrew in 1984 when I was a relatively young student in my second year at the Wharton School's finance PhD program. Andrew was teaching his first course as a newly minted PhD graduate from Harvard—and he was even younger than me. I learned an immense amount from him both in and out of the classroom. We kept in touch over the years as I called on him to fill various teaching and keynote speaking opportunities.

In the early 2000s, I had a year off from teaching and I decided I'd write a textbook, directed toward an executive MBA audience. I was quite naïve and I knew nothing about publishing. I reached out to Andrew and he put in a good word with an editor at W.W. Norton. That introduction helped me land my first book, in 2003, *Financial Management: A Primer*. That's where I had the pleasure of meeting Jack Repcheck, who introduced me to the book publishing world. Jack was a New York gentleman who left this world at too young an age. I'm grateful for what he taught me about publishing and I miss our musings about the travails of the Toronto Maple Leafs.

In 2011, I reached out to Andrew again, this time with a book idea that involved profiling academic and practitioner luminaries who contributed intellectually and practically to the investment industry during the past 60 years. I was thrilled when he agreed to collaborate on *In Pursuit of the Perfect Portfolio*. It was a fun journey that, at the time, we didn't expect would take a decade to complete. Over that time, we were able to interview our intellectual heroes and trailblazers. I'm grateful to the late Harry Markowitz, Bill Sharpe, Gene Fama, the late Jack Bogle, Myron Scholes, Bob Merton, Marty Leibowitz, Bob Shiller, Charley Ellis, and Jeremy Siegel. I'm particularly appreciative of Bill Sharpe, who also provided comments and encouragement for *Trailblazers, Heroes, and Crooks*.

The opening chapter of *In Pursuit of the Perfect Portfolio* covered a brief history of investing, from 9500 BCE to 1950. I had uncovered a lot of interesting stories that I felt needed more space. In addition, among the 10 investment luminaries that we interviewed, there were many investing trailblazers with fascinating stories and messages that I felt needed to be heard by a broader audience. I further immersed myself in their stories and uncovered new ones. Tim Harford's excellent podcast, *Cautionary Tales*, provided the inspiration for two of the stories. Also, an article by Mark Higgins made me aware of Hetty Green, one of the best female investors of all time.

I've had a fabulous career at Ivey and I'm fortunate to have had wonderful colleagues. I learned a lot from the old guard, long retired, including Dave Shaw, Larry Wynant, and Jim Hatch, my main mentors, as well as Rick Robertson. More recently I've enjoyed my collaborations with Craig Dunbar, Saurin Patel, and Felipe Restrepo, and I've learned a lot from them. I'm also grateful to the library staff at the Ivey Business School who helped with my research, in particular with tracking down old books.

When I had nearly completed a manuscript for *Trailblazers, Heroes, and Crooks*, I started along the process of finding a home for it. I reached out to Robin Wigglesworth, author of the delightful book *Trillions*. I'm thankful to Robin for putting me in touch with the amazing Julia Eagleton. She was one of the first people to provide some feedback, suggestions, and encouragement for this book, for which I'm grateful.

I'm indebted to Robert Mackwood, to whom I then reached out to get his reaction to the manuscript. He admitted to being a sucker for stories of financial shenanigans and false assumptions about stocks and investments, and put his faith in me. In turn, he introduced me to the wonderful Judith Newlin, editor at Wiley, a fellow long-suffering sports fan (for her it's the New York Mets). How could she not like a book with a chapter devoted to the Mets' Bobby Bonilla? I've also enjoyed working with the Wiley team and associates including managing editor Vithusha Rameshan, freelance editor Amy Handy, senior product manager Sharmila Srinivasan, product marketer Jean-Karl Martin, account manager Katie Helm, and editorial assistant Delainey Henson.

I'm thankful to my children, Jennifer, Christopher, Thomas, and Melanie, who tolerated my dad jokes over too many years, and put up with unsolicited financial advice like "Diversify, diversify, diversify!" They were also my first audience for storytelling. I'm particularly grateful to Christopher, who provided feedback on the manuscript and gave me a great perspective from a next-generation reader.

Finally, I'm grateful to Graeme and Sue Hunter for their unwavering support and friendship. And as a fellow author, Graeme was the best informal editor one could have, telling me what I needed to hear and helping me to become a better writer.

ABOUT
THE AUTHOR

Stephen Foerster is an award-winning author and professor of finance at the Ivey Business School at Western University in London, Ontario, Canada. Foerster's most recent book, *In Pursuit of the Perfect Portfolio: The Stories, Voices, and Key Insights of the Pioneers Who Shaped the Way We Invest* (with Andrew Lo, MIT Sloan School; Princeton University Press, 2021), was featured in the *Wall Street Journal's* Bookshelf column. Foerster has also written two textbooks and over 100 case studies and technical notes in the areas of investments and financial management. He has published over 50 articles in journals such as *Journal of Financial Economics*, the *Journal of Finance*, and *Financial Analysts Journal*. Foerster has served on pension and endowment fund boards as well as not-for-profit investment committees. He received a PhD from the Wharton School, University of Pennsylvania, and has obtained the Chartered Financial Analyst designation. Foerster enjoys golfing and hiking, which in both cases for him often involves a walk in the woods.

INDEX